RUSS & AIKO

THE HORIUCHI STORY

RUSS & AIKO

THE HORIUCHI STORY

Scott M. Hurst

ISBN: 978-1-944200-36-7

Legends Library Press & Publishing, Rochester, NY
www.LegendsLibrary.org
Send inquiries to: info@legendslibrary.com or call 1-877-222-1960

Cover and interior designed by Jacob F. Frandsen

For Grandpa and Grandma,
with all my heart and gratitude.

CONTENTS

AUTHOR'S PREFACE

OUT OF THE CLEAR BLUE sky Apostle Dallin H. Oaks phones Russell, my grandfather, to ask if he's writing his personal history. When grandpa confesses he isn't, Elder Oaks insists, "Why don't you write it?" Grandpa never refuses Elder Oaks but neither does he begin writing.

A few years later, my mother runs into Elder Oaks and introduces herself as the Horiuchis' daughter. Without skipping a beat, Elder Oaks asks again if Russell is writing his personal history.

Fast-forward a few more years and our family sits gathered around the dinner table.

"Dad, you need to write your life story," my mother chides.

Grandpa, in his modest, matter-of-fact way shrugs, "Nothing much to write about."

"Then I'll have to write it," Mom says.

"You'll get it wrong," he replies.

"Well?" Mom throws her hands up as if to say he can't have it both ways.

I am teasing when I remind him that he's disobeying an apostle. Suddenly serious, he turns and declares, "You know what? I'm not going to write it."

"Because you're stubborn," Grandma doesn't miss a beat.

"No," he states like a prosecutor delivering the final blow, "Because *he's* going to write it for me." His finger points at me, arm fully extended, leaving no room for evasion.

I am suddenly faced with the gravity of his charge. Oh, boy. That's what I get for teasing[1] Grandpa.

It's March 23, 2010, early spring in Utah. I'm sitting with my grandparents talking about their experiences, going over the initial draft of this book. Grandpa is 87 and Grandma is 84 and we are batting a yellow balloon around the living room like a bunch of children, laughing and having a ball. Grandpa bats at it in spurts when it comes his way, Grandma eyes it with great intent and focus, springing at it like a young kitten. Warm light pours in through the large picture window that frames the great Rocky Mountains beyond. Flecks of snow still cling to jagged peaks that effortlessly hold up a vibrantly blue sky.

This is heaven.

A few years later much has passed, including my Grandfather, showing that time waits for no man. I have to remind myself that this most definitely includes me. A perfectionist, hence procrastinator, I have stalled and stalled; this book is for my beloved grandparents. I want it to be perfect, knowing it will never be. So I ask my family and my readers to forgive any flaws, inaccuracies or imperfections you may encounter.

If you're reading this chances are you were acquainted with Russell and Annette in some fashion. In all likelihood you know details of their lives I've never heard. How fortunate you are. In the course

---

1. Later I ask Grandpa, "Why me?"

"You have to write it," he answers, "because He (points to the heavens) knows I'm lazy."

If I've learned anything from Grandpa it's the joy of a debate. "I didn't think He worked that way," I retort, "The Lord knows I'm lazy but He doesn't have someone to do my work for me! So if I'm doing your work does that mean someone else is going to do my work for me?"

Grandpa speaks like it's a simple fact of life, "No."

"Dang it!" I laugh. Oh, well, I tried!

of this grand adventure hopefully you will learn a few things about them you didn't before. I certainly have.

Perhaps all of us can be a little more like my grandparents and love one another, not in spite of our flaws, but perhaps, because of them.

Scott M. Hurst
January 2014

RUSSELL'S PREFACE

WHILE GOING THROUGH A VERY thick stack of papers Grandpa had collected, written, and otherwise amassed, I came across the first page of a type-written introduction that he composed himself from my point of view. Here then, in Russell's own words, is the preface to this book:

Grandpa is a hayseed. No. He is my grandfather.

Over the years, one could often see grandpa in his faded cotton workclothes, mowing the lawn and raking leaves in the yard. He is also the G-man of the neighborhood, putting out his garbage can and that of his immediate neighbors for the weekly pick up. If he is around after the pick up, he goes and puts away the garbage cans. His simplistic approach to things may cause people to consider him a real peasant.

He goes to church on Sundays, but he does not wear his religion on his sleeves. He would go to Church and sit quietly and very seldom express an opinion in the Sunday school class or in meetings. People that do not know him or new comers [sic] would look at him and think that the old man is a bit senile.

He smiles when Grandma tells him to stop acting like a peasant, but grandpa's comeback was that he was not acting, he's just being himself since he was descended from a long line of peasants, and he likes fishing because his maternal grandparents were fisherman. His behavior simply reflected his heritage.

Over the years while my parents were in Germany and Washington, D.C., I have lived with my grandparents, and over the years, I have learned about my Grandparents more and more. While I have never been able to fully penetrate into the inner workings of grandpa's mind, I cannot help but feel that grandpa was a unique person. And to write something about him could perhaps be useful ultimately to his posterity and his family.

What I write is not meant to be a biography. Grandpa simply will not sit long enough to give any information that would come close to being a biography. Rather than attempt a biography like approach, perhaps it may be best for me to take the subject matters like education, finances, war and military service and simply comment on Grandpa's ideas and approach. In so doing, one can get insight how grandpa thinks and acts rather than listing the chronology of his life.

Since grandpa is reticent in talking about himself, a lot of . . . [end of written text]

ACKNOWLEDGMENTS

I AM GRATEFUL FOR THE WORK of the many generations that have preceded me. To them I owe everything. Special thanks to Ellen Williams, my mother, the incomparable daughter of the Horiuchis, for all her work and support and encouragement on this project, for transcribing hours and hours of interviews and drafting them into a semblance of order. Thanks to my entire family for their patience, especially Grandpa and Grandma who have endured hours of me poking and prodding into every aspect of their lives. Last but not least, heartfelt appreciation to the friends, neighbors, colleagues, missionaries and students who have contributed to the intangible monument that is the life of my grandparents. To those left unmentioned or unknown, please accept my apologies but also my gratitude. It is all of you who have helped write this story, I've simply had the pleasure of putting it in words.

What is the measure of a man? How do you chart the unfathomable currents that guide our lives?

An old man, once jet-black hair grown white, walks with a slight limp across his lovingly and meticulously cultivated yard, favoring a left foot often swollen with gout. A deeply etched farmer's tan traces his wrists and neck. Long hours in the sun are not the only reason for the dark skin, his Asian heritage, evident in his features, grants his rich tan a head start. Tulips, lilies and marigolds of every hue flourish against the yellow brick house in which he has lived for the better part of his life. He is a self-described *fuddy-duddy*, a modest equivocation belying his true depth and experience. Part of the Greatest Generation, he has walked the earth for nearly nine decades, seeing more than most of us will see in twice as many.

It is a winding, almost miraculous path that has brought him to the gates of these 88 years. But every journey must begin somewhere. And in this, the story of Russell Horiuchi is no different.

NOZOMI

MAUI ISN'T MUCH MORE THAN a speck of volcanic dirt dwarfed by the immensity of the Pacific Ocean that surrounds it. It's not the biggest island in the Hawaiian chain (it's the second); it's not even where the capital sits (that's Oahu). Rising from sea level to over ten thousand feet at its crown, the island is a wide, flat valley formed between two volcanoes. The tallest is Haleakala, the House of the Sun.

The humble island itself may not seem extraordinary but the Hawaiians recognized it as special enough to name it after the god who created their home. They knew something early on that the rest of the world would only come to realize in time.

Interestingly enough the god Maui's symbol and the instrument he used to create the islands is a fishhook, an emblem strangely appropriate to this story.

The earliest inhabitants were Polynesians who migrated from further south in the Pacific. These early settlers lived in relative isolation for several hundred years. That changed in the 1800s with the arrival of the first white men, whom the natives dubbed *haole*. With the newcomers came different customs and ways of life. Eying the economic potential of the lush tropical climate the newcomers quickly established industrial and agricultural pursuits including sugar cane and pineapples.

At first the new proprietors hired Hawaiian natives to work their fields but the more relaxed mindset of the locals didn't mesh well with their western concept of production schedules. Considering the local natives a less than ideal workforce the plantation owners began looking for laborers from outside the islands. People came from places as far away as Germany, Mexico, the Philippines and China, heeding the siren's call of building a better life. The largest group of emigrants came from Japan, predominantly from the southern prefectures of Hiroshima and Kumamoto. Between 1886–1925 over 180,000 Japanese arrived on Hawaii's distant shores.

Under the lead of the Emperor Meiji, Japan was going through the growing pains of changing from a feudal to a modern society. Fiscal and social disruptions had weakened the economy. These factors combined with the new imperative mandating an international search for knowledge created the foundation for a great outreach to the outside world, particularly the west. It was not difficult to convince poor subsistence farmers to migrate to the United States where they were promised good paying jobs.

One such soul was Mitsutaka Horiuchi (1886–1966) of Kumamoto, in southern Japan. In 1905 at the ripe age of 19 he boarded a ship setting sail to Hawaii to pursue his dreams of wealth and adventure.

While emigration was not uncommon, Mitsutaka's departure is notable due to the fact that he was the oldest son, the *chonan*. In Japan the *chonan* is responsible for caring for their parents in their old age. They also inherited all of the family's wealth, thus keeping the property intact and not breaking it into smaller parcels. Typically it was the younger sons who migrated away while the oldest remained in the ancestral home. This tradition began to change dramatically after the second world war but at the time of Mitsutaka's exodus the custom remained in effect. Mitsutaka's father, Kojiro, an avid *sumo* wrestling fan, did not seem particularly concerned that his oldest should leave for parts unknown.

Mitsutaka was born in 1886 on the 9th of December in Yonetomi-Mura in Kumamoto Prefecture. It was the same year Karl Benz patented the first successful gasoline-driven car, Mussorgsky's "A Night on Bald Mountain" premiered in St. Petersburg and the Folies Bergère staged its first revue-style music show in Paris. Grover

Cleveland, the 22nd president of the United States, dedicated the Statue of Liberty, Jacob's Pharmacy began selling the first Coca-Cola (yes, it contained cocaine) in Atlanta and Sigmund Freud opened his practice in Vienna.

America may have been a melting pot for the tired, the poor and the huddled masses but racial tensions were still very much alive in the burgeoning republic. In Seattle federal troops were deployed to restore order after 400 ethnic Chinese were driven from their homes by mobs. Apache Chief Geronimo surrendered near Fort Bowie concluding 30 years of fighting to protect his tribe's homeland and ending the U.S.-Indian wars. And twenty blacks were killed in Carrollton, Mississippi over an incident that began with spilled molasses of all things. On the positive side, the massacre helped garner enough momentum to successfully pass the first Civil Rights Act prohibiting discrimination based on race, gender, color, religion or national origin.

On October 3rd, Mitsutaka arrived on the vessel *Kopuchiku*, with little in his possession save the dream of returning home with a small fortune. He worked various jobs before finally locating in Lahaina, Maui where he began working in the Honokowai sugar fields for Pioneer Mills. Soft spoken and standing a slender 5'2", Mitsutaka was a man possessed of great moral courage and a keen sense of right and wrong. He quickly garnered a reputation in the community as being hard working and honest. Russell adds that his father "liked kids and had a better education than most of the immigrants."

Another Japanese immigrant working at Pioneer Mills and living in Honokowai was Sadashichi Koyama (1876–1957). Originally from Jigozen village near Hiroshima, Sadashichi and his wife Maki Kitayama (1878–1921) settled in Hawaii seven years before Mitsutaka stepped foot on the *Kopuchiku*. Sadashichi rose quickly among the ranks of workers and was the lead irrigation contractor at the plantation.

With the Japanese immigrants came many of their traditions, including *miai kekkon,* arranged marriages. Sadashichi was impressed with the quiet, hardworking Mitsutaka and made arrangements for marriage of the thirty-year old man to his daughter who was only sixteen at the time.

Kikuyo (Aug. 23, 1900–1981) was the second oldest Koyama child. The oldest, Hatsukichi (born 1896), a boy, was left in Japan under the care of his grandparents when Sadashichi and Maki moved to Hawaii. He never followed his parents to America. Kikuyo shares the distinction of being born on American soil, albeit a territory (in Honokowai), making her one of the earliest *Nisei,*[1] American-born Japanese. She attended school until the fourth grade and could read and write, somewhat of a rarity. Like Mitsutaka she was quiet by nature.

On December 24, 1915, Mitsutaka Horiuchi and Kikuyo Koyama became man and wife. Despite their age gap the couple got along well and over time their marriage became a warm friendship. In her later years Kikuyo confided that if she had it to do over again, she would still marry Mitsutaka, whom she affectionately called "Papa." The couple made their first home in a company house in Honokowai across a bridge not far from Kikuyo's parents, both continuing to work in the sugar cane plantation.

Once the children started coming there were three daughters in fairly rapid succession: Hatsuko (called Kay, short for Kathleen) (1916–2015), Misao (Sodetani) (1918–2008), and Namiyo (Fujimoto Oyama) (1920–1996).

In 1921 tragedy struck when Kikuyo's mother died while giving birth to a baby girl, Makiyo, who passed away as well. Sadashichi was suddenly a widower with three children still at home, Kaneichi

---

1. *Nisei* literally means "second generation." Third generation Japanese are technically designated as *Sansei,* fourth generation as *Yonsei,* etc. But the term *Nisei* has come to refer broadly to those of Japanese descent, regardless of when they were born in the United States.

(known as Roy) (1904–1989), Kimiko (Nakamura) (1909–1966) and Sadao (nicknamed Codac) (1912–1976). Being the oldest daughter in the Koyama Family, Kikuyo shouldered the responsibility of caring for her three siblings as well as her father. Amazingly, Kikuyo was never known to protest her lot. She fulfilled her responsibilities with quiet dignity. She was an unassuming example of the Japanese ideal of *sekinin,* filial duty. Russell remembers "she was the disciplinarian—she gave and asked no quarter—she wanted us to do what was right."

The average day on the plantation started at four in the morning with a siren signaling the women folk to begin cooking rice for breakfast and lunch, which was prepared in a large iron kettle heated over a fire. At 5:00 the general signal was given for workers to rise. At six everyone gathered in the staging area in front of the office where they received the day's assignments. Workers walked or were taken to sites in the back of trucks. Sometimes it took a half an hour on the red dirt roads to reach the latest work section. There was a fifteen-minute break at seven for breakfast then work would resume until noon with thirty more minutes given for lunch. Meals usually consisted of a staple of rice and fish with fresh vegetables and *tsukemono,* pickled vegetables. Meat was an occasional luxury, a real treat being Vienna sausage or canned corned beef. Soy sauce and pickled cabbage accompanied most every meal. Once in a while canned sardines were smothered in *shoyu,* soy sauce, or tomato sauce. Much later canned meats such a Spam became a favorite. At four-thirty in the afternoon the final siren blared the end of the workday. This went on for six days a week.

On the seventh day, Mitsutaka could invariably be found fishing. Using shrimp for bait, he usually caught *kukupi,* perch, and *papio,* pompano, with his bamboo rod, line and hook. As he acquired more comfort he was eventually able to purchase a fishing reel.

It was a demanding life but no one complained. With a roof over their heads and food on the table they were very comfortable compared to the poverty they left behind in Japan. There was even a dispensary when they were sick.

Kimiko Iwamura Figuerres, a playmate of Kimiko Koyama's, and later grandmother to Cyril Figuerres,[2] speaks of Mitsutaka as "the most kind person. Very gentle and [he always] helped everybody."

According to Paul Hyer, a close family friend, Mitsutaka "was a leader of the people–a *kahuna*. He would negotiate on behalf of the workers with the administration. He dared to stand up to the bosses."

The plantation manager was a fellow by the name of John Moir, Jr. His wife was a teacher at the local high school.[3] White haired and in his 50s, dressed in work boots, khaki pants and a collared shirt, Moir was a large man who ran the show but "didn't get his hands dirty." At the time all the plantation owners and managers were white and used Asians for what almost amounted to slave labor.

Mitsutaka served as spokesman for the community with the company. Earlier Moir made a promise regarding improvements that he had not kept. At a meeting Moir denied ever having promised anything. The 5'2', 120 pound Mitsutaka stood and faced the 6'5', 260 pound Moir and told him that he was not keeping his word, and that he was dishonest and a liar. Angered, Moir would have struck Mitsutaka, but there were too many witnesses present. Moir never forgave the courageous Japanese man. There was nothing he could do about it at the time but he would have his revenge, as petty as it was.

In 1922 Kikuyo found out she was pregnant. It was a difficult pregnancy. She was bleeding, and had to take to her bed. Her condition was severe enough that the doctor urged them to terminate

---

2. Kimiko was friends with Ralph Shino's older sister as well. They were from Honokowaii.

3. It's not clear which school she taught at. Whether it was Lahainaluna or not Russell said he never had any class from her.

the pregnancy. It was not a matter to be taken lightly, especially after her mother's death only a few short years before.

Kikuyo was Buddhist, although, like much of the community, her practice was more one of tradition than of faith. Mitsutaka was a Shintoist, the indigenous religion of Japan. Kikuyo's health was troubling enough that the normally private and reserved man decided to discuss it with a priest, Otaiyu-san, whom he knew from sparring in *kendo,* Japanese sword fighting. With his friend Mr. Cho, Mitsutaka traveled to the Mantokuji temple in Paia to discuss the matter with Otaiyu-san. The priest prophesied that Kikuyo was expecting their first son, their *chonan,* and declared the child "would make his mark in the world."

Mitsutaka was thrilled they were expecting their first boy, and that their son might amount to something more than a field hand. Kikuyo knew she would carry the baby to full term even though she was bedridden the entire duration of her pregnancy. She was so sick at times it seemed the decision to keep the baby was the wrong choice. With Kikuyo laid up the extra share of the work fell to Mitsutaka. He wasn't a particularly strong man physically but, as always, he carried the added portion without complaint.

Birth is a miracle, but a common one, and rarely accompanied by much fanfare. So it was on January 25, 1923 when a healthy baby boy was born to Mitsutaka and Kikuyo Horiuchi at the simple wooden hospital in Lahaina. Because of the priest's words they named the child Nozomi, meaning "hope." It wasn't until his late teens that he adopted the moniker most of his friends would know him by for the rest of his life: Russell. Weighing over ten pounds the infant was the largest in the family, no small feat for a woman under five feet tall.

Shortly after Russell's birth the family moved from Honokowai to a small plantation owned village called Puukolii roughly seven miles north of Lahaina. It stood *mauka,* or towards the mountains from where the Kaanapalii Beach Resort now stands. Up on the gently sloping hillside, overlooking the vast Pacific, several hundred families nestled together in crudely built company homes surrounded by nothing but cane fields. There was a theater, a church and a store, all owned by Pioneer Mills. The population was predominantly Japanese with a handful of Hawaiians, Portuguese, Chinese, Filipinos and Koreans liberally sprinkled in.

If you asked the locals today about Puukolii chances are most of them have never heard of it, except for perhaps some of the older generation. Less than a ghost town, Puukolii doesn't even exist anymore. Only an empty field of scrub plants and a few sparse trees mark the spot where Russell grew up. If asked where they were from the Puukolii folks answered Lahaina. It was simpler, like someone from Draper saying they were from Salt Lake City or someone from Elmont saying they were from New York.

The family lived in four different company houses while Russell was growing up. The typical row house was made of whitewashed 1x12 tongue and groove style wooden slats with a modest living room and one bedroom (which everyone shared) behind it with wooden floors throughout. The kitchen was a separate building connected by a walkway that many folks later covered. There were slightly better homes with two or three bedrooms but, of course, those cost more money, something the growing Horiuchi clan did not have in abundance.

The "box" outhouse was located outside behind the kitchen. There was running water and plumbing in the kitchen but no sewage system. Refuse was gathered in a collector box until a functional sewer pipe was finally installed when Russell was about four or five. Baths existed only in the form of *sento*, public bathhouses, separated for men and women and heated by crude oil.

There was electricity, the entire usage of which consisted of two drop-cord lights, one in the living room and the other in the bedroom. Ice for the icebox was delivered from town one or two times a week by the Lahaina Ice Company which froze its own ice. All cooking was done on a simple kerosene stove.

Russell describes plantation living as "primitive" with only two double beds in the bedroom and *zabuton,* sitting cushions, in the living room. Russell slept on a *futon* on the floor. The kitchen contained a few chairs and a table, sink and stove, but no cupboards. The entire family lived like this throughout much of his childhood. Eventually when his sisters could earn a few dollars they purchased a chest of drawers for their clothing. Otherwise they remained quite austere with no real decorations. They couldn't afford it, not even curtains.

One month after giving birth, Kikuyo put the new baby, wearing diapers made from rice bags, in a basket and went back to work in the cane fields. Fieldwork was hot, dusty, backbreaking work. Many creatures lived in the closely grown sugar cane including giant millipedes, scorpions, mites, spiders, white flies and rats. Despite the intense tropical sun, workers wore heavy clothing from head to toe for protection. Conical hats were topped with a tied scarf that draped to their shoulders to shield their necks from the sun. Additional scarves were tied around the neck and much of the face leaving only the mouth, nose and eyes open. A large apron protected the front of the women and large gloves with long cuffs prevented contact with any undesirable creature.

According to Russell the family was "not what you would call particularly close" even though he got along well enough with his siblings. He was very fond of his eldest sister, Kay. He remembers her as a studious person, "hard working and what not." They conversed often but "we never crossed swords." Of all the siblings the two remained closest throughout the remainder of their lives.

While Kay went about her own business, Misao, the second oldest, was very domineering. When asked about her, Russell pointed his finger in a stern impression, "Do this, do that." She was also a hard worker but bossy, "like a surrogate mother. Any time she wants me to scrub the porch or what not, she'd get after me." In later years she would say, "Oh, you boy scout, you boy scout," meaning that he should work all the harder. She was definitely the pushiest among the siblings.

Even years later, when Russell was a man grown and married, this family dynamic persisted. Annette noticed the strong favoritism after the war. When the family got together, as they did practically every Sunday, if someone suggested an activity Misao didn't want to do then Kikuyo would say, "We're not going to do that, Misao doesn't want to."

Namiyo was Mitsutaka's favorite so he tended to cater to her. Namiyo and Russell got along well. Russell liked her because she was a nice girl who didn't boss him around.

Takashi (1925–2010), the youngest Horiuchi sibling, was the baby of the family and "had the run of his way." Russell claims his mother favored Taka "all the way down the line" and that his younger brother "ran roughshod on mama." Russell maintains that the preferential treatment didn't bother him, but the clarity of it in his mind so many years later belies his statement.

One of the ways the family saved money was by being frugal with clothing and materials. Nothing was wasted. Kikuyo kept and bleached old rice sacks and then, using her pedal driven sewing machine, turned the thick fabric into shirts and underwear. Making underwear in this manner was a fairly common practice among the villagers but rice sack shirts were somewhat of a rarity. This was, however, the only kind of shirt young Russell owned. He remembers feeling embarrassed wearing it but had no other option.

Despite the necessary frugality Kikuyo always managed to find a nice shirt and gabardine trousers for Taka. Russell remembers rarely owning any toys but Taka somehow ended up with an air rifle, a bicycle, a hunting knife and even a dog. The preferential treatment was obvious. When Russell gathered the nerve to pointedly ask his mother about it she replied, "I'll be the shortest time with my youngest child."

Why the discrepancy? It was plain favoritism. If it was anything more, Russell never mentioned it to anyone.[4]

Russell claimed he wasn't favored by anyone, but that wasn't entirely true, since he got along very well with his father. Mitsutaka never shouted at him or chewed him out. All he ever said was "Son, remember who you are. You are my number one son and I expect the best from you." It was something he never told the other children.

"I knew exactly what he meant," Russell explained, "He meant 'Don't do anything that would besmirch the good family name or bring shame on the family. Always do things honorably that will bring respect to your family. Don't disgrace yourself. Don't disgrace your family name.'"

Kikuyo was the disciplinarian of the home. Punishment was a swift spanking or in severe cases a burnt punk was placed on a finger or even the back of a neck. "It was harsh," writes Russell. The "family was very much concerned about [a] good family name. As the oldest son—I got the brunt of everything. Younger brother did not get the reprimanding or punishment like I did. Of the five kids—I got it." Then he adds, "Perhaps I was a bit unruly."

Russell was a quiet child, who never really did anything bad or got into any "hi-jinx" as a kid. He earned an occasional scolding but was never in any serious trouble for anything. "Papa really trusted me. He expected me to live up to his standard, not anybody else's standard." Mitsutaka admonished his son to "work hard, study hard." The high expectations were a pressure on Russell but ultimately perhaps the highest compliment Mitsutaka could bestow upon his son. By contrast, whenever Taka got into trouble his father would shrug, *sho ga nai*, what can you do? And leave it at that.

Misao remembers her brother as "the intellectual one, always reading. [He was] persistent but patient in whatever [he] did and [a]

---

4. I had to chuckle though: Grandpa complained that he only had 1-2 trousers to wear as a child. And now, by choice, that's all he wears anyways.

rascal too." Namiyo teases Russell about reading so much in the bathroom that he kept the family "waiting with our legs crossed and our bodies contorted from an excruciating need to use the bathroom, screaming for Mom to help us get you out of there." Namiyo nicknamed him "Bug," short for humbug, because of his inquisitive nature, always asking, "why?" and, "how?" adding that everything he did, he did well.

Remarkably, growing up in Puukolii was a relatively happy time. As a child, Russell would wake up in the morning alone, his parents and older siblings all gone off to work or school. He fixed his own breakfast, usually *gohan,* rice, cabbage and eggs. Sometimes they raised their own chickens and grew their own vegetables such as lettuce and ginger. A trip to the mountainside to pick guava for juice and jam was a common activity. Russell also loved eating sugar cane, sucking the sweet juice out of the thick fibers. Even as he matured he never lost his sweet tooth. Other favorite meals were pot-roasted chicken, potato macaroni salad and *saimin* noodles. Most every Sunday the family went to Grandpa Koyamas and ate chicken *hekka* and the occasional special treat of Howdy brand orange soda or home made ice cream.

During the 1920s Mitsutaka contracted a respiratory illness. There is some confusion in family records as to whether it was pleurisy or tuberculosis. Either way he was forced to live higher up the mountains of west Maui in the Honolua area where the cooler climate would help cure the disease.

Financially and emotionally this was a very trying time for the young family. Ever stoic, Kikuyo quietly shouldered the extra burden of being the sole breadwinner. Continuing to work in the fields she also began taking in laundry every weekend. Five or six large kettles were set over fires in their yard to boil the clothes clean, no small task since the majority of the wash was the well-soiled clothes of her co-workers. She then starched and ironed everything (remember there were no electric irons!), even patching clothes when necessary. When the girls got older, they helped in the home laundry business.

As if she didn't have enough work Kikuyo also raised pigs, butchering and selling the meat herself. Her stamina was amazing. Russell often commented how effortless his mother's motions were in completing tasks. When she worked in the kitchen it seemed that meals were ready quickly and with little fanfare. Russell calls it an economy of motion. In the fields the diminutive woman could outwork two full-grown men with seemingly little exertion.

Acknowledging everything his mother did for the family Russell shares, "She had spunk and a tough inner core. She had fortitude and really did well to support and sustain the family. She had about four years of schooling but she was smart." With a glint of distant reminiscence he adds, "[She] really worked her head off. We owe a lot to her."

Highly pragmatic, sentimentality was not a part of Kikuyo's nature. Once, when preparing to move to the new house in Lahaina, she burned years of old photographs. It was simply too much bother to cart them to the new place. She was a tough lady, often with a cigarette dangling from her lip, who didn't allow anyone or anything to push her around.

Kikuyo admonished her young son to "be the kind of person that people would remember when they need help in times of trouble" and telling him that "a true friend is one who enters your home when all others are sneaking out from the back door." It was something Russell never forgot. Another piece of advice she gave her son was "when the boss is making the rounds and comes to where you are working, pause to rest and talk to him. When he is gone you work as hard as you can so that when he comes around again he will see the results of your work. He will depend on you and trust you to get the work done even if he isn't around."

After two years in the hills, Mitsutaka was able to return home. Never noted for a robust constitution, the illness left him frailer than before. Though not well suited for physical labor, Mitsutaka received his high school education in Japan and was one of the few in the village who could read and write. Because of this he was able to procure employment at the Pioneer Mill company store (the only store in town) as a *chumontori,* clerk. In addition to maintaining the store ledgers, Mitsutaka's main job was to take orders from customers in the surrounding villages.[5] For this he was given use of the store's Model T Ford, which he was later able to purchase for himself. Russell guesses his father likely borrowed some money to do so, but doesn't know for sure.

With his newly acquired wheels Mitsutaka also began running a part-time taxi service from Puukolii down to Lahaina, charging fifty cents to a dollar. Occasionally Russell got to ride along on these trips, listening as his father sang folk songs like "*Naniwabushi*" as he drove. Russell enjoyed spending time with his father even though "there wasn't much to see." The young man also helped Mitsutaka in the yard and would "go around and do things with him."

Among his favorite memories are the times his father loaded him into the Model T and took him fishing under the guise of "putting food on the table." Once a month or more on Sundays, they would drive to Honolua, Honokowai or Kahana or wherever Papa felt like going, bait their hooks with shrimp, cast their lines into the ocean from the shore and fish until they caught enough rockfish, *kukupii,* perch, or *holehole* or whatever else sounded tasty to make a meal. "That's what dad did, he helped support the family by catching fish," Russell says. Russell adopted the saying, using it throughout his life as an excuse to go fishing. The tradition of fishing with his father continued until Russell left for vocational school nearly ten years later.

Wearing his best khaki pants and rice bag shirt, Russell began kindergarten at Puukolii Elementary. His first teacher was Mrs.

---

5. Mitsutaka was only responsible for taking orders, but did not do deliveries. His customers spoke mostly Japanese but all of the orders were placed in English.

Mookini, a petite Hawaiian lady. With a student body of just over 100 students, hosting grades 1–8, the elementary was roughly a ten-minute walk from the Horiuchi home. The school consisted of five separate buildings, four classroom units lined in a row and a teacher's cottage off to the side, all made of the same ubiquitous wooden slats. There was no heating or cooling in any of them.

The children were responsible for cleaning the school. Eventually a baseball field was built but the playground was minimal with few swings and a sandbox. There was no cafeteria so Russell either walked home for lunch or brought one to school with him. Papa usually cooked rice and cabbage for the children's meal since his work schedule was more flexible than Kikuyo's. Russell enjoyed his schooling. He shares that he "didn't understand grammar too well [but] did not flunk any subject."

Asked if he ever got into mischief in elementary school Russell explained that they still practiced corporal punishment so he "kept out of difficulty." He did get sent to the principal's office once "for something I did not do and also for teasing a girl. I once had chili pepper rubbed on my [tongue] because I was reported to have used a swear word—I don't know if I did—but two girls reported me."

One of the youngest in class and small for his age, Russell was shoved around quite a bit. At the playground when the kids divided into teams to play ball the older boys liked to play kind of dirty and slap Russell and the other smaller kids around. If he fought back the older boys would say, "Hey, you a small kid, why you want to play so rough for? I'd say to heck with it. I'm gonna get a beating but they're going to get a beating too."

Whenever Russell came home after a fight Kikuyo gave him a spanking. He wondered how she could tell every single time. Finally one day after a scrap he caught sight of himself in a mirror and saw the tell tale dirt scuffs and tear stains. From then on anytime he got into a scuffle he always washed up before he got home. He never got another spanking for fighting.

Russell wrestled with some of the other boys from time to time but describes himself mostly as a loner, often playing by himself, running barefoot around the house and neighborhood. He spent a lot of time at home doing chores such as cleaning the yard or dishes or tending the chickens. Russell's job was to stack the wood gathered from the Kiave trees that grew down by the beach. "Lots of it," he says. There were plenty of chores for everyone, except Taka, who according to Russell, was never given much to do, and spent a lot of his time getting into trouble.

Russell remembers "the old Sears catalog was a source for me to do a lot of dreaming." He spent time looking at the wondrous toys but with no money or allowance he was forced to create his own fun. After school he would dig up worms and go fishing at the reservoir or go for a refreshing dip. Why not the beach? Roughly seven miles away it was too far for him to go and he very seldom made it to Lahaina city, especially as a kid.

For toys he made his own trains by stringing together soup and sardine cans or playing with an old tire. Once in a while he could scrape together materials to make a slingshot and go shoot birds, cats, and dogs or whatever happened to be around the neighborhood. Other times he went up the gulch by himself to pick mangos. He taught himself to swim "dog paddle" at the irrigation ditch and nearby reservoir, doing "quite a bit of 'skinny dipping.'" It could have been dangerous by himself, but one of the luxuries of being a child is not worrying about such things.

Playing marbles was another favorite activity, even though he wasn't very good. Taka was very good and often won other peoples marbles. Russell also remembers on rare occasions getting to go horseback riding at Mr. Okada's.

One highly anticipated event was the Maui County Fair held in Kahului. Russell found it hard to sleep the night before, thinking about the next day, excited about the treasure hunt and the chance to win a bicycle. Trucks took the school children to see the different and wondrous exhibits. Russell enjoyed watching the circus, and if the rare spare nickel or dime were available he enjoyed the treat of a hamburger or hot dog.

In first grade Russell started playing basketball in organized community league teams. At eight years old he played guard and occasionally forward. He continued to participate in community leagues up through 8th grade at the Alexander House Settlement. Named after early Wailuku missionary William Patterson Alexander the charitable organization provided educational and recreational opportunities for the youth in the area.

The leagues consisted of all local participants. The only games anyone traveled to were the championship games which were held on the other side of the island, roughly 40 miles away.

Russell enjoyed reading. There was no library at the time, so he consumed whatever he could find around the house. At one point Mitsutaka purchased a *Lincoln Encyclopedia* and Russell spent a lot of time pouring over the marvelous volumes. A rare but beloved treat was a copy of *Boy's Life*, the magazine of the Boy Scouts of America. Perhaps once a year or so Russell sneaked a ride on a plantation truck into town and bought himself one.

Russell's parents purchased a subscription to *Shonen Kurab*, a popular Japanese youth magazine, providing one of the few luxuries young Russell was able to enjoy. Its exciting adventure stories about samurai, entertaining comic strips and other interesting articles transported his eager mind to new and different places. Written entirely in Japanese characters, it was a credit to the young man that he could read both Japanese and English.

In the 1930s Russell remembers seeing a convoy of hundreds of military ships in the waters between Lahaina and Lanai. There were aircraft carriers, destroyers, mine layers, battleships, cruisers, and hospital ships. "It was quite a sight to see." He didn't know it at the time but it was the entire Pacific fleet coming into anchor. Pearl Harbor was too small for the whole armada so parts of it anchored at Lahaina instead.

Even as a child, Russell was fond of sitting and thinking. He dreamed about the Navy ships sailing around, pondering what it would be like to be a sailor. He never actually wanted to become a sailor, but he enjoyed reflecting on what it must be like. Even at this age he was practicing the ability to understand things from someone else's point of view.

Grandfather Koyama was able purchase one of the first radios in town and possibly the entire island. Kimiko Iwamura Figuerres recalls the Horiuchis "were the only ones who had a radio, a large cabinet type. It had so much static, but it was a novelty!" She and the Horiuchi sisters would lie on *futons* and listen to the miraculous sound of news and music late into the night. Russell remembers listening to programs such as "Hawaii Calls" and "Hilo Hattie." He enjoyed classical music "but did not fully understand it." How much time Russell spent listening is unknown but exposure to the broadcasts could only have increased his awareness of the broader world beyond the plantation.

Russell tells that around this time a vision of a woman's face appeared to him as if suspended in thin air. Later, about the time when he was graduating from high school, he was walking to do laundry and the same face appeared again. He shook it off and returned to work, paying it little mind. But that face would return to haunt him again.[6]

---

6. I teased Grandpa that Grandma had been haunting him since he was a kid. Either that or he was doing laundry and thinking, "Gee, it would be nice to have a wife." He chuckled.

2

NO KA 'OI

As CHILDHOOD ROUNDED TOWARDS EARLY adolescence new challenges and opportunities came into Russell's life. Around 12 he began working in the fields on days he wasn't in school. In the summer it was full time work. An entire day of weeding in the cane fields with a pick, shovel and hoe rewarded him with 20–30 cents in pay. An average adult male earned around 70 cents per day while women earned 50 cents, barely surpassing children's earnings. They were paid in cash once a month.[1]

It was an exhausting schedule for anyone, let alone for a 12-year old boy. One weekend in particular he wanted nothing more than to sleep in. His hopes were dashed by John Moir himself slamming the door open. "Wake up everybody! Kids, go to work! I'm not asking, I'm telling." This sort of thing happened on more than one occasion with Moir literally kicking the youngsters until they got out of bed. The harshness of life on the plantation spared no one, even the young. "They treated you like dogs." Bosses often grabbed people to work even on Sundays.

---

1. The plantations actually paid different nationalities different wages, part of an effort to sow disunity and prevent the labor force from organizing. To this end housing was also kept segregated. Wages were equalized in 1909 when the Japanese workers, constituting roughly 70% of the labor force, went on strike.

In the states child labor laws were a source of political debate off and on for decades. The Keatings-Owen Act was passed in 1916 only to be declared unconstitutional two years later and subsequently repealed. The Great Depression was in full swing causing massive changes in the work force. Grown adults were willing to work jobs even at children's wages. The lack of concrete child labor laws combined with Hawaii's relative isolation made such concerns feel worlds away, which in many ways they were. Moral and political argument aside, having the children work was a matter of practical survival. All the Horiuchi siblings worked and turned their paltry earnings over to their parents to help make ends meet.

And so most days, Russell rose early, dressing himself in the same manner as the other workers, except bare-footed. In addition to weeding he did participate some in the cane harvest, but most of it was done by the older laborers. The burning of the cane was performed by a regular crew dedicated specifically to that purpose. One of the areas the children helped was planting, cutting pieces of cane, placing it in furrows and covering it with the sun-kissed Hawaiian soil. As Russell grew older he also learned how to perform the irrigation as well.

Early adolescence also afforded Russell one of his most cherished pleasures in life. He was finally big enough to become his father's sparring partner in *Kendo*, the art of Japanese sword fighting. Russell grew up watching his father, an avid participant in the sport, practice nearly every morning. Getting to join his father was a dream he'd held since he could remember.

In *kendo*, participants duel using bamboo swords known as *shinai*, wearing armor made of heavy cloth padding and a metal facemask to protect themselves. The gear was costly and while Mitsutaka owned a set, Russell did not. However, to his great excitement, Russell did receive his own *shinai*. During practice the young man could hit his father but his father only tapped him gently.

Notably, Mitsutaka never sparred with Taka. This was one thing shared exclusively between the father and his *chonan*. Their practices were unsanctioned and Russell never trained under anyone but his father, and though he never received a belt, his skill eventually reached the equivalent of a first or second degree.

Both father and son had the opportunity to test their skills against competitors from neighboring clubs, traveling to tournaments in Lahaina and other nearby towns. Russell participated in these events with a borrowed set of armor, pairing up against other children and adults alike. To the pride of his father, Russell showed good promise, winning his share of matches.

Around the house the children spoke mostly pidgin, the lilting polyglot fused from the many languages that inhabited the islands. *You know da kine. Pau hana, time fo quit work!* With their parents the children spoke *Nihongo*, Japanese, and when they were in school it was English.

An important part of Russell's education was after school Japanese language lessons. Beginning in first grade and continuing through high school the classes were held six days a week. It was challenging to attend public school all day and then go to Japanese class from four to five every afternoon including Saturdays. The school was used by the Methodists to hold Sunday school. The one perk of language school, Russell remembers, was they gave presents to the students at Christmas time.

"Hardly anybody went except me," says Russell, but that didn't mean he enjoyed it. The class averaged three to four people and there was rarely anyone his age. Even his siblings didn't go. Out of all his brother and sisters, Russell was the only one who finished. In all honesty, he would have preferred to go play baseball.

One time he skipped class to go and do just that. When Shimamura Sensei, the language school principal, reported to Mitsutaka (another acquaintance through *kendo*) that his son had been truant, Russell received one of the few lectures his father ever gave him.

"Son, I think you'd better go back to school."

"Why am I the only one who has to go?" he protested.

"Because you are the number one son. You must go." Mitsutaka didn't chew Russell out, he spoke in soft tones but Russell knew he would brook no argument. Dutifully, Russell went and studied. He never could figure out why he was the only one his parents made go. "Looking back, it makes more sense," he says. There was no way at the time he could have known the immeasurable impact his developing skill would have on his future.

When he was twelve Russell happened to walk by a gathering of other boys around his age. It seemed interesting so he peeked his head in. It turned out to be a Boy Scout meeting headed by a fellow named Shigeru Omura, who happened to work in the plantation store with Russell's father.

Described by Russell as a "decent man and a good scoutmaster," Omura was a Puukolii native from an athletic family. His younger brother was a powerhouse *sumotori*, a sumo wrestler, and Shigeru himself was an excellent pole vaulter. Omura, who would serve as scoutmaster for over a decade, encouraged young Russell to join. Russell modestly claims he "sort of fell into things just by chance." His humility no doubt belies a keen interest once he got involved.

He later wrote, "Boy Scouting was a salvation." Blessed with a sharp, intuitive mind the young man found the opportunity to gain new knowledge appealing. Despite the fact that there were not many kids from his community he really enjoyed it.

Meetings were held weekly, and they occasionally went camping either on the beach, which he particularly liked, or in the nearby mountains. With only a blanket in lieu of a sleeping bag he "got cold at night" but enjoyed himself anyway.

Mitsutaka and Kikuyo were never actively involved in Russell's scouting career but they did make sure he was able to go to summer camp, one of the highlights of Russell's year. Usually held in Wailuku Valley at Camp Maluhia, scouts came from all over the islands to participate, some traveling several hours by ship. Some even traveled overnight. It was a great time to mingle with other scouts and work on merit badges. Russell earned most of his merit badges at these camps.

Through his own volition Russell began advancing through the scouting ranks, earning his Eagle when he was nearly seventeen. He was the first in Puukolii to do so, beating out even Omura, the scoutmaster, to the prestigious rank. Russell felt his Eagle opened doors of opportunity for him later in life. A proud Mitsutaka had the pleasure of presenting the award to his son. Namiyo still has a book of scouting songs Russell compiled.

Through scouting Russell was first introduced to people such as Eddie Okazaki and Jim Ota. Eddie was not a member of the church at the time. Jim was married to a Korean wife and was a scout executive in Wailuku in charge of scouting on the whole island. Russell served as an assistant scoutmaster with Jim.

Besides scouting Russell also participated in the 4H Club and began to learn the simple joy of gardening.

Lahainaluna High School was located a little over seven miles from the Horiuchi household and it was here that Russell claimed his alma mater. Lahainaluna wasn't the largest of the three schools on the island but it was certainly the most steeped in history. Founded in 1832 as a Protestant missionary school, Lahainaluna claims the distinction of being the oldest high school west of the Rockies.

Consisting of multiple buildings connected by winding walkways shaded by lush tropical plants and trees, the school stands on the side of a volcanic hill. From its vantage point you can see the Pacific Ocean as well as several neighboring islands, including Molokai. Most of the buildings were built of wood but a few were made of brick as well and, according to Russell, "They all looked really old." Lahainaluna is one of the few high schools that receives boarders and some of the buildings served as dormitories.

The student body at the time consisted of a few hundred students. The school mascot, then as now, is the Luna, literally meaning high or above in Hawaiian and colloquially used to mean a plantation foreman or boss. The bold school colors of red, white and black reflect its motto *O keia ke kukui pio'ole I ka makani O kaua'ula*, meaning "number one in pride and spirit since 1831" in Hawaiian. "O ka Malu 'ulu o Lele (No e ka 'oi)" goes the first line of the school song, one which Russell never forgot.

Since there were no buses, families with students commonly pooled rides to school, with everyone pitching in two to three dollars a month. People with cars, including Misao's husband, Masayuki Sodetani, took turns driving. Mitsutaka never drove the children in his Model T because work began too early in the morning. Carpooling was a bit of a luxury and something the family couldn't always afford (students also paid for their own books), so Russell often made the long walk on foot. Still, he considered himself lucky because some people walked every day.

According to Russell he was not an exemplary student (although his sister Namiyo's account differs!). Although most topics came easily to him he says he didn't like most of his classes, sometimes due to the subject and sometimes due to the teacher. He did well in his math and history and he studied hard for his civics teacher who was also the football coach because "he was hardnosed and [Russell] was scared of him." As for the rest of his courses, he said "hang it." He never brought his homework with him after school, instead finishing what he could in class then leaving the rest. "No place to study," he shrugs then admits using that as an excuse for not really caring at that age.

His meager efforts didn't slide by unnoticed. His physics teacher pulled him aside one day and chewed him out. "What's a matter?" the teacher spoke to him in pidgin, "You score da 90s on that test. All da rest in the class in the 50s. I know what you doing, you not studying."

In all likelihood Russell is being modest about the amount of work he finished during school hours. Despite never bringing his homework home he managed passing grades and made it into the Honor Society his senior year, the only one in his family to do so.

Russell remembers Mrs. Sherwood, one of his English teachers. She liked him because he did well in her class. "She was a real *Haole*," Russell recalls, "blonde and stately." Years later she moved to Indio, California and, quite by chance, became a good friend of Hisako Mori Shibata, Russell's future sister-in-law.

Another teacher that stood out in Russell's memory was Mrs. Hattie Foster. She taught English and Social Studies and her husband worked on a submarine. Russell didn't do "all that great" in class but Mrs. Foster liked the young Japanese boy and he respected her because he felt she was his best teacher.

Born Hattie Jane Dimond, Mrs. Foster was from a far away and exotic sounding place called Ogden, Utah. When people learned that she was Mormon, "Everyone was shocked," tells Russell, who wondered how such a bright teacher could be a Mormon. He didn't know anything about Mormons, only heard they were different. That was the first contact Russell remembers with anyone from the LDS faith.

Mrs. Foster also asked Russell to fill the sports editor position for the high school annual. He hardly ever went to the sporting events but she knew he was bright and could do the job.

Although from two completely different worlds, Hattie and Russell's father unknowingly shared one thing in common: both had run-ins with the Pioneer Mills manager. Moir made it clear that he wanted everyone to work on the plantation after they graduated from school. Hattie, outspoken and brave, was gutsy enough to tell Moir off, saying that the kids should go on to college and move on to bigger and better things. Apparently there was a pretty good argument over the matter.

Russell "fantasized all the time of being a great athlete but knew [his] limitations." Feeling he was too small to participate in high school athletics Russell instead chose to play basketball and baseball in the community leagues. The divisions were made according to size and weight and Russell was assigned to play lightweight. He was small but fast and enjoyed it. Baseball was a particular favorite and Russell followed the Saint Louis Cardinals when he could.

The coach of his community team was Russell Eldridge. Of mixed Hawaiian descent, Mr. Eldridge was a Lahaina local and a good friend of the Horiuchi family, often helping the family around the house doing yard work and other chores. A year younger than Mitsutaka, Russell remembers him as "an athletic football player," a sport Mr. Eldridge played along with his brother. And, although young Russell didn't know at the time, Mr. Eldridge also happened to be LDS. The strength of Mr. Eldridge's friendship, his loyalty and kindness stuck with Russell for the rest of his life.

Russell never dated in high school, mostly because he didn't have any money or a car. He attended school dances and girls sometimes passed him notes and he passed them notes back but nothing ever really came of the flirtation. When asked if he remembers any girl in particular he shrugs and says he doesn't think those things should be written.

One of Russell's friends from this time was Hideo Kanetsuna, who was his neighbor across the street in Puukolii. It turns out Hideyo was also LDS and eventually wound up serving as a missionary in the Tokyo temple. Russell also used to play occasionally with Ralph Shino, though Ralph grew up in Honokowai so they didn't get together often outside of grade school. He and Ralph would run into one another in Tokyo again as well.

In spite of these friends, Russell mostly remained a loner. Drinking and gambling, popular indulgences of his peers, held no interest for him. He didn't care for the taste of alcohol and "saw too many make fools of themselves" under its influence. He hated smoking, especially cigars because of the stink, even though his mother could often be found with a cigarette. He confesses to trying a rolled Bull-Durham once but was put off by the foul smell. He felt the kids who were drinking or smoking were doing it to show off. Besides, he claims he was too busy working in the yard or cleaning up the house.

Overall high school "did not thrill" Russell, who says he made it through because he thought that it was the end of the road. One thing was for certain: by the time high school graduation rolled around in 1940 Russell knew he wanted to get away from plantation life and its "oppressive regimentation" as he called it. Even the graduation ceremony itself served as a reminder why—neither of his parents came, having to work instead.

Looking back Russell expresses deep felt gratitude to his parents. They didn't have much but they did everything that was necessary to provide for their family. They may not have been able to buy toys or fancy clothes but they put a roof over their family's heads and food on the table and they made way for Russell to attend vocational school and expand his future.

Russell made the choice to attend Honolulu Trade Tech on Oahu and was pleasantly surprised when his parents supported his decision. If his parents hadn't agreed he would have stayed on the plantation and worked. He was nervous about leaving the comfort and familiarity of home but felt that it was the right thing to do.

The first hurdle was passing the entrance exam. Russell wasn't even sure if he could get accepted. Roughly one hundred and fifty people took the test. He surprised himself by earning one of the highest scores.

The second and larger challenge was paying for everything. The vocational school was state run so tuition was free but room and board cost $25 a month. It was a lot of money and difficult for Russell and his parents to come by. Russell's oldest sister, Kay, came to his rescue. By this time she was running her own beauty parlor in Lanai and was earning enough that she could help. With her generous offer in place, Russell packed his bag and headed out into the wide-open future.

At age 17, now grown into his full adult height and weight of 5'6", 160 pounds, Russell boarded a ship bound for Oahu. Kikuyo went along with him, the two of them riding overnight to reach Honolulu. It was the first time he remembers his mother showing active interest in what he wanted to do. She had always supported Russell but even more so now that he had expressed intent to make something of himself.

Russell spoke with relatives and others about the school before enrolling but he still left Lahaina without knowing what he was going to study or even where the school was.

On arrival they caught a streetcar to the Nakamura Hotel on Beretania Street. The Nakamuras were relatives on his Koyama *Oji-isan*'s, Grandfather's, side who kindly set up an apartment where he could stay. Even with Kay's generous help cash was tight. To get around Russell walked everywhere. Sometimes Russell could find an odd job here or there and save enough to buy lunch, but just as often he went without.

Russell stayed at the hotel for several months before moving in with Auntie Kimiko, his mother's sister. Kimiko was newly married and she and her husband, Jiro, were living in a cottage in the backyard of Jiro's sister's house on Vineyard Street, about a block from Punahou High School. Jiro's sister was married to Dr. Seto, a Chinese-American thyroid specialist.

The cottage was austere but Russell was glad he could stop borrowing money from Kay. He still paid a little bit to Kimiko and Jiro, whatever he could at the time. Once he started working he paid full, even helping to pay half of the expenses for the birth of the couple's first child.

It was here in Honolulu that the young man from Puukolii began going by the name Russell. The name Nozomi, whether intentional or not, often ended up as *nezumi*, meaning mouse, an unflattering nomenclature for a boy already sensitive about his size. The name was chosen because he respected Russell Eldridge from Puukolii and he liked the name.

Once in school, Russell was finally able to think about what discipline he was going pursue. He opted to enroll in the two-year electrical equipment repair program where he learned to rewind motors and the intricacies of wiring. His fingers were thin and strong, perfect for the job and Russell discovered he had a natural ability for working with his hands.

Russell's most memorable instructor was the electrical teacher, Ernest Kanderson, a 5'8" Latvian immigrant who spoke English with a slight accent. He was not a very outspoken man, perhaps because of his broken English, but he was highly skilled. He quickly recognized Russell's talent and took special interest in the young man When difficult jobs came through, Ernest would call on Russell because he knew he could handle it.

The school featured several different programs. Russell remembers the dress making area of the school was host to some pretty Chinese girls. He never spent much time there, but he definitely looked as he passed by. Russell says he never interacted much with them, but some details stick with you, no matter what your age.

When student body elections rolled around, Norima Horimoto, a fellow student majoring in auto mechanics made a bid for student body president and asked Russell to run as his vice-president. Norima was from Honolulu and the two *Nisei* got along well. Russell realized he was doing all right in school, so he thought, "Why not?" The pair won the election and Russell got his first experience working in a leadership position.

The school traditionally held an annual speech contest. Students addressed an audience of a little over 100 people including the instructors, who acted as judges. On a lark, Russell decided to enter. It is unclear whether the theme was assigned or if he chose it of his own accord but he spoke on the topic of patriotism.

The year was 1941, two years since the German war machine began its relentless march, and the world was in turmoil. The U.S. was not yet involved in the war, but bloodshed was raging across Europe and brewing in the East. Even Hawaii, isolated by thousands of miles of ocean would not avoid it for long. The tides of war seemed far off, but they were rising.

Russell's oration must have hit the right chords. He outshone the other contestants for a clear win. The four-foot cup standing in the school trophy case now proudly bore his name. His eloquence was evident from an early age, but where it came from no one knows. He didn't get it from his parents, both the strong, silent type. Perhaps it came from being small as a child. When he got mad he wasn't able to rely on his physicality, so he was forced to rely on his verbal skills to deal with situations. Ultimately, Russell credits the Lord for giving him "the gift of gab."

Academically, Russell did very well. In high school he hardly cracked his books. "Study for what?" he asked, "To go work on a plantation?" He could never see the point of it. Now in community college he had both reason and interest to apply himself to his studies, which he did, earning himself the top spot in his class.

Russell also continued to be active in the scouting program. The local scoutmaster was a man named Jack Hirano, a *Nisei* who did well as the owner of a typewriter repair shop. Jack was impressed with the 17-year-old Eagle and asked Russell to become assistant scoutmaster. Occasionally Jack treated Russell to lunch, something the young man really appreciated.

During Russell's first summer in Honolulu, Ernest Kanderson found a job for him canning pineapple at the American Can Company. It was nothing glamorous but it was an actual, honest to goodness job. For the past year he had survived on very little, often skipping lunch because he couldn't afford the expense. Now that he was working he could manage things much better.

NO KA 'OI

Between school, work, and scouting, Russell's life was an extremely busy one, but at least he was off the plantation and heading in a direction he felt good about. Possibilities for the future filled his mind like never before and in time he would indeed go on to greater things. But not before a day of infamy would come, changing the face of the world forever.

A young girl, no more than five, her jet-black hair cut in a short bob, darts across a dirt road into a rice field. She bears the distinctive light tan and beautiful almond eyes that mark her Japanese descent. The year is 1930, fifteen years before the cataclysmic events that will alter the course of her life.

There are wars and rumors of wars in far off places, but none of that is of any concern to her now. Her mind reels with a fervent curiosity and joy of life that will remain with her for the rest of her years. Flush with the bliss of innocence, her boundless energy carries her as she runs, playing games in the warm, humid air of a summer afternoon in Tokyo.

3

AIKO

T ODAY THE TOWNSHIP OF YAGUCHI Machi lies in the middle
of Ota-Ku where it has been absorbed into the greater Tokyo megalopolis. Formerly known as Kamata-ku, the name was
changed after the war with only the local *eki*, train station, still
bearing the original name. Like most of the urban sprawl that
makes up the Tokyo region it is a twisting maze of train tracks and
narrow roads tucked in between densely packed and seemingly
endless stores and homes.

But when Yoshio Mori (1890–1972) was growing up in the early
part of the twentieth century Yaguchi Machi was an agricultural
area filled with *tanbo*, rice paddies, and plenty of wide-open
spaces for a child to roam. Buildings were sparse and only a sprinkling of homes stood scattered between fields.

Yoshio was an orphan. The young boy knew he was born in the
Minami Higakubo, Azabu district of Tokyo on March 18. The remaining circumstances of his birth, including his parentage remained a mystery.

Shortly after his birth Yoshi was fostered into the Tozo Mori family.
The Mori family name is a very old one. There are three different
clans, centered in Kagoshima, Sendai and Musashi-no-Kuni, now
known as Tokyo. Tozo's family was an offshoot of the Chotaro
Mori family, which hailed from the Tokyo and Kanagawa Prefec-

tures and was known as the *honke*, meaning "original family." They were very wealthy with extensive properties reaching as far as Okurayama, which they rented out to tenant farmers. The *honke* also opened a post office near the train station.

When Yoshio was ten years old, an *atotsugi*, adoption to perpetuate the family name, was arranged. His name was changed to Yoshizo and he was officially adopted by Hachigoro Mori (1866-1936) and his wife, Mume Saji (1867-1927). The adoption also served to revive the Toyemon Mori household, a line threatened with extinction due to having no heirs.

Never having children of their own, Hachigoro and Mume were not always understanding of Yoshizo's youthful behavior. One time Yoshizo and his foster brother Kintaro went to a festival and, as youth are wont to do, lost track of the time. They returned late to find that Hachigoro had locked all of the doors. Yoshizo pounded on the door, but his parents never answered and he spent the night in the shack behind the house. He later confessed he was so young at the time that he didn't have the sense to go back to Kintaro's house for the night.

Yoshizo attended school in the next village until the fourth grade, which was the mandatory minimum at the time. He took the high school entrance exam and was accepted but Hachigoro was not supportive. Yoshizo persisted and was finally told he could go to school but he had to pay for his own uniform, a mandatory item. As Hachigoro undoubtedly knew, Yoshizo didn't have the money and was compelled to give up his dream of an education.

However, Yoshizo's desire for learning never faded. On his own he studied English and was able to speak the language, something very rare for the time. Throughout his life he carried a curiosity and a desire to learn, both traits he passed on to his descendents. He often mentioned that he wished he could have continued his schooling.

Yoshizo and Hatsu encouraged all of their children to attend school, even when it was difficult with several children going at the same time. Ultimately, all of his children not only graduated from high school but also earned college degrees or post-secondary training.

At the time, young men were obligated to serve time in the military. Yoshizo served in the *Konoe kiheitai*, Imperial cavalry. His daughter Aiko remembers a photo of him hanging in her parent's room, her father looking very handsome in his uniform riding on a horse.

As a man Yoshizo was regarded as well built and at nearly six feet was taller than most others. This no doubt lent to the general air of distinction he carried about him. Aiko remembers riding on a streetcar with her father. There was a bench designated for five people but only four were sitting, taking up the entire space. Yoshizo told them to make room and he sat his daughter on the seat. She remembers being embarrassed but everyone complied without protest.

Volunteer work and civic duty were also important parts of Yoshizo's life. There was no fire department nearby so the neighborhood organized their own. Yoshizo served as assistant chief, responding whenever there was a fire. Once, when a fire destroyed a nearby house, the area was cordoned off with a policeman set to keep curious onlookers out. Yet when Yoshizo stepped across the rope to look around he moved with such authority that the policeman didn't protest.

Early on, Yoshizo helped his father on the farm but developed an interest in real estate, eventually becoming very successful at negotiating properties for large companies.

In keeping with tradition, Yoshizo's marriage was arranged through a *miai kekkon*, matchmaker. On March 14, 1914 he was married to Hatsu Kitajima (1896–1974).

Hatsu's father, Fusasaburo (1860–1930), was a Mori, though from a different bloodline than Tozo. His wife was Aka Kitajima (1864–1943). In Japan if a bride's family has no male heirs, often the groom will take her family name instead. This tradition, which originated to preserve family lines, is called *mukoyoshi* or *yoshi* for short. Aka had two brothers who both passed away very early, so when she and Fusasaburo were wed he became a Kitajima.

Even though Yoshizo and Hatsu both shared portions of the same patriarchal lineage they were not blood relatives. The exact details of how Yoshizo's and Hatsu's match was initiated are unclear but family lore suggests that since Hatsu's mother and Tozo's adopted mother were sisters they made the arrangement. Because there were not many people living in the village it is likely the young couple at least knew of each other growing up. Hatsu mentioned she attended sewing classes in the same neighborhood where Yoshizo lived and they might have met around that time.

Standing about 4'11" with large, deep-set almond eyes, Hatsu was the fourth child of seven with three older brothers and two younger brothers and a sister. Her name means "the first," given because she was the first girl in the family. Hatsu's father Jiroemon was a successful farmer and her grandfather on her mother's side was a sword merchant before the Meiji period. Hatsu was sent to a *gyogi minarai*, or finishing school in Nihonbashi where she learned to use proper language and excellent manners. As a result she was rather strict with her daughters when it came to etiquette. She always dressed in a traditional *kimono*, forgoing simpler western style clothing until well into her later years, and even then only in the summer when it was hot.

Hatsu was spunky and an ideal match for Yoshizo. Like him, her formal schooling ended at the fourth grade because she was needed on the farm. Also like her husband, she thirsted for knowledge and was self-educated, devouring whatever reading she could find throughout her life. She never went to bed without first reading the newspaper or a magazine, feeling it was important to know what was happening in the world.

A devoutly religious woman, evidences of Shintoism were found in corners of Hatsu's home. Each morning Hatsu brought an *o-chawan,* bowl of rice, and water to the small family *butsudan,* shrine, kept in the dining area. Hatsu prayed to her ancestors every morning, lighting incense and clapping. She also frequented the various shrines located throughout the area to pay homage.

Yoshizo, who never complimented lightly, once stated that had she been given the opportunity Hatsu would have become highly accomplished at anything she pursued. Intelligent and motivated, Hatsu worked hard and dedicated her life to her family.

The couple's first child arrived in 1915, a beautiful baby girl whom they named Yae (1915–1939). She was followed by their first and only son Ichiro (1918–2009), their *chonan.* Two more girls followed after: Hiroko (Kikuchi) (1921–1979) and Shige (Mori) (1923). Keeping with tradition Yoshizo's parents lived with the family as well. With four children, grandparents and frequent guests the home was always brimming with people.

The large wooden house sat next to a garden on a triangle-shaped property surrounded by a fence. The front of the plot faced one road, *omote dori,* while the back faced the other, *ura dori,* while the third side butted up against the neighbors. The family used both front and rear gates as entrances.

On December 27, 1925 a fifth child was born into this busy household. She was aptly named Aiko, or child of love. Japanese names are chosen only after a great deal of consideration. Parents want to ensure their child's name meets divine approval, taking into account a variety of factors including the number of brush strokes it takes to write the *kanji* characters. Oddly, even though Yoshizo and Hatsu made sure that the strokes in their newborn daughter's name carried an auspicious count, when Grandfather Mori filled out Aiko's name on the official records he wrote it in *hiragana* characters instead of *kanji*. Even though it changed the number of strokes he was worried that later on she might not be able write out the complicated lettering herself. Ironically, Aiko went on to study Japanese calligraphy becoming known for her elegantly rendered *kanji* characters.

New Year's is an important holiday season for the Japanese. Families prepared by cleaning their houses and making delicious feasts for family and guests. It was a wonderful time of year but also a busy one. It must have been a challenge for Hatsu, in her last month of pregnancy, working to get everything ready.

In Japan at the time age was counted by the year you were born, not by the month. So when New Year's came, Aiko was counted as one year old, even though she was born only the week before. Hatsu wanted to register her birthday as Jan 1, 1926 but it would have changed the baby's astrological sign so the date was left as it was.

On New Year's Day, family and neighbors greeted each other with *akemashite omedeto gozaimasu*, Happy New Year! In most areas visiting friends and family was common on the first, but in the Tokyo area the day was customarily reserved for the family, while visitors and guests were received on the second.

The Japanese didn't celebrate Christmas but shared a similar practice of gift giving at New Year's. Aiko's family gathered together wearing the new clothes they received to sip *otoso*, sweet rice wine, and eat fresh *mikan*, mandarin oranges. One of Aiko's favorite New Year's memories is seeing the entire living room, the largest room in the house, covered in freshly pounded *mochi* rice cakes set out to cool and dry for later use in traditional *ozoni* soup and other dishes.

After dinner, while the children played *hagoita*, similar to badminton, the adults took naps, read magazines or for an extra special treat, went to see a movie. Only Japanese films were available at the time, nothing foreign, but the theaters made it a point to bring

10 of 442

especially good or favorite films for the holidays. Yoshizo enjoyed a good card game and also liked billiards when given the chance to play.

Other activities might include playing *karuta*, a word matching card game using *hyakunin isshu*, which were poems from the Heian period (794–1193). They would divide into two groups and challenge each other, spreading out the cards while one person read the first half of a poem. Players would then try and pick up the card with the second half on it. The team with the most matches at the end won. You needed to know your own cards as well as the opposing team's, so the children worked diligently at memorizing the poems.

The house was larger than average, constructed of wood with *shoji*, rice paper and wood sliding doors, and *tatami* mats for flooring. There was no central plumbing or heating and the family kept warm during the cold winters by bundling up and using *hibachi* foot warmers in their beds. Ichiro had his own room and the girls shared a room together.

Hatsu was a dutiful wife and daughter-in-law, caring for the needs of her seven children and in-laws. With eleven people under one roof, keeping everyone fed and the house clean was more than a full time job. Her youngest daughters remember being chased out of the kitchen where Hatsu usually spent her time cooking the meals and cleaning for the large family. Her hands were constantly engaged—mending, darning and washing. It was only in later years that her daughters realized how much Hatsu disliked sewing. She would do any job around the house but when it came to sewing she sent it out to someone else whenever she could. Because of this most of the families clothes were store bought.

Hisa remembers their mother got her hair fixed at the beauty shop. Hatsu's mother, Aka, often came over to help around the house but she always left before Yoshizo came home from work, since he didn't approve of his mother-in-law being around when he was home.

Yoshizo was able to provide well for his family and Hatsu was able to convince him to hire some domestic help. Laundry women came twice a week to help with the washing. The family was considered upper middle class. Wanting to ensure that meant classy on the inside as well, Hatsu was very careful to instruct her children never to judge people by their outward appearance and set the example by taking excellent care of the help. Her treatment was such that the help never forgot Hatsu. After the war one domestic who raised chickens brought fresh eggs to the family, a real treat at a time when food was scarce.

Hatsu was very welcoming and her home was open to everyone. Guests were frequent around the house. Once when some of Ichiro's military friends had a few days leave but couldn't afford to go home to Aomori or Hokkaido, they all spent a day together at the Mori household, eating, drinking and laughing.

When Shigeko went to college, she took sewing classes and made clothing for her sisters. One year one of Shige's classmates, a Korean girl unable to travel home for the year-end holidays, stayed with them for New Years. She brought a traditional Korean dress with her, in all likelihood a *hanbok*, and all the girls took turns trying on the dress and taking pictures.

For young Aiko having so many people around was normal. Most of their relatives lived close by and the children played together often. One of her cousins told her she was always excited to go the Mori house because there were so many girls there laughing and having fun. Aiko's memories are filled with happy times playing, fighting and simply being a kid.

Aiko was born in the year of the ox. She cried a lot from colic, but otherwise was a happy baby, even though Hatsu said she didn't really smile until she was almost three years old (she hasn't stopped smiling since!). Three years after Aiko was born another daughter came, Hisako (Jean Shibata) (1928–2013) and then in 1934 Kyoko (Tanaka-Fujiyama Partovi) ((1934-) was born, the seventh and final child.

Hiroko, quiet and introverted, was usually found helping her mother in the kitchen. Kyoko was still a toddler so when Aiko went out to play it was usually she and Shige. Hisa tagged along sometimes as well, but often she was a "chicken" (as Aiko would tease her) and would stay home to play with her dolls.

A self-described tomboy at heart, Aiko never wanted to play with dolls. She preferred climbing trees, running or playing ball. She played a lot of hide-and-seek in the bamboo forest down the hill from the house or *ishikeri*, the Japanese version of hopscotch. She did participate in quieter games as well, playing tea, using pieces of wood or leaves for cups.

Gutsy from the start, Aiko and Shigeko were the only ones who would stand up to their older brother, Ichiro, who Aiko described as "domineering." He didn't hesitate to beat her up, but she fought back through her tears. When asked if she remembers any particular fights with her brother she laughs, "There was a pillar in the house. He chased me running around the pillar, around and around." She doesn't remember what sparked the altercation but she remembers the chase and staying just out of her brother's reach. "He wanted to hit me but he couldn't catch me. Sometimes mother would interfere, usually she just lets it go because it happens all the time. If it gets too noisy she says *yamenasai* like most moms." If the children misbehaved there was usually a spanking but it wasn't a common event. Aiko still bears the scar from a burning punk that was placed on her back in an effort to make her be a quiet and meek girl. In her own words, "it didn't work out." Shigeko fondly remembers Aiko was the only sister she had as a fighting partner since Hisa and Kyoko were too young.

Usually though Ichiro and his sisters got along well. Ichiro learned ghost stories from some English books. The girls insisted he tell them the stories even though it frightened them till they screamed. Aiko says the only thing that scared her as a child was walking down the long, dark hallway to the bathroom at night.

The family was fond of dogs. When the children were young they owned a red, short-haired dog. Aiko went with her sisters and her father to his friend's place to get a puppy. Yoshizo carried the puppy home on the train in the breast of his coat. "Later we had another dog who was killed by a streetcar and everyone cried. Shigeko especially took it hard."

Much later when Kyoko, grown and married, had a dog named Duffy she couldn't keep in her house, she asked her parents to take care of it. Their father loved the dog and spoiled him so much he became overweight. Yoshizo slept in a traditional Japanese *tatami* mat room with his *futon* bed in the center of the room. Duffy's *futon* was kept right next to him where they both slept "like warlords." By this time Hatsu had arthritis in her knees and slept in a Western-style bed in the next room because it was easier to get in and out of.

Parenting was handled in the customary manner of the time. Yoshizo rarely interfered with the children's affairs and the children spent most of their time with their mother. If something needed to be communicated Hatsu would convey the message to Yoshizo. Aiko doesn't ever remember being scolded by her father, only her mother. Still, she has many fond memories of her father.

Yoshizo had a taste for quality. His hair was kept trim with regular visits to the barber. He bordered on being a clotheshorse and enjoyed wearing nice suits, especially western style three-piece suits. Everything was tailored, even in later years his suits were made to fit and often accented by a nice fur collared coat in the winter.

In addition to suits Yoshizo possessed a penchant for fine furniture even though Japanese homes were typically sparse. Aiko remembers having many desks and chests of drawers about the house. Yoshizo purchased a desk and chair for each of the children in addition to his own. Other furnishing included a low, traditional Japanese style black teak wood table in the guest room and a long Japanese style dinner table where everyone sat on *zabuton* floor cushions to eat.

Aiko's father owned a bamboo flute, which he played at festival times, usually with a group performing some type of sacred music.

Yoshizo was also very civic minded. A fairly large, well-trafficked wooden bridge in the area developed a hole in it large enough to break someone's leg. When it appeared no one from the city or otherwise was going to fix it, Yoshizo took lumber and repaired it himself so that no one would get hurt.

He was fond of his garden and worked to keep it nice. He put decorative moss on the grounds and got upset when people walked on it. Every morning he could be found in his yard using a long stick with a nail on the end to pick up fallen leaves from the stepping-stones. A skilled handyman, Yoshizo built a small garden terrace for himself where he could enjoy a cold beer. When a traveling theater came through town and set up shop in the field in back of the house Yoshizo made a ladder and attached it to the persimmon tree so the children could climb up and see.

Some of the relatives were dancers and Yoshizo took the girls to their rehearsals. Aiko remembers getting the nervous giggles once, upsetting her father who told her sternly that, "I'll not bring you any more to this kind of stuff."

Hisako remembers another time, when Kyoko was still very little, their father ordered western style dresses made for each of his daughters with flounces in a soft pink and white chiffon fabric. They looked so stunning wearing identical dresses that he insisted on a photograph.

Yoshizo was well respected and trusted in the business community. Aiko remembers seeing her father counting large stacks of money in his office. The children wanted to go to Yamagata for summer vacation but their father hadn't agreed to it. When Aiko saw the money she asked, "Is that for us to go to Yamagata?" To her disappointment it was for business transactions. There were no checks or credit cards at the time and all deals were conducted in cash. Companies trusted Yoshizo with their money. He built such a reputation for honesty and trustworthiness that in his later years large, respected corporations such as Mitsubishi would send private cars to take him to their negotiations.

Like many Japanese the family never owned a car of their own, relying instead on Japan's superb public transportation system. The nearest station was a stone's throw away and, if the trains weren't sufficient they could always call a taxi.

As for the summer trip to Yamagata, the children were eventually allowed to go, but the funds came from Yoshizo's own pocket.

Another fond memory of Aiko's, when she was eight or nine, is the time her father took everyone to Omori, well known at the time for its seafood. The family dined in a restaurant by the seashore, sitting around a long table cracking open crab shells and gobbling up the tender morsels. They usually didn't go too far from the house, so this was an exciting excursion.

In the summer, Yoshizo would take the family to the nearby Tamagawa river, where Aiko learned to swim. The children would play and pick young *tsukushi* plants, which you could cook.

This was before the factories that would dominate the area were built and the water was still un-polluted and good for swimming. The children swam along with their father all the way across, an experience Aiko describes as "kind of scary, because it was so wide. Maybe because I was small. We had a good time." Still very young, Aiko would hang onto her father, who reminded her of "a horse swimming in the water."

At home in Tokyo, Aiko's grandfather, Hachigoro, always sat near the *hibachi* heater, where it was warm. Aiko remembers being scolded when the ball she and some other children were playing with went into the red-berried *manryo* plant he was raising in the back yard.

Aiko vaguely recalls Hachigoro's funeral. The body, washed and dressed in white, was placed in a traditional sitting pose, not in a coffin. She remembers "white triangle stuff" around his head, likely the headband placed on the deceased in Buddhist tradition. Though cremation was common, Hachigoro was buried, a practice still common before and during the war.

The neighborhood children, including Hiroko and Shigeko, often played in the morning before walking together to Yaguchi-Nishi elementary school, about fifteen minutes from her house. Aiko loved to stop and catch the small frogs that populated the fields along the way, still managing to make it to school on time.

Aiko was a natural leader of children her age both at home and at school, always serving as class president or vice president throughout her school years. One of her duties was helping line up the students in the morning so the principal could greet them before school started.

In third grade, Aiko was occasionally asked by her teacher Arai *Sensei*[1] to find out what time it was. The only clock in the school was located in the small custodial office and she would ask the custodian, "*Ojisan, ima nanji?* What time is it?" This particular time she waited and waited but the custodian never returned. Aiko didn't want to tell the teacher that she couldn't tell time so she returned to class and told her teacher, "Pretty soon the bell will ring." The teacher said, "*Ah, so,*" okay, and Aiko sat down hoping her bluff was right! To her relief the bell rang shortly after.

The class was roughly 20–25 kids in size with one teacher in the classroom. There was a large dirt playground with no playground equipment, but Aiko enjoyed recess playing ball games. She didn't have a favorite subject in elementary school but did well in everything, although she disliked algebra. Once a year, in the fall, the school held *undokai*, exercise/sports day. It was an all day event

---

1. Aiko shares that Arai *Sensei* had two little girls and wanted to make cute sweaters and hats for them like Yae would make for the younger Mori sisters. Aiko also remembers Arai *Sensei* often asking her to wait after class, which she hated.

and parents packed *bento* lunch boxes and participated in the various events including races, baton touch, red ball, and games similar to basketball, but with a much smaller ball made out of white cloth. There was also a *fukei* race, which was a parent only race. Aiko really enjoyed *undokai*. Aiko wasn't the fastest runner but she always got a prize, such as a pencil or something so she was happy.

Another school event Aiko was partial to was the *gakugeikai* or school stage show, featuring singing, and dancing, often portraying popular children's stories such as *Momotaro no onitaiji*, Peach Boy, etc. All the parents came to see the production, and every student played a different role.

Like her mother, Aiko possessed an even temperament and generally got along with most people. There was one teacher, however, she strongly disliked. Every morning the students held their hands out over their desk while he checked to see if their nails were trimmed and they had brought a handkerchief, smacking the hand of any student that didn't pass muster with a ruler. It wasn't an uncommon practice at the time but his strictness bothered Aiko. He was from Yamagata Prefecture and she disliked his *zuzuben* accent. More than anything she hated the fact that he played favorites with his students. Aiko's family was well to do and her father was also on the area school board. Because of this she never experienced any problems with her teacher personally but not everyone in the class was so lucky.

The teacher treated children from poor families badly. She remembers one young girl was always a few minutes late because she worked in the morning selling *natto,* fermented soybeans, to help her family survive. The teacher made her stand in the corner of the classroom for the first hour every day. Aiko felt frustrated by the injustice and lack of compassion meted by the instructor.

The memory of this discrimination always bothered Aiko. A visit home in the late 1960s coincidentally lined up with a class reunion and this particular girl, now a full-grown woman, was there. Aiko was relieved to see that she seemed very happy and looked like she was doing well.

The fifth and sixth grades were very busy because of preparations for high school entrance exams. There were after school study sessions followed by more schoolwork when Aiko, now 11 or 12 years old, returned home. Her desk was situated next to Ichiro's, who was in college and he sometimes helped her with her lessons. Other times she'd be sleepy and he would get angry. "If you want to sleep, don't study!" So she would try to stay awake and cram.

When Aiko was in sixth grade, Japan invaded China, initiating the Sino-Japanese War. Aiko wrote an essay about it in school, but with the fighting across the sea in China, life in Japan carried on as usual and the reality of war remained a distant concept.

Things struck closer to home when Ichiro was drafted. The family never knew where he was stationed until after the war ended. In their limited correspondence they devised a simple code to slip through the censors. When Ichiro was in the north he wrote about snow, and in the south about the blossoms.

Hatsu's brother Tsunasaburo Kitajima hired an *o-inarisan,* soothsayer, to come to his home once a month. Whenever he came Hatsu visited to inquire about her son. The soothsayer reassured her that her son was alive and estimated where in China he was. Hatsu was such a believer in the *o-inarisan* that when the mystic went into a trance, she would often start shaking as well.

Whether hocus-pocus or not, the soothsayer accurately predicted that Hatsu's son would return safely because of her faith. And once, when Aiko went along with her mother, he foretold that the teenager's future husband would be three years older than she was, another prediction which eventually came true.

During this time the sight of the Emperor was a rare event; most Japanese lived their entire lives without ever seeing him. It was common practice for groups to go work at the palace. Once when Aiko was there with her fellow students from Aoyama Gakuin pulling weeds outside, the Emperor emerged riding a white horse with his procession. Everyone knelt prostrate, facing the ground as he passed by. Considered a god, it was a punishable offense to look upon him. Aiko, however, her mind fueled by childish curiosity, sneaked a glance and was disappointed to see that he looked like a normal man.

Eventually, as the soothsayer foretold, Ichiro returned from China. He was safe but the family was not able to remain free from tragedy.

In 1939, Yae, who was engaged at the time, contracted consumption and passed away. She was only twenty-four. Beautiful and intelligent, always helpful around the house and skilled at many things, including making clothing and bathing suits for her sisters, her presence was greatly missed.

Hiroko married Tomoya Kikuchi, a shy boy from the countryside of Yamagata Prefecture, then working in Tokyo.

In the Mori house the non-*tatami* sections of the floor, such as the entry and hallway, were made of wood, which was polished by hand using *nuka,* rice husks. *Nuka* is widely used in Japan, its many uses including including pickling *tsukemono* and cooking, washing dishes, and as a beauty treatment for the skin.

Wanting everything spic and span for the returning couple, Shige took it upon herself to polish the floor better than usual, diligently scrubbing the wooden slats to a high sheen. When Tomoya walked in with a "hello," he removed his shoes and, taking two steps in, slipped and fell over, crashing through the *shoji* rice paper and wood lattice that divided the hallway. He was embarrassed, but the girls couldn't help but laugh and laugh.

The older Mori siblings all went to traditional Japanese schooling but every daughter starting with Aiko down enrolled in high school at Aoyama Gakuin-Koto-Jogakubu in Shibuya, about an hour away by train. It was a prestigious Methodist mission school—devotional was held every Wednesday—with a greater emphasis on western science and, importantly, English, which Yoshizo felt would be a useful skill for his children. Most of the students were daughters of English-speaking families, diplomats and some noble families.

Many of the teachers were native English speakers from America and Canada some who didn't speak any Japanese at all. The head of the school was from Philadelphia. Aiko's English teacher was Miss Berry from Canada.

English courses were mostly taught with the teacher standing in front of the class reading from a text and the students parroting back what they heard. Emphasis was placed on reading and to a lesser extent writing with little practice allotted for actual conversation.

Aiko particularly enjoyed her Japanese language classes and geometry. Funny since she claimed to have struggled with math when she was a little girl. The one thing she did not like about high school was the uniform, Navy-styled with heavy pleated skirts and sailor collars, very similar to the uniforms still worn today.

Hisa also attended Aoyama. That Yoshizo could afford to send two daughters at the same time during prewar Japan to a notable private school, and then a third, Kyoko, after the war, spoke of his financial success and also of his intrigue to learn English. Aiko fondly remembers her mother dressing up nicely and going by train to parent conferences in Shibuya.

Aiko thinks her father was expecting the Olympics to come to Japan and was hoping to learn English well enough to work there. Whatever may have been on Yoshizo's mind, the Emperor and his army had different plans in motion that would put English study and many others things on indefinite hold.

4

WAKING THE GIANT

CHANGE IS AN INTERESTING THING. Sometimes it is subtle, small and quiet like the first glimpse of the stranger that will become your best friend. And sometimes it's as unmistakable as a train wreck.

Like many on that quiet Sunday morning, Russell was asleep when the bombs began falling on Pearl Harbor. Wailing sirens and thunderous explosions shook the entire house, jarring Russell awake. It was barely past sunrise, December 7, 1941. The day of infamy had come. Merely wanting to sleep, Russell's first thought was, "What's the matter with these folks making so much noise on a Sunday morning?" Quickly realizing it was more than just a neighborhood racket Russell flipped on the radio to be jolted by the voice of Webberly Edwards, urgent and crackling, "Take cover! Take cover! This is the real thing! This is war! We are being attacked by the Japanese!"

Russell was stunned. He was wearing the same pajamas he'd gone to sleep in, lying in the same bed in the same house in the same city, but the entire world was suddenly a different place.

Slipping into his khaki pants and white t-shirt, Russell stepped outside. The house was roughly twelve miles away from Pearl Harbor but he could see massive black clouds of smoke marring the

Pacific sky. From his vantage no planes were visible but the roaring of the engines tore through the air like angry hornets.

Russell headed towards the Nakamura Hotel to check on his relatives. Two policemen pulled up as he neared Beretania Street. When Russell asked what was going on they told him they were notifying the family next door that their daughter was dead, killed by a bomb on her way to Sunday school. It was the first casualty Russell heard of and the reality of it both saddened and frightened him.

He turned towards Pearl Harbor again as the fullness of what was happening sank in. *"Baka! Nihonjin Baka!"* Stupid Japanese! The more he thought about it, the angrier he became. *"Baka, baka!"* What on earth were they thinking? It was a question he would ask himself over and over for the remainder of his life.

Later Russell candidly posed the question, "Why did they attack Pearl Harbor? They sank only five battleships, basically nothing in comparison to the entirety of the U.S. fleet. What were they doing? They attacked and ran off, no assault or anything. What was the point?" He felt the U.S. government knew some—if not all—of what was going on. But these thoughts only occurred to him much later. For now he was left with little more than shock and confusion. As the day wore on his initial anger sank towards depression.

Instead of going to the Nakamura, he went to the Yamashiro Hotel next door, where a few of his buddies were, all of them wearing the same shell-shocked look on their faces. The owner's son motioned for them to go to the roof so two or three of them climbed the stairs to the sixth floor and went outside. The harbor was still masked behind dark billows of smoke, the drone of planes continuing to permeate the air. Normally jovial, Russell and his friends stood wordless and scared.

When they climbed back down to the street level, Russell noticed a line of people at the market trying to buy food, which disappeared quickly from the shelves. The streets were soon deserted.

Russell returned to his Auntie's house. He remembers hearing several older women crying. No one was speaking. Kimi quietly brought out some rice and pickled vegetables for lunch.

The radio announcer told everyone to stay home, instructing them to turn off their lights after dark in hopes of discouraging a night attack. In a college paper Russell recalled "Motorcycles and ambulances with sirens full blast failed to cover that eery, uneasy calm that began to settle around the area and Hawaii braced herself to spend a long night of expectation, fear and despair with a lingering disbelief."

As the sun sank, noises too disappeared, the chaos of the day leaving an unnatural silence in its wake. The city was blacked out. People stayed inside, shuttering their windows, huddling around their radios waiting for further news. Uncertainty hung over the island, an impenetrable fog almost as frightening as the attack itself. What was going to happen? Would there be another attack? Was this prelude to a full invasion?

Pre-occupied with their thoughts, no one in the house spoke or read, preferring to sit or pace the floor. When sleep finally came for Russell that night it was begrudging and troubled. He and thousands of other Japanese Americans now found themselves in a very uncomfortable position. What repercussions would the attack bring? Would their non-Japanese neighbors become hostile? What would become of them if Japan bombed again or landed troops?[1]

The dirge of the sirens returned the next morning and the streets ran helter-skelter with mobilized American soldiers. All schools and businesses were closed so Russell stayed home, listening to

---

1. In a paper entitled "Aspects of Martial Law in Hawaii 1941-1944," written for Stewart Grow's Political Science 295 class, Russell points out that notably "There were no mass panic or hysteria. There was no looting. There were no mass uprising and mob action against the large segment of Japanese people. Truly, the long training in practical democracy and experimentation in Americanization paid off…human decency and tolerance prevailed and triumphed over bigotry and race baiting."

the radio and fretting the time away. Beyond military and emergency personnel hardly anyone left their homes, Japanese Americans particularly were never seen in large groups. There was a distinct lack of information; no one knew anything. The radio seemed to feed the overhanging sense of fear by suggesting further invasions by the Japanese. Fortunately the rumored secondary attacks never materialized.

Being a doctor, Kimi's brother-in-law was the only one in the family who had anything to keep himself busy. Civilian casualties were relatively low (though it should be argued that even a single casualty is still one too many) so he was voluntarily helping take care of wounded soldiers.

As the days passed, people grew restless staying in their homes and began to venture out to buy food. Schools re-opened, work resumed and some semblance of order began returning to the Islands. But things would never be the same again.

Hawaii, still a U.S. territory at the time, was signed over to martial law by Governer Joseph B. Poindexter. Courts were placed under military control, essentially closing them down, and the Writ of Habeas Corpus was suspended. Russell considered the situation "akin to a totalitarian police state." All non-essential personnel were encouraged to leave Hawaii. Military spouses and children were transferred off the islands. All recreation sites, including theaters, were closed and barbed wire barricades were placed along the beaches, including Waikiki. Guards were posted, the result of which were "indiscriminate shootings . . . at [their] own shadows." More than one farmer woke in the morning to find one of their cows shot dead by a jittery guard in the middle of the night.

Mandatory gas masks were issued to those that stayed and the blackouts continued to be enforced, with military personnel even ordered to shoot out any lights that remained on. Windows were sealed with tarpaper or painted black and curfews were strictly enforced at night. Businesses were told when and how to operate and supplies of all kinds, including food, gasoline, liquor and toilet paper, were rationed.

Even minor violations were severely punished by the military courts. A traffic infraction could net the offender with a fine of several hundred dollars and jail time, often without a hearing of any kind. No such military measures were taken anywhere else along the entire Pacific coast, including Alaska.

Russell understood the nature of the emergency and that people were "reconciled to certain limitations of their civil rights" but felt the extremities of the control exercised were in violation of the constitution. "Aspects of a police state were very much in evidence," he writes, "only brutality lacking but arrogance undiminished." His opinion was shared by many others, including Federal Justice Albert D. Metzer, who challenged the "kangaroo justice" of the military courts, feeling that the suspension of rights was carried out far longer than was necessary. It was an "unjustifiable encroachment of civil rights under the guise of military necessity and expediency."

An announcement came over the radio that all Japanese were to report to local schools and get fingerprinted. Russell and his family walked to the school where a secretary took their names, addresses and fingerprints. They were also issued registration cards which they were required to carry with them at all times. Surprisingly there was little protest from the Japanese community and a willingness to cooperate with the government prevailed. For many, however, registration was the tip of the iceberg.

A week after the bombing a letter arrived from Russell's mother on Maui telling him his father had been taken into FBI custody. At around eight o'clock in the evening of the bombing two Japanese police officers knocked on the door. They were kind, even apologetic when they told Mitsutaka to make himself warm and then he was taken into "protective custody." Mitsutaka offered no resistance, he wasn't even handcuffed when he disappeared with them into the night. This left Kikuyo with only Taka at home, who was at the tail end of high school.[2]

It was several weeks before the family learned of Mitsutaka's whereabouts. He was being held in detention in Wailuku before being sent to Sand Island in Honolulu Harbor. Eventually he was moved to Missoula, Montana in the dead of winter and then on to Fort Sill, Oklahoma. Ultimately he was transferred to an enemy alien detention center in Santa Fe, New Mexico where he would be kept for the duration of the war.

Issued as a "security measure," Executive Order 9066 allowed for over 120,000 Japanese to be moved from their homes and placed in temporary military installations.

Located in remote deserts and desolate mountain areas these settlements were officially titled as "War Relocation Camps." However, with incarceration based solely on ethnicity, they were in fact nothing short of concentration camps complete with barbed wire and armed guards whose guns, as Russell was fond of mentioning, pointed inwards, not out.

An average of eight people shared each "apartment," a 20'x25' wooden structure covered in tarpaper. They were furnished with iron cots using straw-filled bags for mattresses and three-Army blankets each for bedding. Heating was an oil-burning furnace. There were no private facilities. The men's and women's showers were separated by only a short wall.

---

2. Within the government, concern and mistrust of the Japanese Americans (JAs) loyalty began as early as their arrival in the 1920s. Talk of preparations for emergency incarceration circulated even then. To be fair there were also government officials who reported to the contrary, stating that the JAs would remain loyal, which they did. The paranoia had its own repercussions. Anticipating sabotage from local Japanese, all airplanes at Pearl Harbor were parked together to protect against potential threat. The densely grouped planes proved easy targets for the attackers and more were destroyed than would have been otherwise.

Roughly two-thirds of the detainees were born and raised American citizens, second and third generation *Nisei* and *Sansei,* who had never known life in any other country. The remaining third were Japanese nationals, many of whom would gladly become naturalized citizens if not for laws that prevented them from doing so.

Often given less than a week's notice and only allowed to bring what they could carry, they left behind homes, stores, farms, and land. Non-Japanese neighbors often gathered like vultures, purchasing properties for a tenth of their value. After the war most Japanese Americans returned to find they had nothing left. Even estates left in the care of trusted neighbors were often ransacked and liquidated. In 2014 dollars the loss of Japanese American goods and properties is estimated at over $6.2 billion.

The vast majority of Japanese Americans incarcerated were from the West Coast. In fact, out of the 120,000 relocated almost none were from the Midwest or eastward and only an estimated 1,290–1,875 were from Hawaii. In the islands only those perceived as the most prominent or influential among the Japanese population were taken. The 135,000 Japanese Americans living in Hawaii comprised 37% of the state population and the majority of its workforce. If the Japanese had all been taken, the economy of the state would have collapsed. Since this could not be allowed to happen in a spot of such vital military importance, most of the Japanese were left in place. The government clearly had its priorities.

It is interesting to note that construction on the camps—numbering ten in total—actually began before the bombing of Pearl Harbor, included as part of plans to mass evacuate certain portions of the population. In fact President Roosevelt was given a list of all *Nisei* from the previous census created well in advance of any Japanese aggressions towards the U.S.

The camp Mitsutaka found himself in differed slightly from the others in that it was a Department of Justice Detention Center, created to house citizens who were considered to pose a greater potential threat to national security. All in all 7,000 people were kept here, including some German and Italian inmates, but the vast majority of the inmates were of Japanese descent.

There were several reasons for Mitsutaka's arrest. First he was still a Japanese national, not an American citizen. Several laws blatantly discriminated against Asians, barring them from becoming naturalized citizens, owning land or voting. These rights were reserved for "free white persons only."

Secondly, he was educated. One of the few who could read and write both English and Japanese, he handled most of the correspondence for people on the plantation. Literacy in Japan is one of the highest in the world (no small feat if you have ever seen their alphabets) but many of the immigrant workers were from poor regions and were not schooled properly.

One of the charges levied against him was having contact with the Japanese consulate in Honolulu, which indeed he had. Mitsutaka served as the head of the local *Nihonjinkai*, Japanese Community Association, and had written to the consulate on behalf of two young Japanese immigrants who, ironically, were seeking to renounce their status as Japanese citizens and expatriate to the United States.

Third was retribution by Moir, who never forgave Mitsutaka for standing up to him. When hearings for detention were held, Moir was head of the community committee and his testimony was ultimately responsible for Mitsutaka's arrest.[3] By contrast, when another Japanese man in Honolua was to be detained his man-

---

3. Japanese were ranked on what was called the ABC list, sorting them by threat potential. Most of those classified as A threats were community leaders or those with ties to Japan. No writ of Habeas Corpus was ever produced for any of the detainees nor were any ever brought to trial. In 1980 the Congressionally formed Commission on Wartime Relocation and Internment of Civilians (CWRIC) determined that the root causes for JA incarceration were 1. racial prejudice, 2. hysteria generated by the war, and 3. failure in political leadership.

ager, a Mr. Flanning, stood up for him and helped prevent his incarceration.[4]

Mitsutaka was held until the end of the war, once again leaving Kikuyo as the sole provider. "I got to see papa only once during the war," says Russell, speaking of a pivotal experience that would not happen until years later. The news of his father was naturally upsetting but there was nothing Russell could do.

The FBI made searches of every household identified as having key Japanese people. Kimiko Figuerres remembers when they came to her house she told them her family belonged to no group. Still, once the FBI left, her family burned anything and everything that might connect them to Japan—books, papers, photos—just in case, a common occurrence across the islands. For people with so little to begin with, burning such valuables must have been a great loss, but they were afraid.

Kikuyo was not home when her house was searched, but she knew someone had been there. No search was ever announced or formally declared but she returned from work one day and found the tin foil from a cigarette package lying in the house. Kikuyo herself smoked but was fastidious in keeping things tidy. Whether the searchers had a warrant or not, no one knows.

Even with these deprivations, the Japanese islanders didn't suffer as much as the Japanese Americans on the west coast who encountered tremendous prejudice. Russell doesn't recall any Japanese ever being beat up or any other negative action being taken towards them in Hawaii.

Russell remained enrolled in school and working for the American Can Company, which had converted over to canning soldier's rations as part of the war effort.

---

4. Russell's exact words were "really went to bat for him." It is a phrase he used often and shows, even on a subtle level, how sports and baseball in particular were part of his make-up, something easy to forget to those who only knew him in his later years.

The vice-principal of the vocational school, Mr. Frack, was of German ancestry. As a wounded veteran from World War I he had first hand experience with the bitterness of racial discrimination. Anticipating any potential reprisal on his *Nisei* students he assembled them together and told them to be "thick-skinned and don't take crap from anyone" and encouraged them not to despair. His words lent Russell and his fellow students a great amount of reassurance at a time of confusion and fear. Happily Mr. Frack's worries were needless, at least in the islands. The relatively few whites that lived there either had no trouble with the Asians or were wise enough to keep their mouths shut.

The U.S. Department of Engineering (U.S.E.D.) called Ernest Kanderson at the vocational school asking if he could recommend a capable electrician with motor repairing and rewinding skills. Russell came immediately to mind. The canning company was considered part of the defense industry and employees were not supposed to change jobs but Kanderson gave them Russell's name and he got the job anyhow.

Russell didn't know how well things would work out, having never even worked as an apprentice before. It turns out there were other first class journeymen at the department but none had Russell's training or expertise in rewinding electrical motors. Russell was hired and given a full journeyman's rating, earning top wages for the time, almost two dollars an hour. In addition to electrical motors Russell also did considerable work in repairing welders and generators, earning in a single hour nearly twice as much as a plantation worker made in a full day. And he hadn't even graduated yet. The pay was higher but the ten-hour days, seven-day week schedule was also more demanding. Russell was pleased that he was able to start saving some money during this time. It was a habit that he would enjoy all his life.

At work Russell was required to wear a badge, a black circle indicating he was of Japanese American descent. (Apparently it wasn't obvious enough by looking at his face.) Everyone else simply wore a white name tag. Russell felt no animosity for having to distinguish himself. He tackled his job diligently, quickly outworking others who had been there longer.

One day a "cute young gal . . . made a pass" at Russell so he asked her out to the movies, one of his few dates at the time. The war came before the relationship ever developed but this does illustrate that Russell wasn't the total social pariah he tries to conjure when you talk to him.

Despite the disruption of the war Russell finished out the last bit of his schooling, graduating valedictorian. Why the sudden improvement? "I had to do it," he says, "I wasn't preparing myself to work on the plantation." He may not have known exactly what direction he wanted to go but he knew it wasn't back to the fields.

Russell spoke at graduation but didn't think much about it. Perhaps graduation speeches seemed trivial in contrast to what was happening around him. While the world outside was rapidly changing, Russell was beginning to change on the inside as well.

Working ten-hour days and finishing school absorbed most of Russell's energy and focus but he decided that he wanted to expand his social life a bit. One day he casually asked Norima, the student body president, what he did on weekends.

"Oh, I go to church on Sundays."

"Which church?"

"Oh, the Mormon Church."

"What?"

Norima's answer surprised him. The only things Russell knew about Mormons were that they were polygamists and gave away ten percent of their money. Russell's shock must have shown in his voice.

"What's wrong with that?" Norima asked defensively.

Russell didn't mean to offend him. As an apology he quickly suggested, "Hey, can I go with you some time?"

"How about this weekend?"

"Okay, I'll come to your house Sunday."

Religion wasn't a large part of Russell's home life. The family attended services occasionally, more out of tradition than anything else. Once, when Russell asked about Buddhism, Kikuyo indicated it was a matter of feeling inside of you. That was the entire extent of the conversation. As a youngster Russell also attended a Methodist Sunday School in his village. He was never baptized but he did enjoy the hymns and the Sermon on the Mount.

Sunday came and Russell got up early to make the 8:30 morning meeting. The walk to Norima's house took about thirty minutes but when he arrived Norima said he couldn't go because he had to run errands for his mother. The truth is that Norima wasn't a member at the time either although he did eventually join.

Russell started walking home, annoyed that he'd gotten up early on a Sunday for no reason. The more he thought about it the more upset he became until he decided he was going to the meeting even if Norima didn't. Russell had never been to a meeting, but he and Norima drove by the meeting house once before, so he knew where it was. Dressed in a white t-shirt and slippas (flip flops, the only shoes he owned were work boots) Russell took it upon himself to walk to the Lanakila Chapel off of Nuuanu Road.

When he arrived, Russell was greeted by two *haole* missionaries, Elder Joel Moss and Elder Grant Clyde.[5] They shook his hand and he walked into the one room chapel where a handful of people sat. No one else greeted him. He sat on a bench in the back and waited for the minister.

---

5. Another interview states that Elder Clyde's (who was from Springville) companion was Morris Bushman from Provo.

No minister ever appeared. There was no church choir. After a few minutes a young man about Russell's same age got up and conducted the meeting. Although Russell wasn't introduced until later, this young man was Sam Shimabukuro, who would eventually be called as a mission president in Sendai, then precede Russell as president of the Tokyo Temple. Sam was later called to serve in the Second Quorum of the Seventy. The congregation sang a few songs. Russell couldn't help but wonder what strange kind of church this was.

Russell decided to attend Sunday school. All classes were held in the chapel and taught by the missionaries, with a few people breaking off into separate groups. The only other person in the class with Russell was a Hawaiian lady. The class was taught by Elder Clyde. The lesson was on the United Order. "Isn't that communism?" Russell asked and was set straight.

Church ended with the congregation gathering together again to sing a final hymn. A closing prayer was offered and everyone left. No one said goodbye to Russell or offered an invitation to come again.

On the way home Russell says he felt very empty. He wasn't mad, he just couldn't figure it out. "What gives anyway? I was practically ignored. What is this all about? Aw, forget about it." It was just strange, a funny "oddball" church. Certainly nothing like he'd imagined.

Russell explains that his early interest in church—any church—was simply for social reasons. "I wasn't going to join the church or anything like that. I was lonely. It was a war time situation, you know." There was another church he passed on his way to work, the Harris Memorial Church, that caught his interest because it always seemed to be full of young people, many of them students from the University of Hawaii. Russell wanted to go but they were all so well dressed and he didn't have a suit, so he gave up on the idea and went to the LDS church.

The following Sunday he got up early and returned to church again by himself. Russell didn't think he was looking for a church, but something inside compelled him to be there. He didn't know why but he felt at peace. "Why in tarnation did I decide to go back?" It was a question for which he had no answer.

There were a few more people there this week and Russell began to get to know some of them. Although his attendance was irregular, Russell continued to go, dropping by church when his demanding schedule allowed. Still he was never fellowshipped to attend activities and never invited to hear a missionary discussion. He didn't even own a bible.

After a few months of hearing people talk about this *Book of Mormon,* Russell became curious enough that he went to the city library to check out what he could find on the Mormons. He managed to find a copy of the *Book of Mormon* and began reading, "and it came to pass . . . and it came to pass . . . and it came to pass . . . Hogwash!" He closed it, unable to understand a thing it was saying. (Russell chuckles fondly at this memory.)

Russell put the book back and looked around for something else. On the same stack he saw a good-sized volume about the Mormons entitled *No Man Knows My History.* He picked it up and began reading on the spot. Unbeknownst to the curious young man, the author, Fawn Brodie, was David O. McKay's niece and one of the harshest critics of the church.

Russell read on for several hours, enough time to finish most of the book. It was "very, very scurrilous on Joseph Smith. And I got really mad."

Russell remembered his teacher, Mrs. Foster, saying she was a Mormon. She was someone he really respected and was very decent. How could she be associated with a church as horrible as the book said it was? It was too great a contradiction in his mind and he found himself breaking into a cold sweat, growing agitated and angry. How could it be so bad? Russell tells, "That's the thing that converted me."

Following a "strange, persuasive feeling" Russell kept going back to church when he could, also trying to attend the weekly Mutual Improvement Association (MIA) meeting. He became acquainted with people like Sam Shimabukuro, Susumu Arima, Adney Komatsu, Allen Ebesu,[6] Fred Takasaki and others that would become lifelong friends.

Russell's contact with the church was sporadic at best. One Sunday, right after work, he hustled over to church, still dressed in his work pants and a t-shirt, showing up in time to catch a fast and testimony meeting, his first ever. He sat, watching as people stood in front of everyone, weeping and crying and saying "this and that." It was a different experience than anything else he'd seen so far and he couldn't make heads or tails of it.

Suddenly, he found his feet taking him up to the podium. The next thing he knew he was standing in front of the congregation. And he was completely speechless. "What am I doing here?" he thought in sheer panic. Everyone was looking at him. Nothing would come out of his mouth. He tried and tried. For what felt like hours he stood, mouth sealed shut, feeling like a thoroughly "stupid fool." Embarrassment finally overwhelmed his immobility and he rushed from the chapel. Outside he sat on the steps and burst into tears. "It was an asinine thing to do," he recalled.

After a few minutes one of the girls (who Russell liked but she was sweet on someone else) came out. She told Russell not to feel bad. Russell left without saying too much.

In hindsight, Russell says he had some semblance of a testimony without even recognizing it. Eventually he realized, "Hey, I must be interested in the church. I don't know what it's about, but I'm interested." And with that he began his spiritual journey. "Conversion comes a long way. When I start looking back, at mission calls

---

6. Also spelled Alan in some records.

and what not I realize that the Lord's hand was in it, definitely. Joining the church was not an accident. I was lead by the Lord."

His first impressions of the church were not very good. He was often left wondering "what kind of crappy organization is this? I didn't know what it was all about." Despite this Russell felt a strong desire to be affiliated with the church, even if he was unsure why.

"I didn't get into the church because I believed. I never had a missionary discussion. Never had a *Book of Mormon*. I was talking to a missionary who said 'Hey, you have a testimony. Why don't you join the church?' Me? You think I should? Sure." The missionary was Kenneth Aubrey, who Russell would meet again later in a distant land, almost a world apart.

Here Hideo Kanetsuna, Russell's neighbor who later joined the church himself, challenges Russell's humble claim of being a constant loner, saying that lots of church girls were interested in him but he never gave them serious thought.

Ever the dutiful son, Russell wrote to his mother regarding his desire to join the church, fully knowing she would say no. Penned by his sister Misao the reply came back claiming that Russell was an "unfilial" son, wanting to join a church they knew nothing about, throwing away his ancestral religions of Shinto and Buddhism.

Hideo shares that Kikuyo and his mother used to meet in the early evenings to cool off on their veranda. Kikuyo conversationally mentioned, "*Uchi-no Nozomu (sic) wa hen-na Kurischan no kyokai-no memba ni natte so da.* Looks like our Nozomi has become a member of a funny Christian church."

It upset Russell, but he persisted. After several more letters from Russell, his mother relented and gave him permission to join the church, but only on one condition: once he joined he could never quit! "You stay in, you don't get out, that's it." She knew her son would not make empty promises. As for Mitsutaka's thoughts on the subject, he never really said anything one way or another.

More than a matter of religious choice, Mitsutaka approved of the idea of his son's commitment to something he believed was right.

On February 14, 1943, Elder Kenneth Aubrey baptized Russell at the Honolulu Tabernacle. Elder Merlin Nielsen of Utah gave the confirmation blessing. Russell was ordained to the office of priest. There weren't any formal discussions then, and although general lesson guidelines existed, outside of a few Sunday school classes Russell never heard any lessons.

One of his coworkers chided Russell that now he was a member of "the Legion of 10 Percent Suckers (tithe payers)." "And I have been paying tithing ever since I joined the church. But I have no regrets," says Russell.

If you asked him at the time why he joined he couldn't have told you. His conversion was a gradual process, not one singular event. Russell claims he was "not a very faithful member of the church. But still yet I've stuck with it. It's all I know." His testimony was still in its infancy but the impression that he was meant to join was undeniable. The reasons wouldn't become clear for years to come. In the meantime, he didn't worry about it, he just did what he felt was right.

5

THE RISING SUN

FOLLOWING JAPAN'S ASSAULT ON THE United States, Aiko and the rest of the students at her school walked to the Meiji Shrine, roughly thirty minutes away. She remembers everyone carrying national flags but admits that might be her imagination. She does, however, vividly remember the crunching sound everyone's shoes made as they walked across the gravel covering the grounds of the shrine, where they assembled to pray for Japan's victory.

That evening, fearing a retaliatory air attack from the United States, citizens were told to cover their lights and windows.

Aiko was still too young to really understand what the news meant. Her first impression was, "Well, I hope we win." Then she didn't give it any more thought. She remembers feeling a little anxious about the war, but not scared.

Japan was already at war in China but didn't feel affected because the fighting was still far away. Aiko's brother was drafted but little else seemed different. The war simply didn't feel close enough to concern them. So when the attack on America was announced, to many, it sounded like more of the same.

Aiko finished her high school diploma in the nick of time. The government began rationing coal for military use and schools operated by foreign entities, such as Aoyama, were the first to be cut off. They still had electricity but there was no heat and the students were forced to finish out the year in cold classrooms.

The nation was now under military control and using English was forbidden. Aiko never actually saw anyone get arrested but you could be imprisoned for even owning an English book. Most of the faculty at Aoyama were American and Canadian and were all sent home at the onset of the war. Aiko remembers her "dean of girls took the very last boat home after being in Japan for 40 years, return[ing] to Philadelphia." This of course put an end to any further English studies in school. Anyone below Aiko's grade, including her younger sister, Hisa, never finished their courses.

In retrospect this seems severely shortsighted on the part of the government. Win or lose, Japan would need English speakers after the war and people with English skills became high in demand. Aiko's studies would indeed pay off, in ways neither she nor her father ever imagined.

After Aoyama Aiko attended Yoshizaki Home Economics School, which taught sewing, cooking and poetry reading, among other skills. In short it prepared girls to become brides and wives. It was not a good fit for the self-described tomboy, who considered the school "too girly." Aiko confessed, "I can't behave [there], like *hai, hai,*" she feigns an overly polite, feminine bow, "that kind. I hated that school. No fun."

Aiko preferred to attend English school at Tsuda Juku, which was the best English college for girls at the time. Because of the strong reputation of Aoyama's English program any graduate that applied was almost guaranteed acceptance. Aiko would have been easily admitted but her parents worried that no one would want to marry a tomboy, especially one who was better educated. So Aiko dutifully enrolled in Yoshizaki. Ultimately Aiko wouldn't have finished at either school as any further studies were soon to be interrupted by the war.

Although Yoshizaki wasn't Aiko's first choice she did make friends there. She shared the daily train commute with the daughter of a well-known movie producer and also met a very nice girl from Manchuria. Unfortunately she lost contact with both of them after the war.

After Aiko's first year of junior college the government ordered that all able bodied people, including students, were to begin working in factories. Aiko gladly quit school and went to work at Yoshizo's friend's company doing light clerical work in the office.

Later Aiko moved to the Hokushin Company, the same place her brother Ichiro had worked before he was drafted. The president of Hokushin also knew her father well. Working in the office Aiko never knew the details of what they were making, only that it was some type of manufacturing related to the war effort.

Aiko says she had it easy, especially compared to her younger sister Hisa. Hisa's high school experience was interrupted when she and the other students were conscripted to work in a military factory making bearings and other parts. The schools eventually awarded diplomas to those who went to work, so at the very least Hisa did receive her diploma. Usually the girls were given a photo album along with their diploma, a yearbook of sorts, but Hisa only received her papers.

The young women usually didn't work a full shift but they kept tough schedules and odd working hours. The factories operated twenty-four hours a day, so working swing shift till two in the morning was not uncommon. The trains didn't run that time of the morning and the girls were forced to walk home after work.

Education replaced by manual labor, days in the sun replaced by the grime of factories, the cost of Japan's war effort was beginning to affect the lives of her children. The war was moving closer to home.

6

EXPATS AND PATRIOTS

NITIALLY JAPANESE AMERICANS WERE NOT allowed to serve in the military and their draft status was switched from 1A to 4C—that of enemy alien. Many Japanese Americans already serving in the armed forces before the onset of the war were stripped of their guns and some were even locked up in stockades or expelled.[1] This was all reversed in February of 1943 with the creation of the 442nd Infantry Regiment, an all *Nisei* unit.

Burning with patriotic fervor and the opportunity to prove themselves as true and loyal Americans, young Japanese American men signed up by the thousands. Asking for 4,500 volunteers the Army was flooded by over 10,000 applications, most of them from Hawaii. With the motto of "Go for Broke!" the 442nd quickly distinguished itself fighting through Italy into the heart of the Third Reich. Of the *Nisei* who fought during the war General Joseph Stilwell later remarked, "They bought an awful hunk of America with their blood. You're d*** right those *Nisei* boys have a place in the American heart, now and forever. We cannot allow a single injustice to be done to the *Nisei* without defeating the purposes for which we fought."

---

1. There were notable exception to these actions. There were Japanese Americans already deep undercover in places such as the Philippines. These men, such as Arthur Komori and others, remained in place and proved invaluable in their service. No one ever said war made any sense.

For the *Nisei* the war was fought on two fronts. One was for democracy on the front lines across Europe and the Pacific. The other was against racism at home. The Japanese American soldiers were well aware that the outcome of the war would determine not only the political make up of the world but the way their families would be treated in their homeland whether they came back alive or not. If they or their future generations were to ever truly participate in the American dream, they had to fight this war and they had to win it. President Truman acknowledged the truth of this in an address given in July of 1946 when he said, "You fought for the free nations of the world. You fought not only the enemy, you fought prejudice, and you have won."

Like many of his contemporaries, including good friends like Arthur Nishimoto, Russell was quick to volunteer. While there were many reasons to join, Russell, as always, followed a very practical approach. He could imagine people asking what he did during the war while his father was in camp like a traitor. Knowing that having army experience would be better for him once the war ended, Russell also hoped that joining might make it easier to get his father out.[2]

In order to volunteer Russell had to take time off to go to the office in Honolulu. When Mahoney, Russell's superintendent at the Engineering Department, caught wind of it he personally called down to Draft Board No. 6 and ordered the recruiters to leave Russell alone. Mahoney gave Russell a "royal chewing out" when he got back. "Do you have any idea how valuable you are to this country?

---

2. I asked him why he joined and he only half-jokingly answered, "Because I was *bakatare* (idiot or fool)." Also a note on Arthur Nishimoto: He was one of the "three little pigs" the nickname given to Russell, Arthur and Adney Komatsu, because they were such close friends. For the rest of his life, whenever Russell met up with Arthur he snapped a salute with a "Hup!" and called him Colonel, a rank which Arthur earned fighting in the 442nd. Russell also mentioned, "I think [Arthur] received the same blessing that I received from Joseph Fielding Smith: That he would not be harmed." A blessing that was proven true in both cases.

Not too many people can do what you are doing. You are valuable to the defense of the country!" And so Russell was forced to wait out the next two years working at the shop, while his friends were fighting and dying in Europe.

Russell might have been blocked from volunteering but he was still in the draft system. He knew his number was coming up, but kept quiet about it, saying nothing to his boss. Two days before reporting for duty, he notified Mahoney that he was cleaning out his locker and joining the army. Mahoney called up the draft board but it was too late. The Irishman vented his frustrations on Russell with another royal scolding but there was nothing he could do.

At the draft board Russell was told to step forward, which he did, and with that he was in the Army. He soon learned that much of the military experience was hurry up and wait. He spent ten days in the Fulton Replacement Barracks, near the Schofield Barracks, getting his clothing issued, doing drills and "essentially playing Boy Scouts." The barracks were a real sampling of the ethnic flavor of the islands, filled with all kinds of Portuguese, Filipinos, Hawaiians and *Nisei*.

On the morning of departure, the platoon rose at 2 a.m. and assembled with their duffle bags in a large hall. They were told to pull out their mess kits and eat breakfast. After eating they waited and waited and waited until noon when they were told to get their mess kits out again for lunch. Finally at 4 p.m. they left, traveling to Honolulu Port in an old cattle car where they were hurried aboard a ship which didn't budge from port until 4 p.m. the following day.

Even though the war raged to the west in the Pacific, the troops turned eastward instead, heading towards California for training. As they passed Diamondhead the ship leaned heavily to portside as the soldiers crowded to watch it pass behind them. Some were quietly crying, saying *sayonara,* goodbye, *aloha*. For many it was the last time they would ever see their beloved island home.

Only one day out to sea the alarm klaxon blared to life and the ship began to zigzag furiously. "All hands on deck! All hands on deck! All crew to your battle stations! All troops put on your life jackets and stand by your bunk. Repeat, put on your life jackets!"

The ship carrying Russell was alone, unusual for wartime. Japanese submarines lurked in the Pacific waters making any crossing dangerous. In 1942, attacks from submarines sunk two fleet carriers, one cruiser, a few destroyers and other warships and damaged several others. Though not as widely publicized subsequent to Pearl Harbor, submarine attacks remained a threat in the Hawaiian waters. The worst case on record was the sinking of a military transport with a loss of all sixty or so on board.

Beyond this tragedy there was a single attack against Hilo Harbor resulting in only superficial damage with no loss of life and another attack on the port of Kahului which destroyed a chicken coop and killed two chickens. While this is laughable now, at the time the threat of submarine attack was a real fear.

When asked why there was no convoy for their ship, the men were told they could outrun a submarine. Cold comfort to a lone ship surrounded by an ocean with no land in sight.

Russell, on the bottom level of the ship, knew if they were hit that he would never survive. All he could do was put on his life jacket and wait helplessly by his bunk.

The evasive maneuvers continued for what felt like an eternity. Suddenly there was a huge explosion that shook the entire ship to its core. Recruits began screaming and crying. Some rubbed rosaries and a few even wet themselves.

Then the ship straightened out again, the klaxons died down and the comms relayed, "All clear. All clear. Crew report to your regular stations." The explosion had been a test firing of the ship's main cannon. It was only a drill, but more than enough to shake them up. The young recruits sighed with relief and began to rib each other with post-adrenal macho bluster.

You weren't scared were you?

Me? No. Were you scared?

No.

The remaining voyage was mercifully boring. After a week on board with "nothing to see but water" the ship arrived in San Francisco. Russell was transferred to Angel Island on the north side of the bay, where he and the rest of the men stayed. After a few days of sitting and resting they were shipped back across the bay, south to the Presidio, where they continued to stand by. The only thing Russell remembers about the Presidio is that he and a couple of soldiers peeled 11 bags of potatoes.

Despite being next door to the city by the bay Russell never made it into town but the smell of sardines, presumably from Fisherman's Wharf, was "all over the place." After a few more days the battalion and some 442nd soldiers were put on a military train and shipped off for Camp Hood in Texas.

The trip was non-stop, running through the night, and the soldiers remained crowded together in train cars with seats but no bunks. Traveling through the Mojave Desert with no air conditioning for nearly a week, packed much like the sardines Russell smelled at the Presidio, the trek was a miserable one.

There was a mess hall on the train that served a lot of coffee and toast and other "lousy food," according to Russell. But at least they didn't go hungry.

Russell also remembers their train pulling to the side to let a slow moving freight train pass. Near the end of the trip they ran out of water and "everything else." They were able to get water at a way station so they didn't suffer too long without.

Camp Hood, the island boy's first foray into mainland America, stood in the middle of the Texas flatlands surrounded by a ponderous amount of nothing. Coming from lush Hawaii, Russell's first impression of Texas was that it was a dry and ugly desert. Still, he was glad to get off the train and be able to shower and have a bunk to sleep in.

Named after Confederate General John Bell Hood, Commander of the Texas Brigade, Camp Hood was created in 1942 as a testing and training area for tank destroyers. Located near the rural town of Killeen, the camp was originally built to hold 38,000 troops. By the time Russell arrived the population had ballooned to almost 95,000.

Nearly forty years later Russell returned to visit the same grounds again in 1996. Renamed Fort Hood, it is now home to over 65,000 persons and headquarters for the III Corps, the 1st Cavalry Division, 4th Infantry Division, 13th Corps Support Command, 3rd Signal Brigade, 89th Military Police Brigade, 504th Military Intelligence Brigade, 21st Cavalry Brigade (Air Combat), and the 31st Air Defense Brigade. Despite the growth the original wooden barracks that Russell stayed in as a GI were still standing.

The first thing that stood out was the "Whites Only" sign on the bathrooms. This was a culture shock, especially to the boys from Hawaii where Whites were the minority and segregation hadn't been an issue before. With one set of bathrooms labeled "Whites Only" and the other "Blacks Only," where did the *Nisei* go? The Asians weren't considered Blacks so they used the "Whites Only" bathroom. Only those of African descent were allowed to use the "Blacks Only" bathrooms.

Even the Post Exchanges, the base grocery stores, were segregated. Russell remembers some of the *Nisei* getting kicked out of the "Blacks Only" PX. He also vividly recalls the time some Samoan GI's went into the "White's Only" PX and were greeted with, "Hey, you N*****, get out of here!"

"What did you call me?!" One islander answered back in true Samoan fashion and punched the guy out, starting a big riot.

The next day the battalion commander came in and yelled at the entire lot of them, Russell included. "You guys stop fighting, stop doing this, doing that." The verdict was reached that the Polynesians were to use the "Whites Only" services too.

Ultimately, it didn't matter what race or color you were, if you were Black you used the "Blacks Only" bathroom. Everyone else—white, tan, yellow, red, purple or chartreuse—used the "Whites Only" bathroom. (No, segregation doesn't make any sense.) The *Nikkei* thought they were mistreated but quickly realized the Blacks had it much worse.

Sometimes the *Nisei* went into town to shop. Killeen was still very small and they were often asked, "Where you guys from? You guys speak good English."

Once Russell and some friends were reprimanded by a commander for going to a Black bar in Killeen. When the officer asked why they went there Russell answered honestly because the place hosted the best jazz in town.

Another time, while on a weekend pass, a Caucasian man approached Russell who was dressed in full uniform, waiting for a bus. "Aren't you sorry for what your country did to America?" he asked, clearly drunk. It was everything Russell could do not to slug the guy. "Even with the uniform on, people were not about to let me forget my Japanese ancestry," says Russell, "At best I was a Japanese-American—a hyphenated American."

Training was rugged. "They were really running us through the mill, trying to get us ready." The average day started first thing in the morning and went until sundown. The recruits participated in combat training, learning to shoot a Browning automatic rifle, M1 Garand. Russell never fired another gun during his entire training and threw only one hand grenade. By his own admission, Russell was a lousy shot. With the Browning Automatic Rifle he didn't even hit the target. As soon as he squeezed the trigger, the fire caused the barrel to jump up and bruised his cheek. Russell may not have cared for shooting guns but he did enjoy the bayonet practice, perhaps because it was similar to *kendo*.

At one point Russell's unit did a 25-mile forced march in full gear. There was another unit ahead of Russell's (the big pioneer unit, he called them) and their men kept falling out by the wayside, beaten by the unrelenting Texas sun. At the end of the march not one *Nisei* or islander had fallen. Despite blister covered feet, through sheer guts, grit and *makejidamashi*, unyielding spirit, every single man finished.

The incessant marching reminded Russell of a song he used to sing as a child. *Heitai san ga manju kutte he o tareta!* The soldier chows on *manju* bean confections and it makes him fart! It might have been juvenile but the thought of it lent a bit of humor to him during the long hikes.

Everyday at noon, announcements were made reading bulletins of what was happening on the warfront, what fighting was going on and what the casualties were.

It felt like most of the news was regarding Europe and the forces grinding their way towards Germany in Northern Africa, Italy and France. Russell remembers hearing about tanks fighting and feeling things were going badly in Europe.

The Pacific theater was active as well with Naval forces engaged in some of the bloodiest fighting of the war across the islands dotting the path towards Japan.

Once in a while Russell would hear from home. "We didn't do much writing," he explains. Russell also got his driver's license while he was in the army. He learned when he was much younger by watching his father and "fool[ing] around on [his] own" but never received any formal classes. So while he'd been driving for years, now he was finally legal!

It was late December when Russell heard his name called out before reveille. He was to report immediately to the company commander's office. Russell trudged out, groggily wondering what he did to be singled out.

Upon arrival Russell was told by an officer to clean and oil all his combat equipment and turn everything in then pack all his uniforms and other items and stand by for further orders. Russell was being pulled from the 442, which he'd signed up for, but didn't know why. He was the only one in his company. No one bothered to mention what was going on, where he was headed or when. And, of course, he never asked. For a week he stood by without further word.

Christmas day 1944 found Russell pulling sentry duty watching a desolate road, ostensibly guarding a battalion being shipped out to Europe. The cold wind cut him straight to the bone. Winter in the Fort Hood area averages in the high 30s, freezing for a boy from Hawaii. As it turns out, Texas would prove balmy compared to Russell's next assignment.

On New Year's Eve Russell was again told to pack his bags and get ready to ship out. Because of his poor performance on the shooting range he was afraid he was getting sent to cook school. After sunset a truck came by and picked him up along with about two dozen others from the battalion. They were all Hawaii boys. Russell was vaguely acquainted with some of them from the scouting program back home. No one knew where they were headed. They simply kept quiet.

No explanation was forthcoming even as they boarded a train and shipped out for parts unknown. As before, this train made no stops, rolling continuously through the night. There was little to see from the train and what they could see they didn't recognize. War raged across both oceans, the young men were being taken from basic training and shipped out to parts and purposes unknown. It was a scary feeling.

After traveling around the clock the train came to a halt and soldiers were told to disembark. The bewildered island boys stepped from the train to find themselves in St. Paul, Minnesota. It was New Year's Day 1945 and the temperature was seventeen degrees below zero, the coldest temperature Russell ever experienced (the hottest was 120 Fahrenheit in Indio, California). The vast majority of *Nisei* had never seen a real winter or snow before. "It wasn't a magical wonderland," says Russell, who didn't care for it, "It was cold, cold, cold."

Russell and his group were taken to their barracks, which were literally old turkey shacks converted into temporary housing because the regular barracks were already overcrowded. In an uncanny echo of concentration camp housing, each of the wooden framed coops was covered in tarpaper and featured a single coal potbelly stove to provide warmth for the six men bunked inside.

At first the use of the stove was a real mystery to the Hawaiians. Even after they figured it out the contraption still didn't give off much heat, especially for boys raised in the tropics. After a week they were transferred into regular brick barracks with proper heating but not before some of them suffered from frostbite.

Tired from their long trip, Russell and the others quickly settled in, looking forward to some sleep but were instead sent to go do KP. The other units there had the day off so Russell and his compatriots had to forego sleep and wash dishes.

Finally someone asked, "What's this place anyway?"

At last they were informed that they were at Fort Snelling, home of Military Intelligence School (MIS). It was the first they'd heard of their new assignment.

When Russell and other *Nisei* enlisted in Hawaii they were asked if they spoke Japanese. If they answered affirmatively they were given an aptitude test. Though they didn't know it at the time the results of the test were used to determine if they could be considered for service in Military Intelligence. Russell initially volunteered for the 442nd but because of his linguistic prowess, unbeknownst to him, was chosen for intelligence service instead.

The ironic thing, Russell tells, is that those fluent enough to teach in Japanese language schools before the war were now under suspicion and some were taken into custody. Meanwhile "a few of us that only had rudimentary Japanese language training were now being ordered to learn more of the Japanese language and culture."

Life as intelligence officers presented unique difficulties to Japanese-Americans (JAs). They were often the only Japanese-American in their units and endured harsh comments and cruel jokes from their fellow soldiers. They never went shirtless lest they be mistaken for the enemy. MI officers in Hawaii were not allowed to set foot inside Pearl Harbor Naval Base, instead they worked out of a converted furniture store in downtown Honolulu.

As much as the JAs put up with from men on their own side what they faced if captured was infinitely worse. Japanese soldiers harbored no love for the men with Japanese faces wearing American uniforms. They were considered traitors and often received harsher treatment by their captors.

Despite the tension the MIS soldiers saved lives through their vital work and helped lay the groundwork for peace between the US and Japan. Their presence, particularly during the occupation, helped dispel the Japanese rumor that the Japanese-Americans removed from the west coast had all been murdered.

Russell was put into Company I with several hundred other men, mostly *hakujin,* whites, all going through basic MI training. The company commander was Masayuki "Spark" Matsunaga, who was recuperating from wounds sustained in Italy while fighting with the 442nd where he was, in Russell's words, "shot up pretty badly." The company's first sergeant was also a recuperating 442nd member. Eloquently spoken, Matsunaga would go on to graduate from Harvard and serve as a U.S. Senator years after the war. Russell remembers him as "good, straightforward and tough. No monkey business."

At Fort Snelling the recruits were given another battery of tests and further divided up according to their skill. Along with twelve to fifteen others, Russell was placed into the highest rated group. It wasn't long before he began to distinguish himself in that class as well, earning recognition as a top student not only with the staff, but among his fellow soldiers who often came to him with their questions.

Russell's Japanese was masterful, essentially native, with a bit of an island twist. As much of a trial after school Japanese classes had seemed, Russell was now grateful his father made him attend. "I am glad I went. When I was in the military everything came to [a] focal point. I didn't think I knew enough Japanese but when I took tests I did so much better than others that I stood out."

Still, there was a lot to learn. One unfamiliar term, one he never forgot once learned, came during his final interview. The conducting officer asked if Russell knew the term *mujokenkofuku*. Russell didn't. It meant "unconditional surrender," and whether in Japanese or English, it was a phrase the entire world would be familiar with soon enough.

Russell's group attended daily classes developing their Japanese reading, writing and grammar skills. Monday through Friday the day began with reveille at six. Classes began at eight running till lunch at noon. They ate lunch at their billet then back to class from two until four. After dinner, classes resumed from six until nine. Lights went out strictly at ten. Textbooks were classified and not allowed outside of the classroom, although reviewing notes by flashlight under a blanket at night wasn't uncommon. Saturdays they ran military formations and procedures until noon. After lunch they did laundry and polished their shoes. In the evening there was free time and they could go to town and catch a picture show or otherwise relax.

Studies included history and geography. They learned the organizational structure of the Japanese Army, military terms and vocabulary, practiced giving commands and analyzed documents. They even went over the *Sakusen Yomurei* and *Oyo Senjitsu* texts used in the Japanese Military Academy. They also focused on intelligence skills including interrogation. "I did very, very well," Russell states. Brilliance wasn't always encouraged however and Russell was once dressed down by an interrogations systems instructor for using a different approach than was being taught and not following established guidelines. The teacher couldn't say much because Russell always got results.

Russell's Japanese progressed to the point where he was able to recognize differences in regional dialects, which allowed him to pinpoint where the Japanese soldiers were from, what divisions they might be associated with and how their troops were being mobilized.

"[They taught us] language, geography, customs, what they [the Japanese] do and what they don't do. But it is up to you to make the connections and how these things are related. You can really learn a lot if you can see how these things are connected," Russell explained.

In addition to the classroom the trainees were placed in different situations and settings, often in half buried bunkers where they listened to live radio broadcasts and other enemy communications, trying to break codes and gather information. They also spent time going over top-secret documents. They weren't allowed to bring any paper or pencils into the bunkers and their pockets had to be completely empty. They were searched upon entering and upon exiting.

While still in training, Russell managed to decipher one rather cryptic transmission requesting medicine. "*Okuri . . . nanda . . . totsugeki!* (which means to charge) *shoganai. Totsugeki!*" It took some work to figure out but the Japanese weren't talking about charging anything . . . they were talking about venereal disease and needing condoms! Not every day revolved around decoding the proclivities of the enemy but it was always mentally challenging, something Russell really enjoyed.

One constant thread throughout Russell's story is the amazing way people's lives intertwine. Despite the heavy training, Russell's schedule allowed for Sundays off. Russell decided since there was nothing else to do "[he] might as well go to church." There was a colonel who encouraged the boys to attend an Episcopalian church, which Russell visited but felt "they had nothing to offer me."

Russell found out there was an LDS branch in St. Paul. There he happened to meet Sister Amelia Croft and her companion Sister Jenson. Sister Croft eventually married Kenneth Aubrey, the missionary who baptized Russell in Hawaii. It was actually Aiko who stumbled across this fact decades later when she met Sister Jenson while doing Tai Chi at the Senior Center in Provo, Utah. The two women somehow made the connection while chatting. Sister Jenson still had a picture of Russell from Minnesota.

The height of Minnesota's winter chill slowly gave way to the heat and humidity of summer as training and studies continued well into the fall of 1945. The detonation of the atomic bomb over Hiroshima on August 6th was announced over the camp loudspeakers. The soldiers knew a special type of bomb was coming but no one knew where its target would be or comprehended its magnitude.

Russell's initial reaction was a keen sense of relief. Several others shed tears; everyone knew the war was coming to an end. Over the next few days the second atomic bomb drop in history took place over Nagasaki. As reports about the radiation and after effects of the bombing poured in "They sent shivers through me," says Russell.

After months of American B-29s systematically leveling her major cities, bombing was nothing new to Japan. But this new weapon was something else entirely. Faced with the undeniable and overwhelming power of atomic weaponry, Japanese leadership, the emperor in particular, realized that unless drastic action were taken it could mean the annihilation of the entire nation and her people.

The dropping of the bomb was controversial to say the least. Russell would always wonder if it was necessary. Under the circumstances it seemed the most sensible thing to do. The initial cost was atrocious but Russell felt it did indeed hasten the end of the war, saving many more lives in the long run. Still, it was a high price to pay.

Much later, Russell met one of the Mitsuda children, a former classmate of his in Puukolii. Her father worked as the manager of the plantation store in Maui but got stuck in Japan with another of his daughters at the onset of the war. He found work in the Hiroshima city hall and both he and his daughter were killed in the blast. He was identifiable only by a small piece of his pocketknife found in the rubble of the building.

Another friend of the Horiuchis, Katsu Kajiyama, actually survived the same bombing. He remained healthy and went on to teach Japanese in Hawaii.

After eight months of drilling Japanese language and intelligence into his head, the time for Russell's deployment was drawing close. All soldiers were encouraged to take furloughs before being shipped into the field and Russell wanted to visit his father who was still being held at the enemy alien detention center in Santa Fe. Nearly four years had passed since Mitsutaka had been taken into custody and Russell hadn't seen his father since.

Now a soldier with some rank and a top-secret clearance, Russell hoped he might have some leverage. Visiting relocation centers wasn't such a big deal but the detention center was a different story. Russell's supervisor told him he'd need special authorization and not to get his hopes up since he was MI and his father was still classified as an enemy. Despite this Russell wrote to Washington DC—to the head of intelligence—to get permission to see his father.

Russell also inquired with the consul to see if there was any reason for his father to remain detained. The consul admitted that the evidence was meager and reassured him his father would be released when proper arrangements could be made. This apparently meant after the war, for Mitsutaka remained incarcerated until after Japan's surrender.

Eventually, Russell received permission to visit. The request went to the adjutant general's office then directly to the war department in Washington all the way to President Truman himself. Perhaps this is one of the reasons why Russell felt an affinity for the farmer from the Show-Me State. Russell was given a prearranged time and date to visit, so he packed his things and headed west by train.

On the way to New Mexico, Russell stopped for a few days at the War Authority Relocation Center in Rohwer, Arkansas to visit his Uncle Roy Koyama, his mother's youngest brother. Roy and his family had been living in the camp since the beginning of the war. Russell knew Roy in Hawaii but they hadn't seen each other since before Pearl Harbor.

Roy left Hawaii to homestead in Lodi, California, near Stockton, becoming a successful grape farmer. During the hysteria following Executive Order 9066 he and his wife and five young children were displaced to Arkansas.

Like so many other *Nisei*, Roy entrusted his vineyards and properties to one of his *hakujin* neighbors, a fellow by the name of Okey Bennett. While others were robbed blind by their so-called friends, the story of Roy and Okey stands as a bright spot in an otherwise tarnished episode in American history. Okey took over the grape farm, saving the family from holding a distress sale and losing their entire livelihood. Okey managed the farm for the full span of Roy's incarceration, selling the crops and depositing the earnings in Uncle Roy's bank account. Okey also bought knick-knacks, clothing and other necessities and sent them to the family on a regular basis, taking very good care of them.

Okey turned everything back over after the war ended, providing Roy's family with the financial means to rebuild their lives. Roy and Okey's friendship, however strong it may have been before the war, was now unbreakable till the end, when Roy and his family tended to Okey in his aging years. Okey was an honorable man, a shining example of the word "friend."

This was the first time Russell ever met his cousins, who were by now in their early teens. He was relieved to know the family was doing well under the circumstances and striving their best to live a relatively normal life. They talked about the family and other news but they never discussed Russell's military experience.

Following his visit to Uncle Roy, Russell continued his journey to the detention center in Santa Fe. Russell had entertained hopes that his uniform and rank might help him obtain his father's release but it was quite clear that this was not likely. Of the thousands of detainees held in detention centers, Russell knew of only one man who was ever allowed to leave during the war, the father of Lieutenant Maehara, who was killed in action while fighting with the 442nd in Italy. It was such an embarrassment to the government that they released him to attend his son's funeral and then allowed him to remain at home.

While Russell's military status couldn't free Mitsutaka, it at least allowed a chance for the two men to visit. As Russell drew near the detention center the sight of the "tall barbed-wire fence and high guard towers sent a chill through me." Russell entered the desolate-looking camp and reported to the gate office where he'd been expected. His orders from Washington were double-checked and cleared. He was watched every step of the quarter mile from the gate to the administration building. Even though he was dressed in the uniform of the United States Army decorated with the stripes of a sergeant "it was an uncomfortable walk. This was indeed a concentration camp."

In the building was a large room used as an assembly hall or gymnasium for the detainees. There was an area marked off with a rough wooden table and benches. A monitor directed Russell to take a seat facing the hall then wait as they brought his father into the room.

Mitsutaka looked good, although more stooped than Russell remembered. Father and son were forbidden to touch each other so there was no embrace, they could only exchange greetings.

"I saw him coming in from the far end of the hall," recounts Russell, "walking steadily with sure steps. After nearly four years of not having seen him, he looked older with more gray hairs. He came closer and our eyes locked for just a moment. [He] said it was good to see me, and he then turned to [the] monitor and introduced me to him as his number one son and proceeded to take his place, a seat opposite from me. Father was in complete control of his emotions and maintained a very even keel demeanor."

Mitsutaka sat at one end of the long table and Russell at the other, roughly six feet apart; flesh and blood separated by a government who declared them enemies. The son, a soldier headed for the front lines while the father would remain behind, a prisoner of politics. The monitor sat on the corner of their table for the duration of the conversation, which was conducted primarily in Japanese.

"Hello, Papa," Russell asked if they were treating him well.

"*Sho ga nai*," answered his father, "as well as can be expected. How is Mama?" Russell recalls a flicker of gentle affection crossing his father's usually stoic face. It was "an insight into the tenderness and close family unity and love that existed in spite of all the formalities."

Russell explained Kikuyo was well last he saw her and told how the family was faring. Mitsutaka reminded Russell that he was the oldest son, that he wanted to see him get married and be able to hold his grandchildren in his arms. "To him it was always the family," says Russell. Beyond that he didn't have much to ask. He never mentioned anything about the war.

The monitor sat quietly, only moving once to point out an ashtray and indicate they could smoke if they wanted to. Neither man smoked, and both politely declined.

Russell told his father that he was working through the Adjutant General's office to get him released and was a bit surprised when Mitsutaka answered, "If this had been any other country I would be dead now. I have been well treated." While he was innocent of any crime against the country he comprehended that he was nevertheless an enemy alien and understood being taken into custody. There was no animosity in his voice, only acquiescence that life was as it was.

"I learned to play golf while I have been here," Mitsutaka shared, "I made a hole-in-one the other day." Even in the worst of circumstances, Russell's father found the positive. And although the food was somewhat monotonous, he was well fed.

Mitsutaka was resigned to the likelihood that he would remain in custody for the remainder of the war. "Let me tell you something about the United States," Mitsutaka told his son, "It is a tremendous country. I have not been mistreated, I have been taken good care of all the way down the line and I really appreciate what the United States has done for me." He further indicated that even if all the fences were brought down he would remain where he was because that was what was expected.

After a short fifteen or thirty minutes (depending on the record) the monitor signaled time was up. Mitsutaka humbly asked, "Son, can you spare me a few dollars?" Russell took out everything he happened to have on him, roughly fifty dollars, and put it on the table for his father. Both men stood up. Again there was no embrace. In his quiet but firm voice, Mitsutaka gave a final admonition to Russell. "Son, remember who you are. Do not at any time dishonor the good family name. Honor the uniform you are wearing. Serve your country, serve it well."

Mitsutaka thanked the monitor for permitting the meeting. Father and son rose. Both bowed. Mitsutaka told Russell, "*Ki o tsukete* Be careful," then turned and exited the room. He never looked back. Russell knew he was crying.

"I never saw him again until after the war, when I brought Grandma [Aiko] back to Hawaii." This was the only time Russell would see his father between 1940 and 1948. They never spoke much about this experience after the war. Russell later remarked that on his way out "the once formidable looking fence no longer looked so menacing. I knew that no fence could have held my father. Had he not willed it nothing could have contained him. He would have died first."

Some of Russell's Hawaiian friends lived in Salt Lake City, Utah so he stopped there on his way back. Chi Terazawa was there and Arthur Nishimoto arrived a little earlier. Chi suggested Russell and Arthur get their patriarchal blessings before being shipped overseas. In order to do so they needed permission from the Hawaiian mission president; even though the G.I.s were stationed on the other side of the country they still fell under his jurisdiction. Russell and Arthur received clearance by phone to have their blessings given in Salt Lake.

On the appointed day Russell and Arthur went to Church headquarters, still located in the grey granite building next to the Beehive house on South Temple Street. It was Russell's first visit to downtown Salt Lake, but certainly not his last. It struck him as "just an ordinary city. I didn't know too much about the church, I was a pretty lousy member," he recalls.

The two young men from Hawaii received their blessings at the hands of Apostle Joseph Fielding Smith, who later became 10th president of the church. Russell got to chat with the apostle a little bit and described President Smith as "a very serious minded person," which in Russell's way of thinking is a real compliment. Years later Russell would have the opportunity of meeting President Smith several more times after he began teaching at Brigham Young University.

By way of blessing, Elder Smith counseled the young man "there will be many who feel that [being Japanese] in and of itself constitutes an enemy, but I bless you that you shall prove to those with whom you served that you will be faithful to the highest of ideals." He was also promised that he would be "protected from assignments whose fulfillment would conflict with your ideals as a Latter-day Saint" and that he would be "protected in time of danger." Russell was further promised that he "shall prove always worthy." This was both a surprise and a comfort to him.

Arthur was given a similar blessing that he would not be harmed, a bold promise indeed knowing he was being sent to join the 442nd in Italy. At war's end the 442nd would stand as the most highly decorated unit in American history, but this dubious distinction is a clear indicator of the high wound and mortality rate suffered by the men doing the fighting.

Upon his return to Fort Snelling, Russell and one other soldier were asked to go to the assistant superintendent's office where they were commended on their high marks and invited to stay on as instructors. It was "quite a pat on the back" and Russell was happy to accept. He was promoted to staff sergeant, the rank of an instructor, garnering a rocker beneath his three stripes. It was a great opportunity for the young man but a short lived one.

A few days later new orders came in. Russell was to pack his bags and get ready to ship out. As usual the orders didn't state where he was going but Russell sensed he was heading to the Pacific. America was preparing for the invasion of Japan.

7

NOTHING GOOD COMES OUT FROM WAR

Despite the tenacity displayed by the Japanese soldiers, American forces continued to press back the Japanese perimeter in the Pacific. Both sides paid for every scrap of soil in precious blood but by 1944 it was clear that Japan was losing the war. With Allied victory no longer in question, only the final cost remained unanswered.

In June decisive battles were fought against Imperial forces in the Philippine Sea and the U.S. began using forward islands like Mariana and Palau to launch aerial bombing attacks on the Japanese home islands.

The first full-scale air raid on Tokyo was in the northeast section near Asakusa.

There had been previous sorties in other parts of Japan but this one was different. For the first time the American planes carried incendiary bombs instead of conventional ordinance, devastating against the wooden houses and structures that comprised most of the city. The destruction was immense. Many people who jumped into the Sumida River to escape the blasts were still killed by the intensity of the fire surging across the water.

From their house in the southern end of the city, Aiko and her family could see the entire sky lit up in a red glow. It was the first time she realized how vulnerable they were. Her father was worried about his stepsister who lived in the area being attacked. The next day he went to check on her and found her alive. Not everyone was so fortunate. By conservative estimates over 25,000 people were killed in one night.

Yoshizo realized that the family needed a shelter. They had a small one under the straw *tatami* floor mats in the house but he felt it wasn't safe enough so they dug one in the garden outside. It was very small, roughly the size of two *tatami*, around 3x6 feet, deep enough for about four people to crawl in and sit but not enough to stand.

A *totan* metal sheet was placed over the top of it then covered in dirt. It "wasn't much" but at least it was a place to hide.

Aiko recalls that during the bombings her sister Hisa stayed in bed. Aiko always marveled at how brave she was to stay there and sleep. Years later Aiko asked Hisa about it and Hisa told her no, she stayed in bed because she was so scared she couldn't move.

The bombings became so severe that the government ordered the evacuation of all pregnant women and young children from Tokyo. If a child didn't have a place to go they were organized into groups by their schools and accompanied by their teachers into the countryside.

The *honke obaasan*, Grandmother Mori, had one granddaughter, Michiyo, who was seven, Kyoko's age. Both were still in elementary school but Aiko's parents didn't want them to go with the school group so other arrangements had to be made. A distant relative of *honke obaasan* ran a *ryokan*, traditional Japanese inn, in a small town near Yoshina hot springs on the Izu Peninsula, south of Tokyo. It was decided she should take Michiyo, Kyoko and a third young relative to stay there. 19-year old Aiko, who had been working at the Hokushin Company for a year, volunteered to go and help out with the three younger girls.

Yoshizo chose to remain in Tokyo, where he stayed for the rest of the war. He was now serving as chief of the fire patrol in their district and felt obligated to remain in the city. During air raids he and the other volunteers gathered at Yaguchi elementary school as part of an emergency response team.

In addition to his civic responsibilities Yoshizo also established a ball bearing factory to help supply the demand for machine parts. The small factory was located near their home in Kamata. It was bombed out by the Allies before Aiko ever saw it.

Ichiro was drafted for a second time and was sent to the frontline in China. As before, only rare bits of information filtered home, and the family received little or no communication on his condition.

Hiroko, Aiko's oldest sister, was married and lived nearby. Shige was still single and opted to stay in Tokyo to help their mother. Hisa, age 15, continued to attend school until near the end of the war when she was required to do factory work.

Izu Peninsula was very inconvenient to get to but it was far from the bombings and peaceful. From Tokyo the women rode the To-kai train line for an hour to Mishima station, beyond Atami, where they transferred to the Izu line for another hour ride to Shuzenji, a famous historical site from the Kamakura period. Another hour by bus (rigged to run on burning charcoal since no gasoline was available) delivered them to an unscheduled stop from where they had to walk a further half an hour to reach the remote Tofuya Ryokan.

The military had taken over the inns and hotels in the region for housing wounded and recuperating soldiers. With the *ryokan* rooms otherwise occupied, *obaasan's* relatives offered the women two upstairs bedrooms in their private home.

The town was very small—Aiko could count how many houses were in the area—but the location was pastoral. There weren't many people Aiko's age but she kept busy taking care of *obaasan* and the younger girls. She spent time gathering firewood in the mountains, and working to keep everyone's spirits up. Laundry was done in the picturesque and swiftly flowing Kanogawa river nearby.

Surrounded by fields and *tanbo,* rice paddies, Izu was beautiful but very distinct from city life. Even the local language reflected the difference. When Aiko asked a lady where the *otearai,* restroom, was located she was met with a blank stare. The local townsfolk used the more colloquial term *benjo* and never heard the term *otearai* before, even though it was generally considered more polite and commonly used in Tokyo.

One advantage Izu offered over the city was access to a hot spring. During the day it was for use only by the soldiers but at night the villagers could go for free. Fuel was scarce in Tokyo and a heated bath was a rare luxury in the city.

The real difficulty staying in Izu was the scarcity of food. The government was controlling rations and staples such as rice had to be obtained from a distribution center in Yugashima. The families took turns delivering food from Tokyo to Izu, walking a mile to the station to catch the train to the city distribution station, carrying back the supplies in a rucksack. When it was her family's turn it was usually Aiko that went.

After a year the bombings had damaged the transit system and trains from Tokyo were erratic at best, making the trip a haphazard affair. Shipments of food were often delayed or simply didn't arrive at all. As the situation grew more difficult the family decided to return home.

Back in Tokyo, life was dominated by American B-29 bombers. Aiko remembers watching a formation of seven or eight planes soaring with their white tails against the blue sky, smoke and contrails streaming behind them and thinking how beautiful they looked. But any illusion of beauty was dispelled by the rain of destruction the airborne visitors poured out on the city. The raids were so frequent Aiko said it was "almost a regular scheduled part of life."

At first the bombers only came at night, but as the war progressed they grew more brazen, running sorties by daylight as well. The bomber's targets seemed random initially but slowly a pattern began to emerge. People gathered around the radio listening anxiously to hear which direction the planes were headed. *Nishi ni mukatte imasu*, meant they were headed west, towards Osaka in the Kansai area and Aiko and her family could enjoy a little respite. *Tohoku ni mukatte imasu*, meant another fearful night for those in Tokyo. In muted understatement Aiko described the drone of the B-29s hard to sleep through.

Possibly more frightening than the bombers were the American fighter planes, smaller, faster and able to sneak up almost out of nowhere. Aiko recalls standing with her family by their shelter, scared and ready to hide when they heard planes approaching. For years after whenever she heard the sound of a B-29 or any similar noise, a lump would rise in her throat as a visceral reminder of those fearful days.

By this time most of Japan's naval power had been destroyed, including her aircraft carriers and the bulk of her airpower. Only once did Aiko ever see a Japanese fighter resisting the American planes. It was a daylight run and the bombers were hitting what Aiko guessed was central Tokyo. With no immediate sense of danger, her family stood outside their shelter, watching. In the distance, far enough away that they couldn't distinguish who was who, they saw two smaller fighters engaged in a dogfight. The planes darted up and down, in and out of the clouds, almost dancing. Then a white parachute opened and disappeared into the city below, leaving the family to wonder who had won or lost.

On a different night a B-29 was hit by anti-aircraft fire and began to burn like a fireball. The flaming wreckage plummeted from the sky, careening out of control in their direction. It looked like it was going to land right on top of their house. It was one of three times when Aiko believed she was going to die. The plane's momentum carried it directly over their house where it crashed a few miles away.

One of Aiko's most heartbreaking memories of the entire war happened the very next day when news spread that an American soldier had been found dead nearby. She ran to join the group of people that gathered in silence around where the body sat leaned against the fence of a house. A Japanese military policeman stood watch over the body, which had been covered with a straw mat. There was no parachute by the time Aiko arrived but it was assumed he parachuted out of the wrecked B-29, which still smoldered nearby. When enough people came the policeman removed the mat for them to look. The blonde haired soldier was young, not much older than Aiko herself. Except for a small streak of blood on his cheek, he could have merely been asleep. On his finger Aiko saw a single gold band and felt sorrow for his family. It was the first time many of the people ever saw "the enemy" up close and they were frightened. From her time at Aoyama Aiko was used to foreigners; the experience wasn't scary, only sad.

As the war worsened, people continued to evacuate from major cities in droves. The family decided that Hatsu should take the younger girls out of the city again. The problem was Yoshizo's and Hatsu's families were both from Tokyo with no relatives in any outlying areas. Kikuchi Tomoya, Hiroko's husband, was originally from Yamagata and his brother still lived there. This brother was fairly well to do and Hatsu contacted him to inquire if she could rent a room. And so Hatsu took Hiroko, who was expecting at this time, and Kyoko, the youngest, to stay in Myookenji, a village two and a half miles from the Yamagata train station. Hisako stayed in Tokyo long enough to graduate from Aoyama then joined her mother and sisters in Yamagata where she began substitute teaching at an elementary school, a job that ended when she had to be hospitalized with scarlet fever. The illness was quite severe, almost taking Hisa's life and she spent a long time recovering.

Aiko occasionally helped bring supplies to Yamagata but stayed in Tokyo with Shige and her father, who remained in his firefighting responsibilities. Despite food shortages and nightly interruptions by air raids they chose to remain in their home. Tomoya-san also stayed in Tokyo, although Aiko is not sure where. Likely it was a dorm owned by the company where he worked.

Elsewhere in the world, President Roosevelt passed away to be replaced by an unlikely fellow from Missouri by the name of Harry S. Truman. In far-flung Germany, several years too late by any account, Hitler was dead by his own hand. Aiko never really heard much about the war in Europe even when Germany surrendered. It was hard to focus on much else when her entire world revolved around air raids and survival.

Aiko remembers being frightened of the bombings but not of losing the war. Reports came in regularly over the radio announcing the Japanese fleet had sunk this or that ship or won this or that battle, making it sound like they were winning. It wasn't until later she realized it was only propaganda.

"It was all lies," she tells, "Who suffers? The common people . . . Nothing good comes out from war."

It never occurred to her that Japan might lose until a year before the war's end. It was never discussed, even during the bombing. Military influence was so strong in the country that you could be arrested for speaking of it. No one mentioned it publicly but at home, in private, people talked. Even when Aiko realized Japan was actually going to be defeated there was no way to comprehend what it really meant.

On May 25th, a scant eighteen days after Germany's surrender, one of the buildings at the imperial palace was burned to the ground. Some days before, the area on the other side of the *jinja* near Aiko's house was hit, reducing everything around the miraculously still intact shrine to debris. Thus far the Mori's neighborhood remained untouched. That was about to change.

The night was dark when the air raid sirens screamed to life and thunderous explosions filled the skies with hellish red smoke and fire. Their father was gone to the elementary school to help direct traffic, leaving Aiko and Shigeko home alone. Through the keen of sirens the girls could hear the ominous growl of the Wright Cyclone engines driving the bombers above them. They were going to be hit.

So quick was their flight to the shelter that Aiko only had time to put on one shoe. She carried the other with her, along with her bible and hymnbook from school. She had no idea why she grabbed these particular items. She just took them and ran. A huge explosion ripped the air nearby as they scrambled to safety.

Clinging tightly to her sister in the tiny dugout, Aiko distinctly remembers feeling, "I am going to die tonight." It wasn't a sense of fear that filled her but the strange calm of surety.

As the attack continued the sisters resolved if they were going to die, they would rather perish in their own home so they went back inside. A huge explosion nearby rattled the house as they entered, sending more smoke into the smothered sky. The dark and empty house soon became too frightening and they decided to go to *Nitta jinja*, the nearby shrine, feeling it might be safer with its tall trees.

Doing as they'd been instructed, both girls donned a thick quilted helmet that covered their head and shoulders and carried their *futon* mattresses wrapped around their bodies as protective measures.

As they left their house a massive explosion shook the earth, the concussion knocking both girls to the ground. Surrounded by the roar of airplanes and explosions, they brushed themselves off and ran for the shrine.

At the *jinja*, a lone sentry standing among the ashen ruins of the neighborhood, the two girls crawled under a stone bench, tucking their heads beneath it for cover. Aiko later laughed that the bench gave them no real protection at all as their entire backsides were still exposed, but at the time it gave the frightened girls a sense of security.

Gradually the noise of the planes and the bombs faded into the distance and Aiko and Shige decided to return to their home. Thick smoke obscured everything. Aiko remembers it blotting out the sky entirely.

As they drew near to their house a neighbor ran up to them. "Oh! You're alive! We thought you were dead!" It only took a moment to understand why. The place where their childhood home once stood was nothing more than ashes and embers. Ichiro's thick dictionaries still burned in the remains of his room. The explosion that knocked the girls to the ground was caused by the very bomb that destroyed their home. Had they stayed in the house a moment longer they would have been killed.

A small *hinomi yagura,* fire-watchtower, stood on the street-side corner of their property where a watchman could stay to warn when there was a fire. At the bottom of the metal structure was a small one-person room, so the girls stayed there until morning, when their father came back. Yoshizo most likely didn't know his house had been hit until his return. It must have been quite a shock.

Yoshizo had been adamant that the house would be fine. Earlier the girls wanted to take some of the furniture and valuables to Kanagawa Prefecture for safekeeping. There was a farmer there whose son was saved by Aiko's brother during the war with China. The girls thought to ask the family to take the desks for safekeeping but Yoshizo forbid it. The house had survived earthquakes, he told them, surely it would survive the war. Actually the house had been destroyed earlier in an earthquake in 1923 and rebuilt. Regardless Yoshizo remained resolute and the girls left the desks where they were.

After the fire cooled off they began searching through the remains of the house. Sometime before the bombing Shigeko placed the family's dishes and fine China[1] into the bathtub and filled it with water. Placing the dishes in a water-filled *ofuro* was common practice during the war and remarkably the dinnerware survived. Everything else—the furniture, the children's desks, the pictures of Yoshizo in uniform on a horse and all six sisters in chiffon dresses—was lost. It was a great tragedy but the family knew human lives were far more important. And those, so far, had been spared.

One of their neighbors, Mr. Shinbori, brought over *omusubi*, rice balls, which are usually filled with a pickled plum or ginger and were considered a real delicacy during the war. The young sisters really appreciated his kindness. Shigeko, who would live on the same property for the remainder of her adult life, never forgot Mr. Shinbori's compassion, often visiting and caring for him until he passed away.

Because of its corner location, Aiko's house was the only one hit on her block. The other houses on her side were still intact but everything across the street was leveled to the ground. A young man in their neighborhood later told them he'd seen the bomb fall right into the middle of their house. True to the young man's story, when the charred rubble was cleared away they found a slightly concave pockmark almost dead center in the concrete foundation.

Several days after the bombing Aiko's foot began hurting. It wasn't swollen, just terribly painful. In all the confusion Aiko didn't realize she'd stepped on a nail and it had grown infected. Her foot needed tending before the infection turned to gangrene, which meant amputation or even death. No doctors were available, but her brother-in-law said he could cure her foot by pouring boiling

---

1. The fine China was *Aritayaki*, a very nice brand made in Saga Prefecture. Yae's fiancée worked in sales for the company.

oil over the wound. Although painful the folk remedy worked and Aiko's foot healed with no gangrene or even scarring.[2]

The lot next to Aiko's house, which stood vacant for a long time, was also owned by her father. The children wanted to put in a tennis court but Yoshizo built apartments instead which he rented out to factory employees from the countryside.

The building was two stories tall with three small units on each floor for a total of six apartments. The individual units were Japanese style, one small room (four *joo* large, roughly 65 square feet) with *tatami* floors and a wash place with a sink. Everyone shared a single restroom on each floor and baths were taken at the nearby bathhouse.

The apartments were full at the time so Yoshizo fixed up the shelter in the garden and lived there for a couple of months. Eventually, as the factories were destroyed and their workers returned home, the apartments became empty and the family would move into them. In the meantime it was decided that the girls should rejoin the family in Yamagata.

Aiko had been to Yamagata before with her sisters but it was a much different time, prior to the war. The girls wanted to vacation there and begged their father for a trip. Yoshizo finally acquiesced and took the whole family one summer.

Tomoya-san's family was from Yamagata and they stayed at his oldest brother's house. Apparently he was doing well for himself and Aiko remembers the farmhouse, styled like the kind typical to the area, as a very nice one. The *futon* beds were very thick and the blankets were bulky and heavy to lie under because of the fierceness of the winters.

---

2. Miscellaneous details Aiko mentioned during her interview: Even though she did put on her other shoe, the nail apparently went through it. The fate of her *futon* is unknown. She remembers it was quite dirty and soiled and thinks that she and her sister might have left them at the shrine.

The remote mountains, where a person could walk for miles without seeing another soul, were an amazing contrast for girls raised in the bustling city. Climbing the hills and hunting for herbs that grew wild proved to be a wonderful adventure for the sisters.

This time the trip to Yamagata was met more with resignation than anticipation. At this hour of the war the trains were still running, albeit irregularly, and were packed beyond capacity with evacuees fleeing from Tokyo. Everyone one carried large bundles full of their belongings. Some people even carried their *futons* with them. The train cars were so overflowing with humanity that it was impossible for the girls to board through the doors. They finally crawled through a side-window and ended up standing the whole way since there was no room to move even their feet. The girls survived the journey and were grateful to find their mother and family well. Even Hisako had recovered from her scarlet fever and was doing fine.

Once again Tomoya-san's brother took the family in. Both the *ryokan* and the house were already at maximum occupancy and Aiko and her family stayed in a single room storage shed. Mirroring Russell's experience at Fort Snelling, the storage shed once served as a chicken coup but had been cleaned out and converted into a temporary living space.

Because of the confines of the space their *futons* were laid out on the floor side by side essentially forming a large mat where everyone slept. The space was small but Aiko and her family didn't mind. The only real downside to the new arrangement was the abundance of fleas. The girls made a sport of the teeming pests, racing to see who could catch the most every morning. Still they were grateful to have a roof over their heads far from the destruction of Tokyo.

The greatest challenge was scarcity. It was particularly trying for Hatsu who faced the double trial of finding enough to feed everyone and worry about the family still in Tokyo. One distinct memory of Yamagata for Aiko is the potatoes, which they ate almost every day, dried and cut into long strips. The family knew they were lucky to have anything to eat at all but the monotonous diet soon grew wearisome to everyone—except Aiko, who still loves potatoes to this day.

An occasional and welcome respite from dried potatoes came in the form of *konnyaku*, a traditional Japanese food with a rubbery texture that absorbs the flavor of the sauce it is cooked in. Like much Japanese cuisine it is claimed as a health food. The shop of a renown *konnyaku* producer was located outside of town. Aiko was surprised to learn it was made from the powdered roots of the konjac plant, a tuber indigenous to southern Asia.

Despite the less than ideal conditions Aiko always found Yamagata beautiful. Sometimes the girls played by the waters of the large river that ran nearby. More often they explored the countryside, hiking to a nearby *jinja* nestled in the hills to pass the time. Aiko stayed in Yamagata for roughly two and a half months before returning to Tokyo at the end of July to check in on the family. A few days later the course of human history would be altered forever.

August 6th, 1945. It was 8:15 in the morning when Little Boy made its descent through the cool air over Hiroshima. With a flash brighter than the rising sun 80,000 lives were erased in a heartbeat. Another estimated 30-50,000 would follow due to injuries and radiation, most of them over the next few weeks. No amount of words can ever convey the depths of the horror and tragedy. It was devastation of unprecedented proportion in human history.

The news did not take long to spread. Yoshizo informed Aiko that the Americans had dropped some sort of new bomb, not a normal one but something vastly more powerful. He also expressed the feeling that Japan was going to lose the war. "I think Japan will surrender." It was the first time she heard anyone utter the sentiment aloud. Shortly after Aiko returned to Yamagata again.

Allied forces called for unconditional surrender, stating "the alternative for Japan is prompt and utter destruction." Despite the show of force in Hiroshima the Japan government continued to ignore the mandate. On August 9th a second bomb was dropped on the city of Nagasaki to equally atrocious results. This time the message was clear.

On August 15th Aiko and her family gathered around a radio with several other local families and some of the soldiers in anticipation of an important announcement. Through a heavy layer of static the voice of the Emperor emerged from the small speaker. It was the first time most people ever heard the Emperor's voice. Aiko was startled how high pitched and thin it sounded.

In truth the emperor's announcement was actually a broadcast of a phonograph recording made the day or so before. Unbeknownst to many was that the Emperor had survived a coup d'état to give the message. The night before the broadcast nearly a thousand military officers attempted to raid the palace in order to destroy the recording but the Emperor and the phonograph survived.

The Japanese spoken by the Emperor was a high-class dialect of such formality that Aiko couldn't understand what he was saying. When the Emperor finished speaking the room was silent. Aiko didn't know what was happening. Finally someone declared, "We lost the war!"

Aiko's first thought was not of surrender, defeat or disappointment. It was simply that—after months of bombs, fires and anxiety—she could finally get some sleep! Most people's feelings were similar. They didn't feel anger or shame, only relief that the war was over. At long last they could begin rebuilding and attempt to return to some semblance of a normal life.

In retrospect Aiko noticed that the surrender produced the interesting effect of bringing the Japanese people closer to their emperor. Before the war the emperor was considered a god, even speaking a different level of Japanese. Afterwards, the emperor began to travel more among his people and speaking in the common language, gradually transitioning from a distant deity into a beloved figurehead.

It wasn't much later when Aiko saw a man walking up the road in the evening with a sword slung across his back. As he drew closer she recognized him as her cousin, Agu-chan. Agu chastized Aiko and Shige, telling them young girls shouldn't be out at twilight and to get back to their house. Agu-chan's mother (who was Yoshizo's step-sister) and little sister fled to Yamagata from Tokyo when Asakusa, where they lived, was bombed out. Agu-chan worked as support crew for *kamikaze* pilots in Kyushu and had returned north to find his family. Not finding his mother in Tokyo he'd tracked her down to Yamagata.

With contact interrupted it had been months since Aiko and her family heard from Tokyo and they were worried about her father. When Agu-chan said he was going back to Tokyo to find out about his own father, Aiko announced she was going with him. At first everyone agreed how brave she was, then someone suggested it might be dangerous for a young girl to go back to Tokyo. Propaganda was heavy on both sides during the war and the Japanese citizens were fed a steady diet of how barbaric and uncivilized the Americans were. Suddenly everyone opposed the idea of Aiko returning, fearing hostility towards her. Strong willed and earnestly wanting to know her father's welfare, Aiko determined that she was going regardless.

The compromise was reached that Aiko would wear all black so that she looked more like a man. It was also suggested that she should put soot on her face but she refused. Dressed in a *monpe*[3] jacket, trousers and a hat Aiko accompanied Agu-chan to the train station.

Aiko was the first member in her family to return to Tokyo. Others had begun making their way back to Tokyo as well and it

---

3. A *kimono*-like jacket with short sleeves. Simple to make and often home made, *monpe* were commonly worn by women during the war and were decidedly less feminine than a full *kimono*.

was standing room only again on the train. It was an almost surreal experience as they approached the city, seeing the sprawling metropolis leveled except for a few scattered and broken cement buildings. It wasn't a total shock as the city was well demolished before she left to Yamagata but the extent of the destruction was still astounding.

Her head filled with horrible rumors of how dangerous Tokyo had become and the terrible things the Americans were doing to the Japanese, Aiko's anxiety grew as they advanced into the city. As the train neared Yurakucho station,[4] Aiko saw several Japanese children playing with what were clearly American military police and realized at once everyone's fears regarding the Americans were unfounded.

The American occupation in Japan was to be the first of its kind in the history of modern warfare. Instead of destroying the culture of the conquered, America was intent on rebuilding the country, committing time, money and manpower to do so.

As the train continued on, Aiko saw other young Japanese girls walking on the street wearing regular, beautifully colored dresses. Aiko felt embarrassed to be dressed in such rough, dirty clothes, wishing she had worn something else.

Aiko went with her cousin as far as Ueno station where they said goodbye, Agu-chan heading to Asakusa while she took the Keihin line home to Yaguchi.

Aiko found her father still living in the bomb shelter in their yard, even though the apartments were empty by this time. Aiko supposes he felt the shelter was safer. "*Ah, kaette kita*," he said, "You've returned." Both father and daughter were very relieved to see each other. Yoshizo inquired after the family and was pleased to hear that everyone was fine.

---

4. The buildings in the area were being used for American housing at the time.

Over all, the Mori family had been very lucky. They lost only one person during the war, an uncle in Nagoya, married to Hatsu's younger sister, who was killed by the force of a bomb blast as he was entering a shelter.

The postal service soon began running again. Deliveries took longer than before but it was a step towards rebuilding. Aiko and her father sent a post card to Yamagata telling everyone Tokyo was peaceful, Yoshizo was fine and that they should return home, which Hatsu and the girls quickly did.

Here providence smiled on them yet again. Word spread quickly throughout the country and soon everyone was trying to return to Tokyo. The influx was so great that in September, shortly after the family arrived home, the government barred the return of more refugees since the bombed out metropolitan area didn't have enough food or housing to accommodate everyone.

The Japanese phrase *shikata ga nai*, stemming from Buddhist ideology, means roughly "it can't be helped." The war was over, Japan had lost. *Shikata ga nai*. What else were they to do? Without anger they resigned themselves to cleaning up after the war, collecting scraps and rebuilding.

"No sooner after the war ended," writes Russell, "the people, especially the older ones were out cleaning up debris. Even with the future unknown they were out . . . ready to lay the foundation of a new Japan."

Aiko's family moved into their apartments overlooking the remains of their home. The house was eventually rebuilt but that wouldn't be until the early 1950s, well after Aiko had left Japan for the next phase of her life. Her family remained in the apartments until that time.

Yasuko Ide, one of Aiko's best friends from Aoyama lived in Kojimachi, near the center of Tokyo. The Ide family lived in the United States before the war and Yasuko was born in Seattle. Yasuko attended school there until the sixth grade and she and her sisters all spoke English. The Ides moved back to Japan after the tragic, early death of Yasuko's father.

When Aiko learned that Yasuko's home had been bombed out she asked Hatsu if her family could move into the apartments. The four girls and their mother moved into the room on the west side of the building. It was a tight fit but after everything they had been through there were no complaints.

Because they both spoke English Yasuko encouraged Aiko to seek out a new job working for the incoming American occupational forces. Looking at the immediate needs of their families—their earnings would help support them while the younger siblings returned to school—the decision would also bring them into contact with their future.

8

LAND OF MY FATHERS

HURRY UP AND WAIT. FROM Fort Snelling, Russell and the others were shipped out to Camp Anza in California then to San Pedro. It was two in the morning when Russell and his group were rushed to pack then rushed aboard their ship where they sat and did very little for the next month as they worked their way to the Far East. The ship itself was large, holding several hundred soldiers, 60–70 bunks stacked four high in each compartment, offering the men very little privacy. There was barely enough room to store the single duffle bag containing all of their belongings. The tight quarters and lack of privacy extended even to the showers and toilets, which were arranged side-by-side in an open line.

Though Russell and the others didn't know exactly where they were headed they knew that they were part of the invasion force destined for Japan. It was an anxious time. The Japanese were ferocious in defending the islands across the Pacific. How much harder would they fight when backed into a corner on their own homeland? The cost would be high and paid for in blood. This was the anticipated state of things on the ship when word of the surrender came. The sense of relief was palpable.

The ship made brief stops at Enewetak, the atoll that would later become home to extensive nuclear testing, Corregidor Island, used for defending the entrance to Manila Bay, and also Bataan Peninsula, the site of the eponymous death march only a few years earlier.

When the ship finally weighed anchor Russell found himself at Luzon near Manila. American forces had controlled the bulk of the Philippines since the beginning of the year although scattered fighting still continued on some of the outlying islands.

The soldiers were told to remain on board where they sat for several more days. Russell described life onboard a troop ship as "terrible" because it was so boring. The other soldiers entertained themselves by shooting craps or playing cards but gambling never held any attraction to Russell. More often than not one fellow wound up with all the money or the game would end in a fight or both.

To alleviate his own ennui Russell took a needle from his sewing kit and bent it into a small hook, which he attached to some #10 thread. Using bread from the cafeteria for bait he began fishing, dangling the makeshift tackle from his finger down the side of the ship. Before long before he felt a tug on his line and he hoisted up a fish. It wasn't much, only a small *holehole* about four inches long. "I didn't keep it but it felt pretty good. I caught a fish in Manila Bay!"

After several more mind numbing days, orders came in, as usual, without much warning. The soldiers were told to dress for combat, pack their equipment and assemble on deck. From there they climbed down rope ladders onto assault barges, which took them to shore where they were ordered to fall into formation. Then they began to march. Where they were going Russell would never find out. They hadn't gone very far when the command was given to halt. A voice yelled, "Horiuchi, drop out!" He alone was moved to the side of the road while the column continued on.

Russell's memories of his time in the Philippines get a little blurry. The days were monotonous and he spent a good deal of time out of direct contact with other personnel, doing very little. Looking back Russell figures he was under observation, to see what he would do and how he would behave.

He quickly made adjustments to his situation. Scouting around on his own to find things Russell soon located the outhouse. There was a water bag for drinking a stone's throw from there. Russell never filled it himself nor did he ever see anyone else put water in it, but it stayed full so there must have been at least some people around but he never saw anyone. There were no baths but it was the tail end of monsoon season and Russell found that by lifting the flap of his tent he could gather enough of the copious rain for a makeshift shower.

Russell was also told there was a mess hall, which he found after walking around a bit, but after sampling it once, he decided the food was worse than the K-rations he'd been eating and he never went back.

Continuing his walk about, Russell came across a tent with a Filipino guard posted outside. Upon inquiry he was informed it was a POW camp (in his writings Russell calls them PW camps) for Japanese soldiers.

"Can I go in?" Russell asked.

Glancing at Russell's rank the guard nodded, "Sure, you can go in anytime."

Russell is sure that the relative proximity of his tent and the POW camp was no coincidence, an arrangement set up by Military Intelligence, although nothing to this effect was ever specifically mentioned to him.

After removing his dog tags, jacket and other identification Russell went in. Most of the prisoners were out on work detail and the first person he came across was the cook.

Russell struck up conversation with the man who spoke with a *zu-zuben* dialect and Russell quickly and accurately deduced where he was from.

"Which part of Tohoku are you from?" he asked the cook.

The cook was shocked. "How did you know? I didn't say anything!"

With his ability for sensing things and picking up on details, Russell could have made a great psychic. A story he often related was his interrogation of a POW. Nothing like the harsh and overly dramatic portrayals in the movies, Russell walked in and simply offered the man a mandarin orange.

"*Mikan, oishii, ne?* Mandarins are pretty good, huh?" Russell asked him. "*Mikan dekite iru tokoro o mita koto ga aru ka?* Have you ever seen a place where they grow them?"

When the man answered *mita koto aru yo* that he had indeed seen such a place Russell could infer where he was from. From there Russell made what he described as "interconnecting linkages," combining the information from the interrogation with other gathered intelligence, and could decipher what unit the man belonged to and that he'd received his training in China. Through subtle questions and keen attention to detail Russell would unfold critical information such as troop concentrations and movement.[1]

Russell asked the cook if there was any food. The cook was surprised. "Don't they feed you? You're American." Russell demurred explaining how awful the food was and that he was surviving on K-rations. The cook brought out rice and chopped ham and offered it to the *Nisei*. "It was good!" Much better than what the American troops were eating.

While Russell ate, the two began to discuss the cook's eventual homecoming to Japan, a prospect he was astonishingly not excited about. The cook had passed out after being shot in combat and woken up on an American operating table. He was grateful for the skill and kindness of the American surgeons who saved his life but the fact that he surrendered was considered a shame on his honor and his return would be a disgrace to him and his family as well.

---

1. Author's note: when it came to my grandfather, I never got away with anything as a child!

Russell didn't see a lot of the POWs since they were always being put on different details in different places. But he would often head over to the camp, giving the cook his tobacco ration, which the cook shared with the other POWs. Once Russell was even invited to an *engeikai*, a play the POWs were holding. It was Russell, one Filipino guard and the 30 Japanese POWs who put on the show. Overall this first group of POWs seemed well treated and resigned to their situation.

Sometime later Russell got a notice to report. Dressed in his khaki's he was picked up along with three or four other men and taken around Manila. Among the places they stopped was St. Thomas University located in the lower boroughs. Once the religious center of the city it was now "all banged up, destroyed."

As Russell and the others crossed the street they met a Filipino guard who glared at the *Nisei* soldiers in American uniforms.

"You Japs?" he challenged then patted his rifle, "I shot six Japs with this."

There was no right answer. The *Nisei* walked away without a word.

St. Thomas was now being used as a civilian POW camp. Like everything else so far, the purpose of the excursion was never made clear to Russell or the others. "They never told us why [we visited there]. I can only suppose we were supposed to get an estimate of the situation."

Russell was dropped off at his camp again, once more alone. Somewhere beyond him the war continued to be fought but in a little tent in a swamp near Manila nothing was going on.

One day when Russell went to the small shack by the latrine to get some water there was a notice tacked on it for him to report for duty. As usual he saw no one post it and no one mentioned it to him. He was given two hours to pack up his belongings and report to a nearby roadway that served as an airstrip. No further details were given.

This time Russell was not alone. Fourteen other *Nisei* MIS members were there as well. Among them was a young man from southern California named Charles Shibata. Charlie, as he was known to his friends, was attached to counterintelligence and had been in Fort Snelling at the same time as Russell although the two weren't acquainted at the time. That would change down the road. As Staff Sergeant, Russell was the highest-rank present and thus in charge but he was given no information to share with the other men.

They were ordered to go through their duffle bags and get rid of all their combat gear including helmets and bayonets. They were allowed to keep their rifles but no ammunition. When they asked why they were simply told, "We don't want any incidents to occur, that's why."

Besides their combat gear, they were told to get rid of everything else they didn't need as well. By this time they realized enough to know they were being shipped out, but not knowing where made it difficult to know what they would need. They didn't even know if they should prepare for hot or cold weather. Some discarded their blankets but Russell kept his and his jacket. The circumstances felt funny to him so he kept everything he could, which ultimately turned out in his favor.

Russell and his group were herded aboard a DC-3 transport plane. Minutes later the rumbling engines lifted the fourteen *Nisei* into the dark of night.

A few hours later Russell's plane began to descend, touching ground in blackout conditions. None of the *Nisei* knew it yet but they had landed at Naha Airbase in Okinawa. The *Nisei* had come full circle to the land of their ancestry—they were in Japan.

After one night in Naha the intel officers boarded the plane again. Before long they could see the unmistakable view of Mount Fuji growing in the distance. Recalling the experience Russell wrote, "The outline of Mt. Fuji was simpl[y] majestic and breathtaking— more beautiful than the pictures that I had seen."

As they approached the metropolitan Tokyo/Yokohama area the picturesque farmland they were flying over butted up suddenly against "the ugly scene of bomb pockets." This was the first Russell had seen of the city and he was taken aback by the totality of its destruction.

Russell wrote: "With the war in Europe over the full force of American destructive power decended [sic] on Japan. Unless one was actually there and saw the devastation and destruction, no amount of photos or description could fully show what had happened to Japan. It was unbelievable."

Like many historians, Russell felt Midway had been the real turning point in the war. The U.S. lost two aircraft carriers but Japan lost almost everything. When the four Japanese carriers sank they took over three thousand planes and all the pilots that went with them. With the bulk of Japan's airpower buried at sea there was next to nothing left to defend her skies from the onslaught of Allied airpower.

As the intelligence officers crossed the landing strip at Atsugi airport where they touched down, Russell and his fellow *Nisei* came across another group of Japanese POWs who stopped their work filling in bomb craters to watch the *Nisei* pass by. He could hear them muttering amongst themselves. "*Ano hito, Nihonjin no kao ja nai ka?* What are those Japanese faces doing in American uniforms?"

These prisoners presented a completely different attitude than the ones Russell met in the Philippines. The Japanese soldiers in the Pacific were forced to surrender in defeat. The soldiers here were told to surrender by their officers and their emperor. They felt no sense of shame like the POWs near Manila. It may have been Russell's imagination but it felt like there was some hostility as well—to the prisoners he and his companions looked like little more than traitors. Fearing trouble the intel officers hurried on. They decided to wait by one of the hangers. It was about three in the afternoon. No one came by or spoke to them until about nine that evening when a canvas covered truck pulled up and they were told to get in.

The truck delivered them to the courtyard of the *Oukurashou*, the government finance building in Tokyo. Compact and constructed almost entirely from stone, the building escaped most damage during the bombings and was initially used as grand central for the entire American occupational force serving as barracks, headquarter's offices, PX and every other use the military might need. As the surrounding buildings were repaired and rebuilt the different offices were gradually relocated.

MacArthur's forces had only been in Japan about two and half weeks by this point and everything was still in disarray. Showers (which Charlie Shibata describes as "ice cold") and toilets were still being set up and the soldiers were living on rations since there was no cafeteria. Sleeping quarters weren't designated yet either so they found a place that looked suitable and slept there.

Riding in the back of the canvas-covered truck at night afforded Russell very little chance to see outside. The sight that greeted him in the morning was staggering. From the air the damage was bad. On the ground, up close and personal, it was overwhelming. While the death toll wasn't as immediately horrific as Hiroshima or Nagasaki, in Russell's estimation the ruination inflicted on the Tokyo/Keihin area was more extensive. "They had nothing left. Everything was flat," says Russell. He understood why Japan had agreed to unconditional surrender. "I was not prepared for the shock after landing in Atsugi. Destruction was everywhere . . . I saw ill-clad people, looking emaciated and my heart cried . . . The situation seemed so hopeless for the people, and I wondered if the Japanese people would ever be able to get themselves out of the hole."

The *Nisei* found their way to the HQ offices where they were given assignments and disbursed. Russell would remain at headquarters and was assigned to ESS, the economic and scientific research section.

Russell worked with Arthur Tiedemann, an officer of Jewish decent, a "brilliant guy" from Columbia University. The two spent the better part of a year translating Japanese finance and banking laws and the Imperial Household laws.

Filled with legal terms and other difficult terminology, the translation was slow and difficult, really pushing the skills of both men. Russell remembers coming across the word *kyoshitsu*. In common Japanese the word means classroom. But Russell knew from context that it wasn't classroom. Both men were stumped, pouring over the dictionary but still coming up empty handed. Finally Russell asked a native who was able to clarify the word for him. In this case *kyoshitsu* was a term used only during the war referring to the mandatory quota farmers were required to contribute.

Years later the family learned that Aiko's grandfather had been minister over the imperial household. It is likely he was involved in drafting the very laws Russell was now translating.

Occasionally Russell was called in to discuss the finance laws with officials, but most of the time he and Tiedemann were left alone to their work. Once Russell went to the Bank of Japan. He remembers seeing gold bars lying all over the place. It was more gold than he'd ever seen but for a national treasury it was "pathetically small."

Eventually Russell was re-assigned to two Naval officers doing reparations work. These assignments sent him on excursions to various parts of Japan to ascertain the condition of the country's industrial capabilities. He was often shipped out alone. Even the times he was accompanied by an officer the officer usually disappeared to parts unknown and Russell was left to assess the situation by himself.

A great deal of Russell's time was spent looking over bombed out manufacturing plants. Haunting images of acre after acre of half built and destroyed fighter planes at Mitsubishi Heavy Industry remained with him long after the war. Similar sights awaited him at Tokyo Shibaura, Panasonic and Matsushita Denki. There wasn't a single defense mechanism left intact anywhere. "Perhaps my coverage and visits were not extensive enough, but I did not come across a single plant in operation[al] condition. I had not seen anything so reduced to rubble."

The further Russell assessed Japan's pre- and post-war resources and reserves the less he understood why Japan went to war in the first place. It was obvious their ambitions far exceeded their assets. "It was like," he later wrote, "a self-imposed national suicide mission."

At Matsushita Denki, yet another wrecked plant, Russell found a number of workers gathered in a small shed. With materials scavenged from whatever they could find they were endeavoring to manufacture radios for sale. Russell was impressed that the workers were not sitting around lamenting their situation but were busy applying themselves. He was proud of the Japanese determination to rebuild and was concerned with Japan being able to get itself back on its feet.

When a power plant was slated to be dismantled and parted out to other countries, Russell encouraged the Naval officers to keep it in country knowing that with Japan's infrastructure already in shambles her people needed all the help they could get.

Ultimately, for the Japanese economy the real saving grace proved to be the advent of the Korean War. Japanese manufacturing for the U.S. military kept the country from running into debt allowing it to rebuild faster than it could have otherwise.

The military didn't arrange for accommodations and Russell slept wherever he could, in railway stations and burned out factories. He described it as "worse than camping." In the military's defense there weren't a lot of places left where Russell could have stayed.

Russell's work attracted some outside attention. He was once approached by a Japanese man representing a business group seeking inside information. They knew Russell was familiar with the country's current industrial capabilities, the American plans for them and that he also had some say in the proceedings. Russell dismissed the man by returning his gifts and declining an invitation to a company party where he was told, in effect, there would be pretty women and anything else a single GI might be interested in.

"Look, I know what you are after," Russell told the man, "You get out of this office before I throw you out." When the man protested Russell stood up and chased him out of the room. They never bothered him again.

At Fort Snelling the men were told they were forbidden from fraternizing with the native population in Japan. This was a security measure that also prevented them from writing, publishing or discussing anything for the next 25 years. Russell was unable to use any of his military experiences in his schooling or teaching until 1970. The military wanted no information leaked. One result of this was that Russell couldn't even take notes on his excursion trips and instead had to commit everything to memory.

Russell also wasn't paid for nearly seven months. He was on the move so much after Fort Snelling that his pay records couldn't keep up with him. Russell could have sold his ration cigarettes on the black market but he chose not too. Instead his sister Kay loaned him some cash by postal money order, which he paid back as soon as he was able.

The young Hawaii boy considered these some of the loneliest times in his life and he eagerly counted up his slowly accruing discharge points.

9

SEEING GHOSTS

THE FAMILY WAS STILL IN the middle of cleaning up their neighborhood when Hatsu suggested to Aiko that she should go back to school. Aiko didn't enjoy finishing school the first time around and wasn't eager to return.

Because of her English skills Yasuko, Aiko's friend from Aoyama, was hired immediately by a photography shop, which served a lot of Americans who came in to develop their photos. Partly out of practicality and partly in order to avoid school, Aiko decided to go to work as well. So when the *Gaimushou*, Foreign Office, announced they needed people who could speak English, Aiko applied. She and four thousand other applicants were tested on their English conversation skills. Aiko was one of the few who passed.

Aiko was assigned to work with five other women. Four of the other girls were married and still waiting for their husbands to return from the war. It turned out that everyone in the group besides Aiko were former English teachers. Aiko was also the only one who wasn't a college graduate. Her diligent study at Aoyama had paid off.

Aiko was detailed to work for the Post Exchange (PX) at General MacArthur's headquarters (GHQ) temporarily located in the *Oukurashou*. The supervisor of the temporary PX was an American civilian named Miss Berry. (A different Miss Berry than Aiko's teacher at Aoyama.) She was bilingual although Aiko didn't know where she learned her Japanese.

The PX was roughly twenty square feet with a U-shaped counter, although the shelves were mostly empty at the beginning. Customers would ask for an item from the clerk who picked it off the shelf for them. Most of the goods were daily use items such as toothbrushes, toothpaste, shaving lotion and other sundries. Many of the beautiful and expensive looking items with their colorful boxes were unfamiliar to the Japanese clerks. "Nothing like it existed during the war for the Japanese," said Aiko.

The women worked late morning to early evening. With few streetlights remaining the walk to the train station after work was usually in the dark. Concerned about safety Aiko asked her boss if her sister, Hisako, could join her. An Aoyama graduate like her sister, Hisa could also speak English. Miss Berry agreed and the two sisters began working together at the first PX in Tokyo.

So as not to attract any undue attention to themselves on their way from work the girls donned simple clothes, like the *monpe* Aiko wore on her return to Tokyo from Yamagata. Once inside GHQ they changed into *kimono*s. Amusingly, Aiko, ever the tomboy, didn't know how to wear a proper *kimono*, so her mother and Shigeko had to help her. Later on as the rebuilding of Tokyo progressed and the streetlights were returned to operation the girls felt more comfortable wearing their *kimono* to and from work.

Monetary transactions were conducted in Yen even at the American PX. Currency exchange was restricted in order to help preserve the shattered Japanese economy but the general rate at the time was roughly 360 Yen to one American dollar.

After a while the U.S. Military issued its own temporary currency in the form of large, brownish colored bills. Aiko doesn't know how long these bills were circulated but they were still in use as late as 1948 when she and Russell left for the states.

At first Aiko didn't handle any actual cash. Miss Berry handled all the transactions. After the PX moved from the *Oukurashou* into GHQ, Aiko began handling money as well, slowly taking over the responsibility from her new boss. There was no cash register at the PX so Aiko calculated all the transactions in her head.

One day a pair of GHQ staff bigwigs came in together. Aiko didn't know what rank was what but remembered they had "lots of gold stuff on their uniforms, ropes and braids, the works." She doesn't remember who they were but one was the highest ranked *Nisei* in the military at the time. After Aiko helped them with their purchases the two debated if she was an American or not. The *Nisei* thought she was Japanese but the other thought she was an American. They asked and she politely answered in Japanese that she was, indeed, Japanese. Aiko often deprecates her English skills but they were enough to make the officers question her nationality so she must have done better than she liked to admit.

Russell had just returned from an excursion trip when he heard that the PX was open. He and a friend decided to go see if they carried anything he needed. As they turned the corner Russell froze in his tracks. His blood drained from his face, and he stood rooted to the floor. The woman's face he had seen as a child in Maui stood before him in the form of a petite Japanese girl in a *kimono* working behind the PX counter. He felt as though someone had kicked him in the stomach. All he could do was stare.

"Hey, you okay?" Russell's buddy nudged him to his senses.

"That face! That face!" was all Russell could say.

They left the PX without buying anything but Russell resolved he was going to meet this young lady although it would take some time for him to build up his courage.

Russell wasn't the only soldier to notice the girls behind the counter. Charlie Shibata remembers he and his fellow soldiers going to the PX "mostly to see the girls, who we thought were pretty cute." With relatively few women available and GIs arriving by the hundreds, Russell had a lot of competition.[1]

Every day after Russell walked up to the PX but he could only gaze wordlessly at the girl behind the counter. Finally he mustered up enough guts to approach Aiko. "I told her she had a nice kimono on." Russell remembers it was a red one.

Aiko doesn't remember what she was wearing but she does remember thinking that this GI had a cute baby face. In a very Japanese gesture, she put her hand over her face, thinking this soldier was very forward talking to her without any introduction. At first Aiko mistakenly thought that this fellow was perhaps Yasuko's boyfriend.

Still holding tightly onto the his nerves Russell mentioned, as casually as he could, *"Konya geeto no tokoro de matte iru kara ne.* After you finish work I'll wait for you at the gate." It was a pretty gutsy move for him. Aiko nodded politely then dismissed it thinking he was joking and that he wouldn't really be there.

When Aiko finished her shift and changed into her trousers, she stepped into the cold night with Hisako. True to his word Russell was waiting there chatting with an MP, the frigid wind sweeping around his ankles. It was a clear night, but very, very cold. "She met me, so she felt a chill," laughs Russell.

Was Russell nervous? "Sure I was nervous! I just wanted to get better acquainted with her is all." He was a bit surprised that her younger sister was there as well. "So no monkey business," he jokes.

Russell decided to walk them to the railroad station, Shinbashi Eki, fifteen minutes away. The streetlights were still out and Aiko and Hisako were grateful for the extra protection Russell provided

---

1. In a letter to Russell and Aiko 40 years later Charlie winks, "Russell had it over us with his mastery of the language. He virtually had the pick of the group and he chose Aiko, of course."

through the bombed out city blocks. They didn't talk much on the way to the station, just moderate chit-chat.

The lights at the station were working so at least they didn't have to wait for the train in the dark. While they were standing on the platform Russell brought out a letter from his father written in Japanese and asked if Aiko could read it for him.

Didn't Russell know how to read the Japanese? "I could," he says with a sly grin. But it was a good chance to talk and ask questions. In his defense Russell said it was written in *sorobun*, old classical Japanese. He could read it but it wasn't entirely clear. At least that is what he claimed. Whatever extent this might be true, one thing was clear: the young man from Lahaina was a pretty good flirt!

Aiko read the letter for him. Mitsutaka didn't go into much detail, just one-page encouraging his son and explaining that he was home and everyone was well. The return address was from Hawaii. This was how Russell first knew of his father's return from the detention center.

Aiko folded the letter and handed it back to Russell as the train arrived. They said goodbye and parted. Aiko thought to herself, *Kanari kawaii ne?* He's pretty cute!

The sisters returned home and told their mother about the soldier who walked them to the train station. Ever welcoming, Hatsu told Aiko that she should bring him to their house, since there was nowhere else to go. There was never any concern expressed about the girls associating with a GI, most likely assuaged by the fact that Russell was a *Nisei*.

The next day Russell met the sisters again after work and an invitation to the Mori house was extended. It was something he hadn't anticipated but "*Ureshikatta!*" he was very excited. A few days later, unsure of what to expect, Russell made the trip to the Mori household with Aiko and Hisa. Both Yoshizo and Hatsu were home when the trio arrived.

With most of Tokyo destroyed there were no theaters or restaurants to speak of, nowhere to go for a more traditional date. So most of Russell and Aiko's courtship took place at the Mori house. Russell and the family got along very well from the start. Both Yoshizo and Hatsu were impressed because Russell seemed so relaxed, a real departure from Japanese formality. The young GI also joked a lot, which kept everyone laughing and having a good time. Russell knew immediately this was no ordinary family. They were a relaxed, open household, which suited his style, so he liked them very much.

For their part the Mori family found it interesting to learn about the foreigners now occupying their country. Russell explained all kinds of things, including what a GI's life was like. Much to everyone's delight he even demonstrated how to thumb down a jeep by standing up and motioning with his hand.

At one point Russell told them part of his job was keeping records of everything. Hatsu misunderstood and thought Russell was a musician. The girls explained her misunderstanding and everyone enjoyed a good laugh.

Because of the restriction on fraternization with foreign nationals it wasn't often Russell escorted Aiko to her home. But he went whenever he could. Everyone would return late, around eight or so, then have dinner together. It was usually a simple affair but it was Japanese style food which Russell enjoyed.

Looking back, Aiko realized her family had food on their table every day. She never thought about it then, but on reflection wondered how her mother was able to find enough food even with wartime rationing. Hatsu was a most resourceful woman.

Russell did what he could to help out. When he visited he would bring some *omiyagi* or goods from the PX or market such as a watermelon or vegetables or other hard to get items. He brought a lot of animal crackers, which Aiko really liked, or Almond Roca candy, a family favorite to this day.

Almost four months after the war's end there was still no word from Ichiro. The family knew he had been somewhere in China or Southeast Asia. Choking up as she told the story, Aiko recalled the cold winter night of Ichiro's return. Hatsu was cooking outside. She thought it was a ghost when Ichiro walked through the gate and quietly called out "*Okaasan* Mother."

By this time Russell was coming to the house regularly. Worried about any possible animosity between the two opposing soldiers, Hatsu sent Shige to meet him and Aiko at the *Musashi Nitta* train station, warning of Ichiro's return and that Russell shouldn't come over that night. He obligingly turned back.

Later, Hatsu mentioned to her son that the family had become acquainted with a *Nisei* soldier who visited the house occasionally. Ichiro merely shrugged indicating no objection so a few days later Russell came over again. The two men got along fine, but it was better safe than sorry. Remarkably little acrimony existed in the Mori family regarding the war.

Ichiro recounted the story of his steamer ship stopping at Shanghai during the war. At the last minute he was pulled ashore because they needed an accountant. The steamer continued without him and struck a mine several miles down river losing every man aboard. He considered himself very lucky.

Another time after the war a farmer family came by the Mori house with a wheelbarrow full of vegetables as a humble gift of gratitude. Ichiro's platoon was strafed by fighter planes while marching in Indochina. Ichiro's friend was hit and unable to get cover on the side of the road. Ichiro dashed out and covered the wounded man with his own body as the planes made another pass. Both men lived to tell the tale. The farmers could not believe that the oldest and only son of the Mori Family would risk his life to save their third son.

Several months later the GHQ offices were relocated to the nearby *Dai Ichi* Building, a former government structure located across from the Imperial Palace. The building would serve as MacArthur's permanent headquarters during the occupation.

Russell continued to be billeted at the *Oukurashou* and every day made the brief walk to work. His office was a "small cubbyhole" on the mezzanine level overlooking the main floor of the building, the same floor the war crimes lawyers were located.

Being Japanese American made Russell's position fairly unique, acting as a bridge between the two cultures but not fully fitting into either. While both sides treated him well he sometimes struggled more with his fellow Americans because of "the attitude they had towards me from Hawaii and elsewhere. I got pushed around quite a bit but the people from Japan were very decent, very nice."

Most of the Americans behaved respectfully but a few were insensitive to the situation and culture around them. Once a Colonel from Wyoming asked Russell to interpret for him. Some Japanese workers were making license plates using small wooden boards painted black with white numbers on them, something the officer didn't approve of.

The Colonel said, "Why don't you use more imagination? Stupid people. [This is an] ugly looking thing [meaning the license plate]. Back in Wyoming we have a metal plate with a bucking bronco on it, really nice. Why don't you do something like that?"

He motioned for Russell to translate. Russell was dumbfounded. Anyone in country at the time should have known that materials of all kinds, metal in particular, were in short supply and people were forced to make do with what was available.

Unable to say anything to the officer, Russell turned to the workers, "*Ne, kono taisa wa baka dakara na, De watakushi wa iu koto* . . . This Colonel is an idiot. What I'm saying now, you take as if I'm saying what he said and just nod your head. What's the matter with this guy? He knows you don't have the material. Just keep doing the best you can."

The workers nodded politely and the placated Colonel left them to their task.

The PX moved with GHQ to the Dai Ichi Building and Aiko, Hisa and another woman named Emi all transferred with it. Eventually three more women were hired, bringing the total again to six.

Along with a new location the girls got a new boss. Paul Cockrell was a military man from Mississippi in his mid-30s. A Baptist and the father of two beautiful little girls, the oldest about eight years old, whom he proudly showed off in photos. The thing Aiko remembers the most about him is his kindness. Having been through the war he knew first hand what people on both sides had suffered. He occasionally brought gifts for the girls working for him. With decent clothing and food so difficult to come by, the gifts, even small things like lipstick, meant a lot to the workers. Once Paul even asked his wife to send some high heel shoes for all of the girls. It must have cost a lot but "we were so happy we wore them even though our outfits didn't match the shoes. They were so beautiful," says Aiko. The girls all loved and appreciated him. When he returned home to the states 18 months later, the girls all cried.

Many years later, in the mid-60s, Paul contacted Russell and Aiko through Hisa and came to visit them in Utah.

American soldiers and native Japanese were still not allowed to fraternize under threat of arrest by military police but, as Russell puts it, "we were inside GHQ. The guards were outside." This allowed him and Aiko to see each other on a regular basis.

If the MPs ever stopped them Aiko was able to show her GHQ ID and Russell, of course, had the GHQ badge on his uniform. The Staff Sergeant's three stripes and rocker bar didn't hurt either. Often soldiers who gave him guff would snap to as soon as they saw his rank and station. "They never slammed on me, they never talked bad, they never said anything bad about me," told Russell.

Eventually Russell would be given one more rocker and the rank of Sergeant First Class.

The ban on fraternization kept Japanese out of certain American only areas and also prevented Americans from entering certain Japanese only areas as well. Russell sidestepped this by changing out of his uniform into civilian attire, allowing him to mingle freely with the Japanese. Still it was difficult for Russell and Aiko to really date. Sundays they saw each other, usually meeting at Aiko's house with her family. Even though they had only been seeing each other for several months Russell was really enamored. One day, while waiting at the edge of the train platform, Russell suddenly sneaked a kiss on Aiko. Quietly, she dug her handkerchief out and circumspectly wiped her lips. They were both surprised.

At lunchtime Aiko would meet Russell on the mezzanine level. From this vantage point they watched General Douglas MacArthur leave the building for lunch at his residence in the American embassy. Ever the showman, MacArthur knew his audience well. He would come out from the elevator, straighten his hat and uniform, place his pipe in his mouth, tuck his walking stick under his arm, and stand erect before walking out the front door to the several hundred curious Japanese waiting outside to see him each day.

Aiko felt the Japanese respected MacArthur because of the way he handled the people and culture during the occupation, wisely retaining the emperor as a figurehead and keeping key elements of Japanese society intact through the transition.

In 2011, Aiko saw an American veteran talking on television saying that he never saw MacArthur. "I saw him every day," she laughed, "Not only did I see him but I was looking down on him from the balcony!"

Russell liked MacArthur despite his showy style. He never had much direct contact with the general but described him as quiet and steady and approved of his general policy and leadership during the occupation.

MacArthur's office was on the sixth floor. It was a surprisingly un-ostentatious room with a wooden desk and bookshelves. Once during lunch when Russell was walking in an adjacent office he saw the door to "Mac's" library was open. Curiosity getting the best of him, Russell peeked in. A large map sat on a table in the center of the room. On closer inspection, Russell realized it was the final plans for the invasion of Japan. There was to have been a feigned attack on the Kanto and Shikoku areas while the main force of 750,000 men assaulted Fukuoka. The assault would in-volve over five thousand ships and all available aircraft. At least one million casualties were expected. Russell knew the only thing that prevented him from being part of the invasion force was the surrender of Japan. He left the room greatly relieved they hadn't gone through with the plan.

Charles Shibata, who flew over from the Philippines with Russell, began hanging out with Russell and Aiko and, more particularly, her sister, Hisako. As a counterintelligence officer, Charlie was at-tached to the CIA translating Radio Tokyo station materials. He was later moved to GHQ on the mezzanine level where he be-came better acquainted with Russell. Hisa came to watch MacAr-thur with them so Charlie would come down as well. They soon became a regular foursome with Charlie also going to the Mori house to meet the family.

After Paul Cockrell left, Aiko and Hisa got a new boss, who was much younger, and, in Aiko's estimation, cruder. He was part of the wave of new American soldiers being brought in to replace those who were finishing their service and heading home. Seeing the war first hand tempered the earliest soldiers who always con-ducted themselves as gentlemen. To Aiko, the latest batch, having never passed through the refiner's fire, were rougher and more brash. When a position opened up at the procurement department Aiko transferred there. The offices were located upstairs above the American Club annex, a short walk from Tokyo station.

There was a large shower room downstairs from the office and when work was slow Aiko was allowed to use it. With no fuel available to heat water elsewhere it was a real luxury. According to Aiko the soap furnished by the Americans "smelled so good."

The other side of the building housed the employment office, which was always crowded with long lines of Japanese men, many who were former soldiers, looking for work. They were all dirty and tired, wearing worn out army uniforms and faces of dejection. Food and housing were scarce but jobs were even harder to find. Holding a good paying American job, wearing clean clothes, Aiko always felt a bit guilty knowing how much she had to be grateful for.

Aiko never learned the proper spelling of her new bosses name. Lt. Haggady is as close to the pronunciation as she knows. Aiko was the only native Japanese at the new office. She worked with two *Nisei* soldiers and a bilingual *Nisei* woman from Los Angeles, Rose Katsura. In Aiko's own words the job was very simple, consisting mostly of some light filing. When Haggady called for a certain file number, Aiko brought him that file. There wasn't as much interaction in this office as there was in the PX, but she didn't care because she was busy dating Russell.

10

GATHERING THE SAINTS

NITIALLY ACTING UNDER HIS OWN volition, Navy Lt. Commander Edward Lavaun Clissold, an LDS member stationed in Japan, began assessing what could be done to reassemble the Latter-day Saints that remained after the war. Scattered meetings of service men and Japanese saints had taken place but nothing formal or organized. The Tokyo group, with a dozen or so Japanese members from the pre-war period, was the largest.

A Salt Lake City native, Clissold served in Hawaii as a stake president then as acting president of the mission succeeding President Jay C. Jensen. Clissold was now billeted with the Civil Information and Education (CIE) section of GHQ. He was originally part of a division created specifically to handle Japan's surrender but because the terms were unconditional the department was deemed unnecessary. Clissold was sent home after two months only to be called back to serve in the CIE.

Clissold first ran a small ad in the one-page mimeograph being distributed as a newspaper.

Urgent Notice—would immediately desire to get in touch with members of the Church of Recent-Day [sic] Saints of Jesus Christ (Mormonism). Lieutenant Commander Edward Clissold, Room 548, Daiichi Hotel.

The ad ran on October 30, 1945, and, despite being poorly translated, was able to reach some of its intended audience. On November 5th Sister Tazuko Watanabe and Brother Fujiya Nara met with Clissold at his barracks in the Daiichi Hotel to discuss the condition of the saints and the possibility of re-opening the mission.

Clissold had studied Japanese but, recognizing the limits of his ability, realized he needed help with translation. He promised to introduce the saints to Russell, who he knew from GHQ. Clissold contacted Russell right away, meeting with him and another soldier in Clissold's office the very next day.

The other soldier turned out to be Kenneth Aubrey, the missionary who baptized Russell in Hawaii. Aubrey was serving as a First Sergeant in the 7th Cavalry in the Roppongi district of Tokyo. Neither Aubrey nor Russell knew the other was in Japan and Clissold had no idea that the two were acquainted.

Russell was an Aaronic priesthood holder and served as go-between for the Japanese and the English-speaking saints. He would not be ordained an Elder until after his return from Japan. Russell pointed out that he didn't technically have authority to do the stuff he was doing but he was still directly involved in helping get things organized and getting meetings going. The church during the occupation was, in Russell's words, "the craziest set up."

A month later, on the 7th of December, Clissold was released from active military duty, necessitating his return to the states. With Clissold's departure responsibilities informally fell to the twenty-two year old Russell, a convert of less than three years.

Upon his return home, Clissold met with President David O. McKay, then a counselor in the First Presidency, to discuss the situation in Japan. Clissold apologized for acting without direction from Salt Lake but President McKay told him he'd done the right thing. This meeting set the wheels in motion towards the re-organization of an official mission in Japan.

With few buildings left standing after the war, Brother Genkichi Shiraishi, a reporter for the *Mainichi Shinbun* newspaper, asked a friend if the church members could use the living room of his house as a meeting place, a request his friend graciously consented.

The first church meeting was held on December 21. It was a very informal gathering with most of the time spent making administrative decisions, including where and how they were going to meet on a more regular basis. In addition to Russell, the meeting was attended by Brother Nara and his wife, Tomoko, who wasn't yet a member, Brother Shiraishi, Kentaro Mochizuki, Tazuko Watanabe, and Preston D. Evans, an American serviceman. As an elder, Brother Nara conducted the meeting. He didn't speak English and relied on Russell a lot, including how to proceed with services.

A few scattered meetings followed and on the 9th of February Brother Nara was appointed the presiding elder of the Japanese saints with Brothers Shiraishi and Mochizuki called as his assistants. The saints were meeting in Brother Nara's office but it was announced that a more suitable building would be rented for meetings as soon as one could be located.

The first adult Sunday School was held on the 14th of April in Russell's quarters. Ten people attended including three servicemen. The group sang hymns, Brother Nara conducted, and the invocation was given by Brother Shiraishi. Both men then spoke with the benediction given by Brother Aubrey.

The sacrament wasn't administered until the following week but was discontinued in May. From then on the meetings took the form of hymns, talks, scripture reading and occasionally a lesson. The informal meetings were held in various member's homes. Other saints held meetings in the Meiji Life Building, but it was primarily an English speaking group, and the language barrier was difficult for the Japanese saints.

In June, Aubrey met a woman named Ko Sakai while waiting for a train. In her 60s, the daughter of a Japanese native mother and an Irish father, Ko was blonde and appeared Caucasian. Aubrey struck up a conversation. It turned out that Ko was a Christian herself and a teacher at the Touyo Eiwa school. When Aubrey mentioned that his church was looking for a place to meet, Ko said they could use the school building in Roppongi.

Eventually Ko Sakai's friend, Mrs. Shirosaki, a rich widow in Gotanda, offered her home to the fledging church community. There were two large buildings on the Shirosaki property, one western style building being used by occupational forces and one Japanese style house that Mrs. Shirosaki lived in with her teen-age daughter. On July 28, 1947 the members began meeting in the Shirosaki *osetsuma,* guest room, for their meetings each Sunday. Attendance averaged between 15–30 adults, including several *Nisei.* Sometimes American servicemen and women came to the meetings as well, even though many of them didn't speak much Japanese.

Like most Japanese, Aiko's family wasn't particularly religious. They went to the *jinja,* shrine, when a baby was born or the *otera,* temple, for *houji,* ancestral commemoration, or an *osoushiki,* funeral. Russell asked Aiko if she went to church on Sundays. She didn't.

"Would you like to come along?" he asked.

She said ok. Then as an after thought she asked which church.

"Mormon."

She'd heard of Catholics, Methodists, Baptists and Lutherans but never Mormon. "*Nan deshou ne? Kawatta kyoukai no namae.* What a weird name for a church," she thought but agreed to go anyway. At work, Aiko asked Paul Cockrell if he knew about the Mormon Church but he hadn't heard of it either.

The first church meeting Aiko attended was early in 1946, after Brother Clissold left but before the meetings were moved to Touyo Eiwa. Despite understanding very little about the church Aiko quickly found herself involved in the fledgling community. She sometimes offered the prayer and even helped teach children's Sunday School.

Aiko also contributed in a particularly unique way—she was the only person with a copy of a hymnbook of any kind and, as far as she knew, the only one with a Bible as well. This was the same bible and hymnbook she rescued the night her house was bombed. The hymnbook was Methodist and Aiko asked if it would still work. Some of the words were different but the melodies were the same, and Brother Nara said it was be fine. Aiko copied the words onto a large sheet of paper pinned to the wall for everyone to read as they sang.

How did she feel about teaching in a Christian church? "I felt like I was a member, was involved like [I was one]," said Aiko. She found out later that Sister Nara wasn't a member either, but came along with her husband like Aiko was doing with Russell. Sister Nara eventually joined the church as well.

Aiko supported Russell then as she would throughout all of their callings and responsibilities. Said Russell, "The amazing thing about it is this: she never voiced any opposition. She came along, and then when we were coming to the mainland, she got baptized a member without one lesson, without knowing anything. Why she put up with me I don't understand."

"I'm the obedient one," Aiko demurs, "I don't think anything, ok. Maybe [I'm] stupid in a certain way. (Laughs) Training from school time, we follow obediently. I don't know." Only in hindsight does Aiko acknowledge that there "was a purpose in life for both of us. When we got to Japan on a mission . . . it becomes more clear."

Some of the GI's found several orphaned children rummaging through the GHQ garbage for food and brought them to church. By 1946 there were 7–9 children attending. Brother Nara decided to hold junior Sunday School in the afternoons at his place in Setagaya. During the war Brother Nara worked for the Manchurian railroad and was now living in company housing in Tokyo. By the

RUSS AND AIKO: THE HORIUCHI STORY

end of 1947 the number of children blossomed to 20–30 attending weekly. Many of them were orphans or children from Nara's neighborhood. None of them were members.

A teacher was needed so they asked Aiko if she would teach, which she did, sharing stories from her Bible. The Sunday meetings in Gotanda and junior Sunday School continued in this manner until Brother Clissold's return to Japan, again in 1948.

Alma Ogata, not yet a member at the time, remembers Russell bearing testimony in church saying he wanted to return to Japan, not in the uniform of the U.S. Army but as a missionary, a testimony which would be heard and answered in time.

By this time Russell's interest in Aiko had grown to the point where he felt, in his own words, "Hey, I could get serious with this girl." Their relationship evolved very naturally into engagement and marriage. There was never a formal proposal although Russell did ask Kenneth Aubrey, who was now stateside, to find and ship a ring over for Aiko, since such items weren't readily available in Japan.

Only a few months remained of Russell's military commitment. He thought of going home to Hawaii and getting discharged but realized he wouldn't be able to come back for Aiko. The governmental restriction on Americans and Japanese Nationals fraternizing forbid any marriages and as a civilian most likely he wouldn't be able to re-enter the occupied country.

Another choice soon presented itself. An officer came to visit Russell one day, not at his office in GHQ, but instead approached him at his billet. The officer wondered if Russell was willing to give up his discharge points for a commission as a second lieutenant serving in Korea. Russell passed it up, preferring to stay in Japan, close to Aiko. In retrospect Russell is certain that he would not have come back alive.

Russell began inquiring after available jobs as an army civilian. Within a short time a position opened up for which he was well qualified. And so, in order to stay close to Aiko, Russell retired from military service and got a job as foreman of the GHQ Utilities electrical division, doing almost exactly what he had been doing in Hawaii before he was drafted. In this new position he would be earning $1.70 an hour. Most importantly the move allowed Russell to stay in Japan and continue to see Aiko.

Russell's new work took him to a different building in Tsukiji. The area was known for having the biggest wholesale marketplace in Tokyo and Russell often picked up vegetables or the occasional watermelon to bring to the Mori house. Shige remembers she was taking a nap once when Russell came over, very excited. "Shige, wake up, wake up! I brought a watermelon for you! *Suika*! Look!"

In all the time he spent fraternizing with "the enemy" as he often referred to Aiko, Russell was only stopped once. Instead of taking the shuttle bus back to work he took a train to Shinbashi and then decided to walk from there with Aiko and her sisters. An earnest MP saw all the young ladies Russell was walking with and got suspicious. He told them to stop, even going so far as reaching for his gun. Russell asked what the issue was and the guard asked what he was doing so early in the day with such a large group.

Even though Russell's job was a civilian position he was still required to wear his military uniform. Russell told the MP he was going to work at the GHQ shop and showed his pass. The guard knew he had no good reason to stop them and sent them on their way. In retrospect, the guard had been right—Russell was indeed fraternizing!

In July 1947, President Harry Truman signed the Soldier Brides Act, extending the War Brides Act of 1945, allowing Asian spouses of American personnel to immigrate to the United States. The language of the bill, "regardless of race," was a major breakthrough in racial attitudes. Public Law 271 temporarily lifted the ban on Asian immigration established by the Immigration Act of 1924. Russell and Aiko filled out a marriage application and a background check was run on Aiko before they received clearance.

Russell wrote to his parents regarding his intentions and Mitsutaka was thrilled that his son was marrying a Nihonjin and an Aoyama Gaukuin graduate as well.

On August 6, 1947, after seeing each other for nearly three years, Russell and Aiko were married in the Yokohama consulate, the first consulate open in post-war Japan. It took them six days to get clearance and the date was scheduled by GHQ.

Aiko was required to take her *kosekitouhon,* family registry, issued by the city and was interviewed by an American lawyer in GHQ. The *kosekitouhon* contained extensive family and genealogical information including birth dates and locations and information on wedding dates and spouses. One of the major reasons these checks were in place was to screen for potential communists, which the government was very worried about at the time. Having determined that Aiko wasn't a communist, permission was given for the marriage.

The couple didn't know what to expect for the wedding. They asked Russell's long time friend from Honolulu, Allen Ebesu, to come along to act as witness. Allen wasn't military but could speak *Nihongo* and signed up as a war department civilian working as a censor in GHQ.

One of Allen's first assignments was to Hakata where he and Russell had their first reunion since entering the service. In a letter to Russell dated 1988 Allen writes "Frankly, I don't remember any of the details of your visit, except one, and that is, you brought me some cans of sardines and Vienna sausages. These were Hawaiian "gourmet" delights only the sons of Hawaii can appreciate." When Allen transferred to Tokyo, Russell was instrumental in helping him get billeted in the Yaesu Hotel where the two became roommates.

The trio arrived at the consulate dressed in western style suits but there was no formal ceremony. Aiko remembers being nervous, still feeling she didn't understand English all that well. Russell remembers having to sign a lot of forms. After putting their signatures on a few papers in the consul general's office and paying the odd sum of two dollars and one yen they were declared man and wife.

If you ask Russell how many times he's been married he'll tell you three times, all to the same woman. The consulate was marriage number one, which satisfied the American government. The next day the couple went to the Japanese *kuyakushou* government offices in Ota Ku and register there as well. That was marriage number two.

Such was the lack of formality that when they passed a Catholic church on their way back to Yokohama station Russell asked Aiko if she'd like to go in and have them perform a ceremony. Aiko said it wasn't necessary so they returned home

Marriage number three took place a number of years later when the couple was sealed in the Los Angeles temple.

The couple took their honeymoon in Yoshina hot springs in Izu Peninsula, not too far from where Aiko stayed during the war. According to military restrictions Russell wasn't permitted to go but he went passing off as a native. Less than a week after Russell and Aiko were married in Tokyo, on August 11, Charlie Shibata married Hisako and he and Russell became brothers-in-law. Charlie and Russell started their paperwork at the same time but it took Charlie longer to get clearance because of his CIA attachment.

Marriages in Japan were traditionally arranged and there was some embarrassment on Hatsu's part that two of her girls found their own husbands. If Yoshizo felt any embarrassment, he never said anything. Surprised but supportive, Hatsu decided to hold an official party to introduce their new sons-in-law. Aiko remembers the small apartment being packed with relatives and *sake* being served to celebrate the marriages. Following custom, only the male members of the extended families were invited, the only women in attendance being the brides and their mother. Many in the family didn't know that Russell spoke Japanese and were pleasantly surprised to find out he was fluent. For his part, Russell remembers the large stack of dishes after, which he insisted on helping wash.

Both sets of newlyweds lived in Yoshizo's apartments in Yaguchi. Russell and Charlie were still quartered closer to GHQ but their wives were not allowed to stay there. Russell's switch from military to civilian status also dictated a move from the *Oukurashou* to new dorms at the Yaesu hotel with a shuttle bus running between the hotel and the electrical shop. After work Russell went to the hotel to shower since there wasn't one at the apartments, eat dinner then return home to Yaguchi. On occasion, if work were particularly demanding, he stayed overnight at the hotel, sometimes for the week, returning home on the weekend.

In November that same year, Shige was married to Iwakichi Mori. Iwakichi was from a different Mori line. This was a traditionally arranged marriage through one of Aiko's uncles who married into Iwakichi's family. So the family had to adjust for not two but three sets of newlyweds, giving one room to each new family.

Russell describes it as an odd marriage situation. Circumstances being what they were, it couldn't be helped. Life continued much the same as when they were courting but now they were married. Russell says early marriage life was calm and he was glad to be married to Aiko. As a military spouse Aiko enjoyed more privileges, including being able to go to the PX. It is wonderful to note that all three of these couples stayed together for their entire lives.

In October of 1947, Edward L. Clissold was officially set apart as president of the newly formed Japanese Mission of the Church. He finally received clearance from the government to re-enter Japan and on the 6th of March 1948 he arrived in Yokohama harbor. He was greeted by 43 members at the Sunday meeting in Gotanda the very next day. According to Shinji Takagi's *The Eagle and the Scattered Flock: Church Beginnings in Occupied Japan, 1945–1948* "With Clissold's arrival in March 1948, a mission of the Church was finally (re)established in Japan, after well over two years of American occupation, and twenty-four years of official absence."

Years before, Russell and Preston Evans had discussed the possibility of starting a real branch in Tokyo and asked Clissold how to get it sanctioned. It may have taken a few years but Clissold's return helped bring that dream to fruition.

Because of his history with the military Clissold received a special privilege to stay in the occupation hotel (coincidentally right across the hall from where he had bunked as a serviceman) but only for sixty days. Clissold needed to locate a permanent residence or he could be sent home because of his legal status.

In addition to preparing Japan for missionary work, Clissold was also instructed to find a suitable location to establish a mission home. Getting right to work, President Clissold began reaching out to contacts and friends he'd made while working at GHQ with Russell helping out wherever he could. The search was made more difficult by the relative scarcity of buildings left standing and the fact that many of these were under military use. Materials were also under military regulation and difficult to obtain.

Through Clissold's contacts at GHQ, they were able to locate a likely property in Minami Azabu, one of the finest districts in Tokyo and home to many embassies. They were able to track down the owner, Mr. Hachiro Shimizu, who purchased it the fall before. Valued at ¥2,000,000 (roughly ten-thousand dollars in the exchange rate of the time) the property had good acreage and the large home on it seemed in mostly good condition.

The largest hurdle was obtaining financing. Foreign exchange controls set in place by GHQ prevented anyone from converting dollars into yen. The controls were established to give the Japanese economy a chance to recover but also had the effect of blocking the Church from transferring any money for the purchase.

President Clissold spoke with Mr. Shimizu and looked into obtaining a loan from the Bank of Japan. Naturally the bank wanted a guarantee, which Clissold obtained, once again utilizing his contacts in the GHQ finance office, who verified the Church would be able to pay the loan.

On the 20th of March 1948, with little more than a verbal agreement in place and an amazing amount of trust Mr. Shimizu deeded the property to the Church, free of any encumbrances, in good faith that he would be paid as soon as the Church was able.

According to Brother Takagi's record, Clissold recounted the event thus: "We left [Shimizu's] office with all the signed papers and I marveled at the trust and kindness of the man. Mr. Yamamoto, a lawyer, remarked he had never seen anything like this piece of business in all his experience!" Despite not seeing a single yen of his payment for almost two years, Mr. Shimizu honored the agreement without complaint or issue.

The house on the property, though mostly intact, had been damaged in three separate bombing attacks. Clissold inspected the building on March 26th with two LDS military structural engineers. The men determined the damage was superficial and that the building could be safely rebuilt and used.

After its restoration the old house served as a meeting place and mission home until it was torn down in 1978 to clear room for the construction of the Tokyo temple.

Russell had remained in Japan, helping hold the church together and providing stability during the time between Clissold's departure from the military until his return as a religious leader. But his time in this capacity was drawing to a close.

Clissold asked Russell if he was interested in staying on as a missionary. However the Soldier Brides Act required all war brides be on American soil by the end of 1948, and so Russell declined.

Russell and Aiko celebrated Thanksgiving of 1947 with their LDS friends. It was the first time Aiko ever smelled cooked turkey. She immediately began to feel sick. It didn't take long for them to figure out she was expecting. News of the pregnancy only encouraged Russell to hurry his efforts to get back to the states.

On April 8, 1948 the couple began their journey across the Pacific. They had been married for 8 months, Aiko was 5 months pregnant. Her family and many of her relatives came to see them off in the morning. Yokohama harbor was still off limits to non-military personnel so Charlie and Hisa drove the couple in their sedan. Allen Ebesu was in Yokohama to wave goodbye as well.

While Russell was glad to be going home, for Aiko the experience was something different. She wasn't melancholy about leaving her family and Japan—it was an exciting adventure—but she would miss her mother. When the car started moving Aiko couldn't see Hatsu in the crowd. Her first thought was "*Okaasan, doko?* Where's mother?" She began to cry, and everyone else teared up as well. Aiko remembers Hisa not lifting up her face because she was sobbing so hard.

Yoshizo later admitted that if he'd known his daughters would live so far away on the American continent he might not have sent them to Aoyama to learn English. He hoped to keep all his girls nearby but three of them wound up leaving the country.

A family picture taken before Russell and Aiko were to leave Japan presciently foretold where each daughter would spend the bulk of their lives. The older sisters, Hiroko and Shigeko, dressed in traditional *kimono* would remain in Japan while the three younger sisters, Aiko, Hisa and Kyoko, garbed in western dress would all spent their adult years living in the United States. Charlie and Hisa followed Russell and Aiko to the states in November, settling in the Cochella Valley area in California.

From Yokohoma, Russell and Aiko boarded a military ship headed for the Philippines. The Navy transport ship wasn't exactly the finest of arrangements for newlyweds but would get the job done. Aiko remembers there were a lot of *Nisei* aboard the ship.

For Russell, travel by military transport was old hat but Aiko re-members the first night being really exciting even though she didn't move around the ship much. Men and women's quarters were separately kept, regardless of marital status. They were al-lowed to see each other but bunks were isolated. They could visit the deck or cafeteria but beyond that there wasn't anywhere to go. Aiko stayed with the other women, about eight or so per room, on the bottom level of the ship. It was fun for her to meet with other war brides, all headed off on similar adventures in a new land.

The passengers were well fed but it was typical American style food and by the time the ship arrived in Manila three or four days later the emigrants found themselves missing Japanese cuisine, especially rice.

In Manila a Filipino cook came aboard ship and to everyone's de-light started making rice dishes. The rice was a long grain, not the usual Japanese short grain, but "it still tasted good," shares Aiko. One girl bought a yellow melon and used the skin to make *tsuke-mono*, which the Japanese really enjoyed.

The stay in port lasted for one or two days. Russell and Aiko took the opportunity to go with another couple by taxi to look around the city. A high level of animosity among the Filipinos towards the Japanese remained so they were told to be careful. Fortunately there were no incidents and the couples were able to enjoy their sightseeing including a visit to the Manila Cathedral.

From Manila the ship headed to Guam. The next morning Aiko was sick. She hadn't suffered much morning sickness at all, so it was seasickness that got her. A nurse came around telling her to do her best to get up and move around and not to lie down. But Aiko felt so terrible that she remained in bed for most of the pas-sage to Guam.

With encouragement, Aiko tried to go to the dining room but the first thick slice of ham she saw caused her to flee back to her room. The only thing Aiko found that didn't bother her stomach was apples. Even so she didn't feel up to eating much. Russell never got seasick but grew very bored of seeing nothing but water, water, water.

After Guam the ship headed towards Hawaii. By now the initial excitement of the trip had worn off. Hawaii boys gambling in their rooms to pass the time became a common sight. The trip lasted the better part of the month leaving everyone little choice but to patiently settle in.

The otherwise calm ocean became rough and lots of people on the ship became ill. Ironically, it was at this point that Aiko began feeling better. She remembers going to the upper deck to watch the moonlight reflecting on the waves with Russell and thinking how beautiful it was.

11

FAITH, HOPE, AND CHARITY

Aloha Tower came into view as the vessel John Pope[1] sailed into Honolulu Harbor. After twenty days at sea, Russell and Aiko had finally reached their destination. For the ever-curious Aiko arriving in Honolulu was a wonderful experience. The air was warm and tropical and the bright sun shone down on people lining the harbor to welcome them. The crowd was singing Aloha 'Oe and she could hear the accompanying strum of ukuleles. The locals brought out handfuls of vibrantly colored leis for everyone. Bombed out and grey, Japan had been very dull after the war. The sunshine and dazzling appearance of so many bright colors was like floating into a different world.

For Russell, who didn't know if he was ever coming back when he left, it was a real homecoming.

Russell and Aiko were caught up watching the crowd when he cried out, "Oh, there is Kay!" His sister had come to meet them. They took a bus from the harbor to Auntie Kimiko's house. Russell and Aiko stayed with Kimi and Jiro again in the cottage in back, the same place Russell stayed before shipping out to basic training. Kimiko had three cute girls, the oldest around six, who would come to Aiko's room and speak to her slowly in English.

---

1. Listed as the USAT General Pope in one of Annette's personal history papers.

The following morning Kimiko served cold papaya. It was the first time Aiko ever tried the "heavenly fruit" and has never forgotten how delicious it tasted.

When they left Yokohama, Aiko was still early in her pregnancy and wearing a regular suit. By the time they arrived in Honolulu she was really starting to show. In the hustle of preparing to leave Japan she didn't pack any maternity clothes.

Aiko got along well with Kay, who took her new sister-in-law to the Liberty House department store. The beautiful dresses in the window were an almost unbelievable sight to Aiko, not having seen such things since before the war. Almost naively she asked, "Can you actually buy these dresses?" While they enjoyed looking, they didn't end up buying anything in the end. Aiko found the abundance overwhelming.

Skilled and resourceful, Auntie Kimiko quickly sewed together three or four *muumuu* dresses for Aiko, which she gratefully wore.

Russell spent a lot of time getting reacquainted with friends, mostly from the church, who came visiting one after another. They were having a wonderful time. The local Japanese newspaper, the *Nippujiji*, even interviewed Russell and Aiko for the beginning of a series about the war brides coming to Hawaii.

After four joyous days in Honolulu the newlyweds headed to Lahaina. Mitsutaka and Kikuyo were so excited to have Russell return, and with his bride, that they purchased a new home in anticipation of the young couple living with them. Russell put up most of the money for the house, along with some from his sister Kay, using up most of his savings in the process.

Russell and Aiko boarded a twin-prop island hopper for the thirty-minute flight to Kahului. As they crossed over the island of Maui Russell pointed down excitedly. "There's Lahaina!" Aiko looked down but couldn't see any town, only cane fields.

Now a large, beautiful airport, Kahului at the time was only a small airstrip. The waiting room was about 25 square feet. Mitsutaka was there to greet the couple. It was the first time Russell had seen his father since their meeting in the concentration camp nearly four years prior. They greeted each other with typical Japanese restraint, exchanging simple hellos.

The three of them drove to Lahaina in Mitsutaka's Model T. With the exception of the paved stretch that ran to the plantation camp, all roads outside of Lahaina proper were still dirt. Wailuku and Kahului were the big towns of the time while Lahaina was still considered quite rural. It wouldn't even have a movie theater to call its own for many more years.

Aiko was impressed with the kind demeanor of her new father-in-law who was slender and tall for a Japanese. And although he didn't express it much outwardly she could tell he was very excited.

Right after the war Mitsutaka was laid off from the plantation by Mr. Moir who still bore a grudge for the small Japanese man. Moir told Mitsutaka if wanted his job back he could go cut sugarcane. Mitsutaka told him to keep the job and instead went to work for Nagasako, a grocer in Lahaina, doing basically the same job he had done for the plantation.

Russell once complained that the only canned goods they ever had at home were dented. "How come we always get these funny looking cans?" Mitsutaka's ethics wouldn't allow him to deliver damaged goods to his customers. Not wanting his employers to lose money either, he would pay full price for the damaged cans himself. The contents were still good, he reasoned, and the store was able to sell proper looking goods so everyone came out better for it.

Along the same lines another lesson his father taught him occurred during a shipping strike. Even though food from the mainland was piling up on the docks there were food shortages. An emergency shipment of ten sacks of rice was sent to the store. With so many people wanting rice, ten sacks would not go far. Mitsutaka was given the responsibility of coming up with an equitable solution to benefit as many people as possible. He decided to divide the large bags into about 200 smaller bags of about 2 kilograms of rice each. Russell saw what he was doing and told his father that he should take a whole sack of rice home with him. Russell writes "He did not look at me or answer me. I then asked the same question again. This time he looked at me with a withering look on his face. He then said, 'Son, what is the matter with you? Can you stand there [with] a full stomach and watch your neighbors and friends go hungry? We all go hungry together.' It was a stinging rebuke from my normally soft spoken and gentle father."

The new house stood in the recently developed Lahaina Homestead area. Despite the name, it was still a one-hour walk from Lahaina town proper. The Homestead was a nice area with much of the neighborhood being made up of doctors, lawyers, teachers and other professionals including the plantation accountant. The house itself was relatively spacious on good-sized property with a large stone *lanai* porch in back. It wasn't large by today's standards but comfortable for its time. The family thought about making the *lanai* into another room by adding a screen but never did.

A welcoming party was organized to greet the newlyweds. People from all over the neighborhood came to wish the new couple well. Kikuyo was there, of course, as were Misao and Taka. Kay wasn't in attendance as she was with Namiyo at their beauty shop in Lanai.

Inside the house was a long Japanese style table, low to the floor. The living room furniture was moved out and long tables were brought in and piled high with all kinds of food. The abundance was overwhelming. Aiko hadn't seen this much food in one place in over five years and grew teary-eyed at the sight of it. Everyone thought she was so happy but her first thought, having just survived the war, was to ship all the food back to her still struggling family in Japan.

The biggest room in the house was given to the young couple with Mama and Papa taking the next room. The bathroom was located between the two rooms. The third and smallest bedroom was occupied by Sadashichi Koyama, Russell's grandfather on his mother's side, who everyone called *Jiisan,* grandfather.

After a few weeks Russell was hired as an electrician at the Pioneer Mill-Lahaina Electric Power Company making good wages. He worked an eight hour day at the plantation then most evenings would spend a few hours more at odd jobs around town, doing home repairs, wiring washing machines or motors in electrical appliances. The days were long but he was happy to have a beautiful wife, a steady job and be home in Hawaii.

Because of her pregnancy Aiko was unable to get out of bed most mornings. She remembers wanting to make breakfast for Mitsutaka but having a hard time moving. To her embarrassment, by the time she got up Mitsutaka had already fixed breakfast and gone to work. Kikuyo took several days off from work in the cane fields to stay and cook for her new daughter-in-law. When Kikuyo returned to work Aiko took over cooking duties but found herself a little overwhelmed in the unfamiliar kitchen—she couldn't even find the soy sauce! The food itself was a challenge as well. It was Japanese food, but Hawaiian style, and Aiko confesses not knowing much about cooking to begin with. She remembers they ate a lot of eggs.

Most of the day the house was empty and quiet even though Grandpa Koyama was home outside puttering around in the garden. Sadashichi enjoyed taking care of the big yard, often spending all day there. The house came alive briefly at lunchtime when Mitsutaka and Ma-chan, Misao's husband, came home to eat. But most of the time Aiko felt pretty isolated.

With everyone gone during the day and having little responsibilities until the baby came, life was pretty boring for Aiko. There was no one else her age around. With little or nothing to keep her occupied her homesickness lingered and she sometimes found herself crying. Her isolation wasn't only physical, it was linguistic as well. A neighbor, Mrs. Sato, invited Aiko to come and visit with her but she was a *Nisei* who spoke only English and Aiko didn't feel very comfortable with the language yet. To keep herself occupied Aiko learned to crochet, making bedspreads and doilies. She also kept busy cleaning around the house, engaged in the seemingly endless struggle against the red dust that settled everywhere.

Overall, life in Hawaii was good, although the cultural learning curve was a big one for Aiko. She was used to dressing up to go shopping, carefully selecting her clothes and wearing stockings. Later she learned that the local women were gossiping about how she wore stockings to the grocery store. Aiko was a big city girl from a prosperous family and the rural mentality was very unfamiliar to her.

Many in the community had left Japan nearly 50 years before. To them the sight of a modern Japanese city girl was a curious one. Inversely most everyone in Hawaii spoke a different Japanese dialect mixed with a heavy dose of pidgin, and Aiko had a difficult time feeling she belonged. She never tried to act better than anyone else, she was only doing what she thought was appropriate. This included wearing dress suits to church, which, in her words, "was ridiculous in Hawaii" where the dress standard was a *muumuu*. Aiko didn't know any better at first.

It was early Sunday morning when the first contractions woke Aiko from her sleep. The baby was coming. The Horiuchis didn't know if it was a boy or a girl, but it was definitely on its way. Despite the early hour Russell and Aiko woke up Mitsutaka who was so excited that he ran to the neighbor's house still in his *nemaki* pajamas. This wasn't the first grandchild—the baby was fourth behind Misao's Patricia (known as Patsy), Namiyo's son Andy, and Taka's

Norman—but Mitsutaka was still thrilled. The neighbor two doors up the hill was Dr. Shimokawa. When Mitsutaka told him the labor pains had started the doctor told him to get Aiko to the hospital.

Mitsutaka gave the couple a ride to the Pioneer Mill Hospital in Lahaina since he was the one with a driver's license and a car. Russell admits he could drive but "I had to go to work."

"So did Mitsutaka," teases Aiko.

Situated next to the beach, the barrack like structure looked more like a wooden shack than a hospital. There was only one delivery room with a single waiting room next to it, attended to by one doctor, a *haole* former military doctor (Russell refers to him as Doctor Tony) who was married to a Chinese woman. One advantage of the plantation system was that it covered the cost of delivery.

Aiko's initial contractions were fairly weak, indicating that the baby might be a long time in coming. Consigned to waiting, and feeling useless, Russell went to work. He would be notified when the baby was close.

Most homes, the Horiuchis' included, didn't have phones. So when the call came early the next morning it went to the neighbors, the Satos. They rushed the message to Kikuyo who woke the slumbering Russell. It wasn't customary to have the husband in the delivery room so Russell waited outside, joking that he was treated like a "*nokemon*" from the Japanese *nokemono* meaning "outcast," because he wasn't allowed inside.

Aiko was in labor nearly 20 hours. She was given a shot in her spine that made her numb but also knocked her out. At one point in her delirium she heard a baby cry and thought, "finally the baby came out." But when she touched her belly it was still full. "My goodness, I'm going to have twins!" she thought before the hazy realization came that the crying was next door. Aiko's labor took so long that a Hawaiian woman, who checked in after Aiko to deliver baby number eight, gave birth in the waiting room instead.

At 6 am on Monday, August 30, 1948 Aiko delivered a healthy 6 pound 11 ounce baby girl. "I saw the cutest baby with nose like [Russell]," said Aiko.

"We were glad because [she] had dark black hair," Russell smiled, "[with a] cute, pink red face. *Yokkatta, ne?* (Great!)" Russell was happy to find both mother and daughter well. Again, following the more pragmatic social practices of the time, after seeing his wife and baby Russell went to work.

Part of the reason Aiko's delivery took so long was because the baby's head was large for her size, enough so that it was difficult to put regular sized baby shirts on her. After her ordeal Aiko was fine but weak. She was not only exhausted physically but mentally worn out as well, not just from the pregnancy but from the entire ordeal of leaving her family and coming to a new and foreign place. The hospital kept her for four or five days and she remained groggy the whole time. She remembers overhearing her roommate, the Hawaiian woman with baby number eight, saying to someone, "That girl sleeps all the time." Aiko could hear them talking but she couldn't even open her eyes.

A reporter from the Lahainaluna paper came and asked what they were going to name the new baby for the birth section but Aiko was too tired to answer coherently. He came back several times but Aiko was never able to answer him.

When Aiko finally came to, the Hawaiian woman expressed that she didn't know why it took Aiko so long. "It's so simple," she scolded, "like taking a s***."

Birth might have been commonplace to her but to Russell and Aiko it was nothing short of wondrous. They named their daughter Ellen in honor of Allen Ebesu. They also gave her the middle name of Nobuko, completing the trio of Faith (Nobuko), Hope (Nozomi) and Charity (Aiko).

Russell was thrilled to be a father. At one point he asked if Aiko wanted to have another child even after such a long labor, and though Aiko doesn't remember the conversation, she said yes.

Once Aiko was back on her feet, she and the baby returned to the house in Lahaina. Kikuyo cleaned and readied a crib in preparation for the baby. It is Japanese tradition to give the baby its first bath, so Kikuyo and Aiko set aside a plastic container in the bedroom with warm water. Both women were nervous. Kikuyo particularly was worried that her hands, so stiff and calloused from years of grinding labor, were too rough for the baby or that she might drop her. Following custom they wiped the baby's face and hair before removing her clothes, wrapping her in a soft towel and slowly setting her in the tub, afterwards making sure to dry her thoroughly so she didn't catch a cold.

Aiko registered for English classes taught in the evening by Reverend Himeno at the local Methodist church. Mitsutaka and Kikuyo were happy to take care of Ellen while Aiko went but Ellen cried everytime Aiko left. She could always tell when Aiko was getting ready to go somewhere and gave her grandparents a hard time, refusing to sleep so Aiko eventually stopped attending.

Other than that Ellen was generally a happy, roly-poly child. She had a healthy appetite and ate everything. Aiko doesn't remember her being picky at all.

Russell never changed diapers. "I was too busy!" he argues, but it really wasn't a fatherly thing to do in those days either.

With work *pau hana* "all finish" by early afternoon Kikuyo usually came home around 3 o'clock, which allowed her to spend time with the baby. When the baby heard the slow *patpatpat* shuffle of Kikuyo's leather slippers on the hardwood floor she shook her crib excitedly in recognition. Aiko warmed up coffee for Kikuyo who drank it while she sat in the living room and rolled her own cigarette for a smoke. For her part Aiko never smoked but admits she liked the smell of a burning cigarette.

Ellen was a very active, precocious child and began walking well before one year. Now, instead of rattling her crib when she heard Kikuyo's slippers, she would run and bring Kikuyo her cigarette box and tobacco bowl. Growing up in the household in Lahaina, surrounded by her multi-generational family, Ellen learned Japanese before she ever spoke English.

The Sato's next door owned a mid-sized dog that Ellen was very fond of. She liked to follow along behind it as it wandered in and out of the bushes and hibiscus trees separating the two properties.

The garage was detached from the house by a long driveway. Russell kept his shop in one half with the other half serving as the laundry room. Aiko would bring Ellen with her to do laundry. Ever outgoing, Ellen was born with a sense of curiosity and wanderlust that has never left her. If Aiko didn't keep an eye on her Ellen would take off and wander down the road towards the main street. Aiko remembers chasing after her several times, fearful of the plantation trucks that came rumbling down the hill.

"Ellen definitely has her dad's nose," writes Russell in his journal, "She is lively—energetic and takes after her mother. There are certain traits that she seemed to have inherited from grandma Horiuchi and Mori—both of whom were sharp—energetic and always on the go."

Russell praises Aiko as a good mother. Aiko, in her humble way, says she didn't do anything but stay home.

Life was good. Aiko marveled at the way plants grew in Hawaii, claiming all a person had to do was stick a branch in the ground and it would be growing leaves the next day.

Kay and Namiyo, both beauticians, asked Aiko to be their model for a hairdresser's competition in Wailuku. She agreed and the sisters came over to Maui. Aiko ended up in the top three and got her photo in the local newspaper.

It may surprise some that Russell didn't do much fishing in those days. Mitsutaka, however, continued to go most every Sunday bringing a handful of fish home, which they ate for dinner. Mitsutaka would sit back enjoying a beer and fried fish as a treat.

When Russell and Aiko first arrived in Honolulu they had the opportunity to meet some of the missionaries serving there, including an elder by the name of Paul Hyer, who was completing two years of service in the Japanese Mission in Hawaii. While they wouldn't see much of each other during his mission, Elder Hyer and the Horiuchis would cross paths again. And again. And again.

The couple also met the first four elders called to the newly formed Japan Mission.[2] Although the mission was officially sanctioned, actual missionaries weren't yet allowed into the country. The elders were waiting in Honolulu until they were given the green light, which came at the end of June. Russell choked up as he shared the conditions of Japan and the Japanese saints.

Back in Lahaina, if Aiko ever saw the missionaries in the neighborhood, she offered them drinks and occasionally invited them for dinner as well.

Russell still attended church when work or family gatherings didn't take him away, borrowing his father's Model T to drive to the meetings in Lahaina. No one was there to force or encourage him one way or another. The chapel consisted of a one-room home near the beach. Despite his self-described intermittent activity, Russell was ordained an elder on August 20, 1948, by Leroy Smith.

Aiko, still not a member, went along as a dutiful wife. Her only real reluctance to participate was lack of confidence in her English. She recalls spending most of her time outside of the building tending to a squirming baby.

---

2. Near Beretania Street. Among their number was Ted Price, who with his wife, Ramona, later served as a mission president in Japan and eventually as temple missionaries in Tokyo when the Horiuchis were there.

One night Russell came home late from a long day at work. Aiko was already in bed. As he crawled under the sheets and cuddled over to her he felt tears on her cheeks. He asked what was wrong.

Aiko remembers her heart pounding she was so nervous. The bottom line was that she was unhappy where they were. Russell was gone to work most of the day, then he'd come home for dinner then work some more in the evening. Most of the time he was gone till about 8 o'clock or so, leaving Aiko waiting at home with a cold supper. The isolation of the rural village was oppressive and she felt there was no real future for them in Hawaii.

One day Aiko saw a man climbing up an electrical pole not too far from the house. It looked like Russell but she couldn't tell at the time, so she asked him that evening. It turned out that it was Russell she had seen. Aiko realized Russell couldn't do this for the rest of his life and that she didn't want to raise her daughter in a small, rural community.

These things weighed on Aiko's mind for quite a while. She wasn't a church member but she was praying every night, knowing they needed to make a change. She didn't want to raise their daughter in these conditions. It took all of her courage but she reminded Russell of the promise he made to go to school on his GI bill. If he wasn't willing to live up to his word, then she was taking Ellen and moving back to Japan.

Russell was stunned. He was working long hours thinking he was building a future for his family. Aiko appreciated his hard work but also knew it wasn't the life for them. With no inkling that Aiko was unhappy, this turn of events broadsided Russell. He agonized back and forth over the decision to the point where he couldn't sleep. He certainly didn't want to lose his family. He already had a technical skill. He wondered if going to school was a waste. He didn't know what to study. Besides he was 27 with a wife and baby. He'd done fairly well in school but he felt inadequate for college level, which was, if he was honest with himself, completely intimidating to him. He was also concerned about his ability to support his family at the same time. Most of his savings had gone towards purchasing the house. Having very little money left, it would be a real struggle even with the $125 a month provided by the GI bill.

After wrestling with his soul for several weeks, Russell decided he would go and earn his university degree. It was through a suggestion by Lee Knell, then serving as a missionary in Hawaii, that Russell decided to apply to Brigham Young University. Lee supported Russell's decision and helped him fill out the paperwork. Russell says that it never occurred to him to apply to any other school. He only put in for BYU.

Much to his own surprise, Russell was accepted. Expecting only rejection, Russell hadn't even considered what he planned to study. At one point Russell thought he might like to be a forest ranger but now he was thinking perhaps he could come back to Hawaii and become a high school teacher. So he went to Lahainaluna to get his credentials sent out in case he needed them.

When Russell informally mentioned he was thinking about going back to school, everyone in the family thought he was crazy to move, leaving behind a good paying job to earn a degree. They thought it was a waste of time.

"My uncles were calling me stupid, you jerk, you jacka** you, why do you want to give up some good profession that you trained for? Why do you wanna go to school? For what? You married, have a kid. Whatsa matter with you? I got really lambasted," recalls Russell.

Only two people, besides Aiko, supported Russell's decision. One was Reverend Himeno, himself a college graduate. The other was Russell's father. Mitsutaka apologized that he couldn't support Russell financially but he encouraged his son to go with his full blessing. Able to read and write, Mitsutaka understood the value of an education and would have gone to school himself if he'd had the opportunity.

Russell felt he was leaving his security to enter a totally unknown world. He and Aiko packed all of their earthly possessions into two metal footlockers, bidding farewell to the family and flying to Honolulu, from where they made the voyage to the mainland.

With tears in his eyes, Mitsutaka embraced his son and shook his hand. It was the last time Russell ever saw his father. "My father and I had a very deep feeling of closeness," said Russell, "More than any other kids in the family." When asked about Mitsutaka, Russell sat quietly for a moment then, in his understated but emphatic fashion said simply, "Papa was a great man."

On their layover in Honolulu, Russell baptized Aiko at the Honolulu Tabernacle on May 26, 1950.

Lee Knell gave the confirmation blessing. After his mission, Lee returned to Utah, living near BYU where the two families remained in contact for over sixty years. He became an architect and is most well known for designing Utah Technical College, later renamed Utah Valley University.

When asked how she made the decision to be baptized Aiko laughingly confesses, "I didn't! They did!" Meaning Lee Knell and Russell. They reasoned that if the couple was going to BYU where the majority of people were members then it would be better if she joined. And so she did.

Still laughing as Russell relates the story, Aiko elbows him and teases, "Hey, you better create a more exciting story!" Ultimately, Russell argues, it *was* faith when she was baptized. Not every life of faith and testimony begins with a great conversion. Sometimes it's more a matter of encouraging and practicality. It took a great deal of faith to be baptized, placing trust in the word of other witnesses of the gospel.

"The reason came out when we were on the mission to Japan," told Russell, "Without her I would not have made it."

12

BRIGHAM YOUNG UNIVERSITY

GRANDPA KOYAMA ACCOMPANIED RUSSELL AND Aiko to California. It was his first time to visit his youngest son, Roy, who was working as a successful grape farmer in Lodi.

After nine hours in a prop plane from Honolulu the trio landed in San Francisco. Uncle Roy drove from Lodi to greet them, bringing out the welcoming committee—Ethel Hatsuko Cho, his wife, and their children (Five at the time. Two more would eventually follow). Even Roy's good friend Okey Bennett, who took care of Roy's farm during the war, was there. The entire entourage took two full cars to move. With Okey driving the second car, they made the two and a half hour return trip to Lodi.

The following day the family, Okey included, hopped into their cars to visit Yosemite National Park and other parts of Northern California. Aiko remembered being in the car most of the time, amazed by how big and wide the country was. Russell remembers seeing the big redwood tree.

Although it was good to see family and they enjoyed the trip, even Uncle Roy mentioned to Russell that he was foolish for pursuing his schooling. While this didn't help to set Russell's mind at ease, his course was already set and with Aiko's patient persistence he stayed on his chosen path.

After three days in Lodi, Russell and Aiko parted with Grandpa Koyama and Roy's family to board a train for Los Angeles to visit Aiko's sister Hisa and her husband Charlie. Hisa and Charlie settled in Charlie's hometown of Indio, a few hours east of Los Angeles. From the time she was small, Aiko liked traveling by train so she enjoyed the trip, taking in the scenery. Russell found it boring. "I hated it," he recalls in his best grumpy-old-man voice. The train was nearly empty with only one other couple on board.

Hisa and Charlie came up from Indio to meet them in Los Angeles, where they stayed with Grace, Charlie's older sister. Grace was a very kind woman and her home was the social hub of the Shibata family, where the family met whenever they got together. When Russell and Aiko were in town, Grace always invited them to join the family gatherings. These visits were frequent over the years and Russell and Aiko got to know the Shibata family well.

From Los Angeles the two couples drove to Indio. At the time Hisa and Charlie were living in a quonset hut on their tomato farm along with Charlie's parents. The property belonged to Charlie's father, although he didn't do any farming. It was said you could make a million dollars in one night farming in the Coachella Valley region. While the rumor may not have been entirely true, the region was indeed well suited to agricultural pursuits. The sandy ground was excellent for tomatoes and the hot climate ensured they grew early, well ahead of many other areas. Later Charlie switched from tomatoes to eggplants.

Charlie had an older brother living in Indio but Charlie was the only one in the family interested in farming. Charlie used only a small portion of his father's land, working hard and raising successful crops.

Nearly every summer vacation Russell and Aiko drove to Indio, spending time playing and helping out on the farm. One summer Charlie built a sorting room. It was large, about the size of a small house and Russell helped by doing the electrical wiring. Eventually when Russell and Aiko settled in Provo, the Shibatas came to visit with their children in Utah as well.

In early August, after a couple of weeks in Indio, Russell went ahead by bus to Provo to look for housing, leaving Aiko and Ellen in California.

In Provo, Russell encountered unexpected difficulty in securing an adequate place to live. At some apartments doors were slammed in his face with the trailing words of "Jap, go home!" For a decorated veteran and fellow member of the Church this treatment was doubly discouraging. He was reminded of the words of his patriarchal blessing that "men shall revile you" because of his ethnicity.

Fortunately this type of reaction was rare. Allen Ebesu, who was going to school a year ahead of Russell, helped him find a suitable apartment near 400 North 100 West.

Allen aspired to become a concert pianist but knew the rigorous hours of practice were not for him. Allen never married but did eventually become a successful elementary teacher in the Los Angeles Unified School District.

Aiko stayed in Indio for a month. As soon as Russell and Allen secured the apartment, Charlie and Hisa drove Aiko and Ellen to Provo. For Charlie it was a bit of an old home week since he had worked in Spanish Fork during WWII.

At the start of the war, the Shibata family was relocated to Poston Camp in Arizona. Some farmers in the area advertised for workers to come pick fruit in Glendale for a month. In the camp Charlie could earn twelve dollars a month. Outside they paid fifty cents an hour. It was better pay and more importantly, more freedom. After returning to camp, Charlie looked for more work. He landed a job in Spanish Fork picking cherries, apples, peaches, and sugar beets for three months. During this time he first became acquainted with Brigham Young University. Charlie's continuing work eventually took him to Chicago for a year.

Charlie's younger brother, Henry, enlisted joining the 442nd. When Henry wound up in a hospital in England, Charlie, full of what he called "patriotic fervor" volunteered. If he hadn't volunteered he never would have been drafted—he later learned the powers that be had lost his records including his draft information.

When the Shibata's returned to California, Russell, Aiko and Ellen said goodbye to their family and got busy settling into their new home. The apartments were unfurnished and the couple rented basic furniture. Located in the rear of the unit, the small apartment still depended on coal to fuel the oven. Allen Ebesu taught Aiko how to use the stove to bake bread, pies and other American style foods. The Horiuchis, like others at the time, were very frugal, not shopping much, preferring to bake and bottle their own food. Harriet Hyer, wife of Paul Hyer, the missionary the Horiuchis first met in Honolulu, bottled about a thousand bottles each summer to help keep their children fed (The Hyers eventually had seven). Ever generous, the Hyers invited people to join them and bottle peaches for themselves.

No store in Provo carried rice and so the couple went without it for the first few months. Eventually they were able to purchase it at a Japanese grocery store in Salt Lake on South Temple Street. In the meantime western foods such as bread, pie and cake became part of their life.

When the front apartment became available, Russell and Aiko moved into the larger quarters. Their neighbors across the street were the Gamett family. Lavell Gamett taught upholstery at BYU. Ellen spent hours with their youngest daughter Joyce in the playhouse her father built.

The Provo area was still very rural. Aiko tells there was "nothing around." BYU consisted of lower campus with the Maeser building serving as not only the crown jewel of the university but also the entirety of the upper campus.

There were several Hawaiians living in the area but Russell and Aiko were one of the earliest Japanese families to move into the valley. There were other Japanese around, but the only other Japanese couple was Mamoru and Mary Iga. Working on his graduate degree, Mamoru was from Kobe. His wife was originally a Matsuura from Idaho.

The Horiuchis' unique and obvious ethnic appearance coupled with the recency of the war led to some dramatic experiences. Once near Christmas time, Aiko sent Ellen, who was about four or five, up to Carson's Market to buy a loaf of bread. A bunch of kids chased her, calling her "N***** girl!" and she fled home in tears.

The next Sunday was fast and testimony meeting at church. Russell stood at the pulpit and chided the members, "You call yourselves Christians, yet you allow your children to call my daughter names." Aiko remembers a lot of ward members bringing food to their home after that, apologizing for the behavior of "poor, white trash."

Not all racism was quite so pointed. Another time one lady in the ward asked Russell if he was a veteran of the Japanese army. She was surprised to learn that Russell was a veteran of the United States Army. She wasn't trying to be mean but the idea of Japanese Americans serving in the U.S. military had never occurred to her.

Russell says such occurrences were part of his experience, stating that when "you are a minority, a foreigner, you come under scrutiny." When you stick out from the crowd, you come under close examination just for being different.

Settling into Provo presented Aiko with a cultural learning curve as well. She was so shocked to see a Caucasian man collecting garbage that she called Russell over to look, wondering if something was wrong. Russell shrugged, he didn't know what the big deal was. For Aiko, whites were honored teachers at distinguished schools or plantation owners. The sight of a white man working manual labor was a novel sight.

Despite these incidents, overall their experience was a good one. Lee Knell's parents were living in Provo and invited the couple over for dinner. Paul Hyer, was living with his family in Provo as well and often came by to check in on them, helping them settle into the new town.

Scared? No. Terrified was a better description of how Russell felt about starting school. At age twenty-seven with a wife and child he was much older than most of the students. He had been a mediocre student in high school and felt intimidated by the younger mainland students, who he felt were more academically sophisticated than himself. More than anything else Russell "didn't want to flunk and go home humiliated to Hawaii." He fully expected to be sent home after the first semester.

Worried sick about failing, Russell buried himself in his studies day and night, hoping to make good on his promise to Aiko. Russell took his first class in education and disliked it so much that he immediately dropped the major and was again faced with the dilemma of figuring out what he was going to study.

On top of everything else Russell still needed to work to support his family. The G.I. bill provided an income but it was meager and had to be supplemented to make ends meet.

Once again coming to their aid, Lee Knell was able to find work for Russell with Carl Miller at the BYU Heating Plant. The work was hard and Russell came home black and grimy but grateful he was able to enhance his income.

When the university built the Comparative Science building Russell picked up extra hours as an electrician running high-tension wires. He was paid the student rate of .75 cents an hour even though he was an experienced electrician. He had earned more in Maui, although Russell admits it wasn't all that much more. Work at the science building led to other jobs including wiring classrooms and even one of the scoreboards at the Smith field house. Nearly a decade later in 1963, Russell also wired the silver domed

Winter Garden Ice Rink, later better known as the Ream's grocery store turtle, a Provo landmark that stood until it was razed in 2006. Russell was working almost full time and picking up extra hours when he could, including Saturdays, on top of carrying a full class load.

Every opportunity to save a penny was used. A board nailed over wooden orange crates and covered with fabric made a vanity chest. More crates covered with fabric made a nice living room table. Life was not flush but Aiko was able to stay home with the baby and they managed to survive. On rare occasions there was even enough left over for them to enjoy a hoagie-style sandwich while walking home from the library.

As word of the Hawaiian's electrical skills got out, Russell often found himself running wires in the homes of faculty as well. This was rarely paying work. He was only "helping them out," he says then adds with a laugh, "I did quite a bit of it!"

Partly because of his skill and his willingness to lend a hand and partly because he was closer in age, the faculty tended to treat Russell more as a friend and equal than the average student.

Russell served as an assistant scoutmaster in the university ward, becoming good friends with Chris Christensen, the scoutmaster. Chris was a botany professor, three or four years older than Russell. He and his wife, Ruth, had small children about Ellen's age. It was Chris that first taught Russell and Aiko how to jar fruit.

Russell had many good professors but four in particular seem to stand out. Elliot Tuttle, in the geography department soon became a mentor for the Hawaii native. Stewart Grow from the political science department and Gordon Taylor, an English teacher also became quite close. Once when the Taylor house needed fixing the Horiuchis borrowed Fred Takasaki's car and drove over. The Taylors served fresh baked bread and milk. Aiko remembers how good the homemade bread tasted.

Always kind and smiling, William C. Carr taught Political Science and his wife, Naomi, taught elementary school. Originally from New Zealand, perhaps William felt an affinity for others, like Russell, from the Pacific islands and often invited the Horiuchis over for lunch, dinner and family parties. Even after the Carrs were grandparents and great-grandparents many times over, they continued to hold a "cousins dinner" at their home on Sunday afternoons. In this case cousins not only meant the literal Carr cousins but was also used in the common Polynesian usage meaning friends and neighbors. Russell and Aiko continued to attend as long as the dinners were held.

The Carrs had six children, many of who have fond memories of Brother and Sister Horiuchi. "He came to our home, not as a professor but in work clothes to help in the process of remodeling our old home," tells Debby Carr Bohman. The Carr children remember the "can do" positive attitude "Uncle" Russ kept even while climbing through a hole in the ceiling to the attic. Young Ellen often played with the children in the front room while Russell worked.

As Russell started teaching at BYU, and the Carr children grew older and entered college, some of them enrolled in Russell's geography classes as well. One of the children remembers earning the high A in the class which they described as a "dubious honor" since it allowed them the option to not take the final or even attend the last few weeks of class. (Russell extended this offer to students who demonstrated they had applied themselves properly and grasped the material so that they could use the last week of the term to focus on preparing for their other finals.) They admit they took up the offer and to this day are "embarrassed and saddened . . . because [Russell] was the best professor I had in my four years at BYU."

Others remember that Russell and Aiko always gave them cards before they left on their missions. At one point, Aiko also gave the Carrs a watercolor she painted as a gift. When one child lost his car in a wreck he was able to catch a ride with Russell and the

Horiuchis' neighbor, Bruce Warren, to school at BYU until he got a new one.

Another time Russell met one of the Carr children in the BYU bookstore. Russell inquired how he was doing and learning he now had six children of his own kidded, "You don't have to populate the earth by yourselves." The Carr grandchildren kept a look out for Russell and Aiko at church because they knew Russell always had candy in his pockets. One Carr daughter remembered Russell for his "cute and playful nature" and felt he and Aiko were part of the family, whose presence was always a blessing.

When Professor Carr was bedridden during the last months of his life, Russell, well aged himself, went faithfully every Thursday to visit with him, watching movies, reading to him and playing his harmonica.

When asked why he liked these particular professors so much Russell shares that "they made me work hard. And they were kind to us. Showed personal interest."

Russell worried about his classes that first semester, English in particular. The first paper he turned in was laboriously written by hand. It was returned with a frightening amount of red pencil corrections on it, doing very little to bolster Russell's tenuous confidence when he turned in the final version. When the paper came back it was marked with an "A." Russell asked the teacher if he had made a grading error but the teacher assured Russell that he deserved the mark. Encouraged but still doubtful of his scholastic abilities and driven by fear of failure, Russell continued to plow into his schoolwork.

Through great financial care, Russell was able to purchase a typewriter and diligently taught himself to type. Aiko remembers him constantly at work on the keys, typing and typing. The first typewritten paper was a real struggle, the manual typewriter predating spell check or self-correcting tape. If you made a mistake you had to start the entire page over again from the beginning.

When the grades came out the end of the quarter, Russell was astonished to find that not only had he passed all his classes (15 hours worth of English, government, political science and botany among others) but that he had earned straight "A"s. He was so happy he couldn't believe it. Professors began asking him where he was going to school to receive his doctoral degree.

The young Hawaii boy had earned himself the confidence to know he could finish college. "It shows he really had something," says Aiko, "Blessed with brains."

After two years, student housing became available for the young couple at Y Mount, at a considerable savings, so they moved their few belongings up the hill. Reminding Russell of army barracks, the wooden two story box-shaped buildings were laid out where the J. Reuben Clark Law School and parking lot now stand, sweeping up to Carson's Market, which is now the BYU Creamery on 9th East.

Church was a wooden bungalow next to the dairy where the Engineering Building now stands south of the Wilkinson Center. During the week a small preschool with student teachers was held on the east side of the education building which Ellen attended.

The Horiuchis' apartment was located on the bottom floor in the middle of the complex. With two bedrooms, a shower, laundry room, living room, and central heating the new place was very comfortable. Aiko couldn't remember if the stove was gas or electric but it definitely wasn't a coal stove and she found herself baking more often. Most of their furniture was still crafted from wooden orange crates draped in sheets. They didn't even own a proper bedspread until Charlie and Hisa gave them a nice embroidered one.

The Utah winter was a bit of an adjustment for the family but they soon adapted. Ellen particularly enjoyed being pulled around the apartments on a sled. During the summer she liked riding her tricycle and later a bike.

Their neighbors consisted of four or five other student families around them. Despite the tight finances, the young couple never really felt poor since everyone else was in the same situation. It wasn't until one neighbor's parents sent them a television that Aiko sensed a tinge of poverty. Not complaining but more by way of conversation she mentioned to her mother that they were poor compared to some. Still living in post-war Japan, to Hatsu being poor meant a very different thing. Worried that is what Aiko meant, she sent a care package. The notion stung Russell's pride and he reminded Aiko angrily that with a refrigerator, a washer and a bicycle they were not poor, especially by Japanese standards.

Around this time Russell had a run in with Mark Benson, the son of Ezra Taft Benson, who was attending school at the same time. There was a "big, splashy article" in the school paper about Mark taking an extra heavy load of classes, well beyond what was usually allowed. Russell's temper flared and he wrote an editorial to the school paper arguing that preferential treatment of the children of general authorities was a violation of school policy.

Mark showed up on the porch of their apartment a few nights later and a lively discussion ensued. Mark explained how his credits worked out and that who his father was held no bearing on anything. The explanation did not meet Russell's satisfaction and he told Mark "to hang it" and kicked him out.

"[Russell] was fearless," tells Aiko, her tone indicating that it wasn't always a good thing, "When he thinks he's right he just goes ahead."

This action would cause Russell a fair amount of anxiety down the road.

Russell and Aiko never owned a car while they were at BYU, opting instead to use a bicycle when transportation was necessary. When friends like the Tsuyas in Salt Lake invited them up for a get-together they would get a ride from one of their friends, usually Fred Takasaki or Roy Smith.

The Hawaii boys stayed in close contact with each other. Fred Takasaki and Tom Nakama from Maui frequented the Horiuchis' apartment, coming over to use the ringer-type washing machine Russell purchased. Others, including Allen Ebesu and Gladys Kondo from Kauai, gathered together to enjoy the cakes and pies that Aiko was fond of baking. As testament to Aiko's cooking skill, Russell began to put on weight!

By his diligent efforts and Aiko's loving support, who "helped by keeping [Ellen] quiet" while he studied, Russell finished school in three years. Despite his hesitation at the start, he earned excellent grades, which in turn allowed him to believe in himself. His only goal had been to finish and he focused on doing the best he could, which turned out to be very good indeed.

About a year before graduation, as the high marks continued to roll in, the thought occurred to Russell that at his current pace he was likely going to graduate valedictorian. This notion was confirmed sometime later when Professor Carr drove them to a small banquet held by the Phi Kappa Phi Honor Society to which they'd been invited. The New Zealander could hardly contain his excitement. At this point he wasn't really allowed to say anything, but he did drop the hint that "a wonderful thing happened today" in faculty meeting. Russell had indeed been chosen as BYU Valedictorian for the Class of 1953. Professor Carr, in his own words "had the signal honor of being asked to speak in your [Russell's] behalf before the voting faculty whos [sic] majority acclaimed you as their representative."

The story is handed down that the opening prayer was given by Hugh Nibley, who, dressed in full honors robe and regalia, began with "We come before thee, Lord, in the robes of an apostate priesthood . . . " He really was a maverick.

Shortly after, Russell was contacted and officially asked to give the valedictory speech at commencement. In addition to being a personal victory, Russell was also the first Asian valedictorian ever at

BYU. He was interviewed by a KBYU announcer who wanted to interview Aiko as well but she declined, still hesitant over her English.

There wasn't much preparation time. Russell's English professor, Brother Taylor, helped touch up Russell's talk. The speech was then taken to University President Wilkinson's office to get his sanction. Wilkinson, who Russell described in a letter as "an ambitious fellow with plenty of drive," paced up and down the room while he looked it over. He wanted to make a few changes and got a bit upset when Russell refused to do so.

Commencement was held in the Smith Field House, the largest building on campus at the time. Allen Ebesu brought flower leis and saved seats for Aiko and Ellen, who danced the hula in the aisle while her father spoke. Russell titled his speech *The Education of a Convert*, telling the story of how he came to join the church and how he reconciled his intellectual pursuits with his religious beliefs. His speech received an ovation so tremendous that it took President J. Rueben Clark a few minutes to get the audience back to introduce the next speaker, President Adam S. Bennion of the Quorum of the Twelve. Elder Bennion opened his remarks referring to Russell saying, "It is hard to follow a man like that." According to Paul Hyer, Russell had "outgunned a G.A."

The public relations corps sent a press release to the local Hawaiian newspaper. It was there that Russell's parents first heard about their son's achievement. Mitsutaka and Kikuyo were extremely proud that their oldest son was not only graduating from college but in the number one spot—not bad for peasant folks. Kikuyo shared the story of how, one morning when she was getting on the truck for work, Mr. Sakamoto (the boss of the plantation field workers) greeted her exclaiming, "*Oban* Auntie, your boy is graduating number one in college!" She already knew but in typical Japanese fashion had humbly kept quiet about it. None of the uncles or anyone who told Russell he was *baka* for going to school ever said a word.

Through the course of his college career, Russell found that he liked political science, law and botany. He performed so well in his classes that the professors approached him saying he had what it took to become a professor or an attorney. Greatly boosted by his academic success, Russell decided to go into law instead of teaching and changed his major to political science in preparation for law school.

Russell's constitutional law class was taught by Professor Paulson, a Stanford University graduate. Russell found that the subject came naturally to him. At the semester's end, Paulson took Russell aside and told him that he had never come across a student who grasped the significance of the various cases as well as Russell. Paulson also said that in all of his years teaching, Russell was the first and only student he'd ever given a full "A" and encouraged the young man to go to law school. There was no law school at BYU at the time or perhaps Russell might have enrolled.

Russell had entertained the idea of going into law only a short while when Henry Ching, another Hawaii boy, invited him to drive to Salt Lake City together. Henry was a highly successful Chinese businessman from Honolulu who Russell met in class. Henry was in his 60s and as far as anyone knows he was going to school simply for pleasure.

Henry was friends with Matthew Cowley, the apostle with a great fondness for the people of Polynesia. Henry felt that Russell should speak with him.

"Why do you want to go into law?" the apostle asked Russell, "If you know a man's guilty, how do you feel about getting him off the hook?"

"I do what I can do," shrugged Russell. Getting a man off the hook was part of the job.

"Stay out of law," Cowley said, pointing at Russell. The conversation was pleasant but Cowley was serious, "I'm a lawyer and not a very good one because if I know a man is guilty it's difficult for me to represent him."

Then he repeated himself, "Young man, you stay out of law!"

To Russell's credit, he heeded the counsel given even though he would have excelled in the profession. Family theory is that success might have turned his head away from service in the Church. When asked what his thoughts on the matter were Russell made his best I-don't-know face and shrugged.

13

BERKELEY

THE HORIUCHIS THOUGHT HARD TO decide where Russell should go to graduate school. Choices included Yale, Cornell, Michigan and Harvard although Russell strongly favored the University of Washington in Seattle. In a letter to Earl Christensen, his friend and botany professor, Russell explained it was "closer to home and strong in the area which I hope to study. There is another angle to that and it's finances. Things are going to be rough but I hope we can see our way through." In the end Russell applied for and was accepted to the University of California at Berkeley. The Horiuchis remember it as a happy time filled with the thrill of having accomplished a major hurdle and excitement about attending another school.

After graduating, the Horiuchis had less than twenty dollars in their savings account.[1] They began saving for their first car, a maroon colored Chevrolet which they purchased for $625. Russell and Aiko initially planned to take a train to California but calculated that the tickets would cost the same as buying a car plus they wouldn't have transportation once they arrived.

In the same letter to Earl Christensen, Russell expresses his feelings regarding moving from Utah: "With the approaching of our

---

1.   One interview says $16, another says $17. Either way it wasn't much, even in those days.

departure from this valley and the school, I feel very reluctant. We have made many friends and we leave some fine memories. Perhaps I may someday return but the future is difficult to ascertain."

In preparation for the move Russell spent time welding a small trailer from scratch that they hitched to the car to haul their belongings. He worked on the trailer every evening after dinner. "He did a good job," tells Aiko, then shares the following story:

South of Provo, near Springville the left-side trailer tire fell off and rolled ahead of them. Aiko remembers seeing the tire rolling along. She thought, "Oh! There goes someone's tire." At first neither she nor Russell realized it was theirs. When they pulled off to the side of the road and surveyed the situation, Russell realized the bolts had stripped off.

There was a junkyard in town and Aiko and Ellen stayed in the car while Russell hiked back to get parts to repair the trailer. After this initial delay they were off.

Traveling through Nevada in early summer with no air conditioning was a challenge, even though there weren't many cars on the road in those days. Still the family enjoyed crossing the desert together. Ellen saw a rabbit and started singing *Here comes Peter Cottontail* and soon everyone joined in.

That evening they slept in the car since they couldn't afford a motel. The car overheated only once, on the other side of the Sierra Nevadas. Russell hiked down the canyon with a canvas bag for water to cool off the radiator. The Horiuchis literally prayed that the car would make it.

The maroon Chevrolet rolled into Berkeley in the late afternoon, its passengers staring out in wonder as the fog rolled in. Despite the summer season, people on the street wore winter coats, a strange sight until the Horiuchis realized how cold it was.

Again, like angels sent to ease the Horiuchis' every transition, the Hyers were there to provide a pillow for the family when they arrived tired and dusty. Paul had graduated from BYU the year before, and preceded the Horiuchis to Berkeley.

Even though the Hyer's were white, they lived in an apartment in the black district of town. It was a poor area but "We had great neighbors," tells "Uncle" Paul. The Hyer's themselves were poor college students with four children, sometimes so financially strapped they had to debate if they could afford an ice cream cone.

The Horiuchis stayed at the Hyer's for a few days until they found a suitable two-bedroom apartment at 2633 1/2 McGee Street (the half is the basement) for $45 a month, which was pretty costly at the time. It was essentially a raised basement with a large living room. It didn't get a lot of sunlight but the rooms were large.

To Ellen, Berkeley was a magical time filled with good friends and adventures such as starting kindergarten at nearby Longfellow Elementary School. For Russell and Aiko it was a little harder. Although they too remember those years with fondness they quickly realized that it wasn't only their rent that was more costly—all of their expenses were going to be higher.

Aiko didn't know exactly how much more things were costing them. Russell wrote the checks and "I didn't worry," she laughs. Russell still had his GI Bill but it was very tight. For a while the couple had difficulty finding work, living strictly on the money earned from Russell's service.

The McGee apartment also happened to have two sets of Japanese neighbors. The Abes, an older couple who lived upstairs, and the Kagawa family next door.

When *Obon*, part of a celebration honoring one's ancestral spirits, was held in Berkeley, Aiko took Ellen and went together with the Kagawas, Abes and another friend, Gladys Hayashi. Dressed in full kimono and obi, Ellen danced with the Kagawa's daughter Margie and other children.

Both the Abes and Kagawas helped the Horiuchis find ways to earn extra income. Mr. Abe gave Russ a few of his clients to cut their lawns. Ellen recalls going along with Russell to the house of a "funny, old lady" who gave the young girl a mirror, which she kept for years. Eventually, Russell also got work as a teaching assistant to Dr. Eugene Burdick who wrote the book *The Ugly American*.

Both Mrs. Abe and Lily helped Aiko find some house cleaning jobs, ideal for Aiko who still felt shy about her English.

Mrs. Abe introduced Aiko to Ms. Cochran, a spinster. She was a very tidy lady who didn't like too many small things cluttering up her home and kept all her magazines and papers neatly stacked. Aiko was paid $1.25 an hour for four hours but had to pay her own bus fare. Aiko only stayed for a month.

Lily had a younger *Nisei* friend who was looking for someone to take over her housecleaning job. Aiko accepted the position, which happened to be cleaning the home of William Prosser, the renown expert on legal torts. The Prossers lived in a beautiful house on the top of Berkeley Hill, which they kept sparsely decorated. Aiko still worked only four hours for $1.25 but Mrs. Prosser also agreed to pay her bus fare.

When Mrs. Prosser had friends over for lunch, she would insist that Aiko join them. Aiko remembers breaking a wine glass once when she was cleaning. She felt very bad but Mrs. Prosser told her not to worry about it.

One day Mrs. Prosser asked Aiko if she could clean the shelves in the bathroom, which wasn't something she usually did. There were four or five very high shelves and Aiko had to climb on a stool to reach them. As she stretched out her arm to the top shelf Aiko's hand brushed against something. When she pulled it down she was surprised to find a six-inch thick stack of $100 dollar bills sitting in her hand. It scared Aiko. She quickly put it back, finished her cleaning and left the bathroom.

Aiko thinks Mrs. Prosser was testing her. If it was a test then she must have passed because the Prossers, planning a trip to Europe, asked if Aiko and her husband were willing to house sit for them and take care of their cat. Between Aiko's cat allergy and Russell's lack of interest they turned the offer down. The Prossers were able to find another student couple instead.

Aiko also cleaned for a woman whose husband was a professor at Contra Costa College. The income from the two cleaning jobs helped out but Aiko didn't clean houses for long.

Aiko began cleaning the house of a Japanese man who was the first representative of Mitsubishi Shoji. On her second visit the man happened to come home early. When he learned that Aiko was an Aoyama graduate he made a funny face, feeling that a graduate from such a prestigious university should not be doing menial work.

The next thing Aiko knew she was being invited to work for the Japanese consulate in downtown San Francisco. The man made arrangements for the interview, which Aiko took and got the job. Her new boss was Mr. Kumamoto who was *kibei*, a person of Japanese descent born in America but schooled in Japan. He returned stateside for college, graduating from the University of Washington. Aiko's coworker was a Mr. Okamoto, a *nisei*, who commuted from Menlo Park. She worked in the legal and visa section. The job consisted mostly of issuing visas and replying to letters sent to Mr. Kumamoto with questions about Japanese law.

It was a definite step up in pay and Aiko, like Russell, was determined to stay out of debt. The only real drawback to the job was the hour-long commute. Aiko took the train from Berkeley, following a route that no longer exists, crossing over the bridge into the city. It wasn't the ideal situation, especially with a young daughter still at home. Aiko remained in the job from 1955–1957. It upset her in later years when other immigrants were picky about the kind of jobs they would perform. The Horiuchis believed you simply did what you had to do to stay out of debt and make ends meet.

Aiko got her driver's license in Berkeley. Initially Russell tried to teach her how to drive but kept yelling at her every time she stalled the clutch. She gave up and went to driving school to finish her lessons.

It was in Berkeley that Aiko received her naturalization as an American citizen. Paul Hyer drove the Horiuchis into San Francisco for Aiko's testing and also acted as witness.

Each candidate's place of birth was verified. Aiko remembers the instructor asking one applicant, "Ma'am, were you born in the United States?" The nervous woman declared, "No, I was born in Texas!"

Aiko studied the naturalization pamphlet diligently, memorizing all the president's names, information on the system of government, etc. After all her worried preparation the quiz was actually pretty simple. She was verbally asked a few questions then told that she passed and that she'd be notified for oath day. Aiko was now a fully naturalized citizen. It was an exciting day but she was more relieved it was over.

Upon naturalization you could change your full name if you desired. Aiko liked the name Annette so she went to Russell and asked, "Did you ever have a girlfriend named Annette?"

"No," he answered.

"Good," she said and took the name.

It was at this time that Russell legally adopted his English name as well. Russell had been going by his chosen name for years, but it was at this time he had it legally formalized.

Annette had worked at the consulate for almost two years when Ellen fell off a swing at school and broke her front tooth.[2] Ellen was all right but Annette decided that the one-hour commute was

---

2. Ellen's only other childhood mishap occurred in sixth grade when she broke her arm while roughhousing with some of the neighborhood kids.

too far and began looking for new opportunities. Many companies discriminated against minorities and it was hard to find a job. At the time Cal State didn't hire minorities so Annette applied to Cal Farm Insurance. In the qualifying exam she excelled at the math portion, scoring 30 percent above average, but didn't do well with the English portion.

Brother Hale, who was in the same stake as the Horiuchis and one of the top men at Cal Farm, recognized the Horiuchi name and phoned Russell to ask if he knew anyone named Annette. Russell replied Annette was his wife. Thus, with a little help, Annette was hired as the first Asian worker at the company. Cal Farm was really looking for someone fast with numbers to work in their fleet department. Annette joined a team of 5–7 other girls, approaching her job with typical Japanese industriousness. Much to the consternation of the other women in the office, Annette usually finished her work by midday and asked for more to do. She was so productive that the other girls told her to slow down. By the end, Annette was doing the jobs of three people including work from the accounting department.

Ellen remembers her mother working at Cal Farm because there was a burger shop down the street where Annette took her from time to time. Annette was there for one and half years.

Through their friend Carl Johnson, Annette learned of a promising job opening with the university accounting department. Carl's wife was an interior decorator and Annette remembers that their entire house was decorated in black and white. She also worked as the secretary at one of the departments at the university. When she heard of an opening in the testing department she told Annette to apply since it paid double her wages at Cal Farm.

The application required a typing test. Annette wasn't a good typist so she spent a whole month practicing every day. She passed it, got the job and then hardly ever used a typewriter again at work. Annette worked at UC for thirteen months. The extra money definitely helped the couple survive but they grew tired of, as Russell puts it, "living on measly wages."

Russell and Annette attended the Claremont Ward where Russ became the assistant clerk under Bishop Ernie Ahlborn, the Chief of the Berkeley fire department. Carl Johnson served as one of the counselors.

Margaret Ahlborn served as primary president and took Ellen to primary class. Up until then, Annette didn't know that the primary program even existed.

The Horiuchis and the Ahlborns became close. The Ahlborn children, Ernest Jr. and Peggy became good friends with Ellen. The friendship even extended to the Ahlborn's two shepherd dogs, which Russell and Annette watched when the Ahlborns took vacation. Ernest gave a tackle box to Russell, which he kept for years. The Ahlborns loved horses. They eventually moved to Provo where they kept a few, then later they moved to Tridell, Utah to a larger ranch.

Bishop Wood and his wife Virginia lived across from the chapel of the Claremont ward. Russell and Annette were good friends with the Wood's son, Arthur. A letter from Brother Wood in 2001 serves as a reminder of Russell's other interests beyond academics and fishing: "I remember the church softball games that were played 'under the lights'. As I remember you were the only batter I knew that could hit a fly ball past the center fielder for a home run and stretch it out to a double."

Russell mentioned one day in passing that he'd met a fellow from Hawaii whose wife was from Japan. It wasn't until later when Annette ran into her at a meeting of Japanese war brides that she realized the man's wife was none other than Yulia Motofuji, an acquaintance from Japan. Yulia was from Omori in Tokyo and also graduated from Aoyama. She was four years younger than Annette and had been good friends with Hisako.

Yulia's husband, Francis, was finishing his doctorate in Japanese Literature and taught at the university. Yulia's mother was white Russian and her father was Japanese, and she spoke fluent Japanese, Russian, and English. She and Annette spent many hours reminiscing about Japan and keeping up on the latest news. It was relaxing for the two women to speak Japanese.

Yulia worked for Henckel's cutlery, supporting Francis through school. Through Yulia, Annette purchased a cutlery set. Costing a little over $30, the set was on the pricey side but Annette still uses the same knives over 60 years later. They still look as good as the day she bought them, testament to the quality of Henckel's workmanship.

In the meantime Russell decided to earn his master's degree in political science. He was enjoying his classes and working as a teaching assistant.[3] To help pay for his schooling Russ applied for the John Hay Whitney Scholarship. He remembers the interviewer asking about his Eagle Scout rank since the man was also an Eagle. They enjoyed a pleasant chat. Later, Russell was awarded the sizable scholarship. He also applied and received a Danforth Academic fellowship. The scholarship and fellowship brought in some much needed cash flow and helped ease Russell's financial worries.

While at Berkeley the Horiuchis strengthened their bonds with friends like Paul and Harriet Hyer while creating new friendships with others such as Spencer Palmer, Richard Wirthlin, Dean Mann, Earl Remington and John Martinez. At lunch time these starving students, who began to refer to themselves as the Berkelyites, got together to "chew the fat," a bonding pastime that Russell claimed help him keep going. Paul Hyer referred to these times as "informal sack-lunch seminars." They spent a lot of time together, supporting each other in their scholastic endeavors, helping each

---

3. Working for either Dr. Belquist or Scalapino but Aiko doesn't remember which.

other when they moved and so on. Over simple baked beans these fellow students forged connections that would last a lifetime.

During Christmas, half a dozen of these struggling students decided to apply for seasonal work at the post office, taking the required civil service exam. None of them got the job. Later they all sheepishly confessed to each other that every one of these brainy masters and doctoral candidates had failed the exam. For years they laughed about being good enough for PhD work but not for the post office!

On the 22nd of August, 1957, Russell and Annette were sealed in the Los Angeles temple.

Ellen was eleven when Annette thought she might be pregnant again. Excited, she rushed to a doctor to find out if she really was or not. The next day Annette suffered a terrible stomach ache that turned out to be a miscarriage. Not a word of this was spoken for years, not even within the family.

In good time Russell completed his Masters in Geography and began coursework for his doctorate. He and Annette found another apartment at 1709 Milvia Street closer to the University. The second story, one-bedroom flat didn't offer a lot of space, and the rent was slightly higher but the location was more convenient to campus and the train station.

Ellen attended Whittier Elementary School, located near the Virginia Bakery, close to Shattuck Avenue. After Ellen left for school in the morning, Annette caught the train to work. Russell finished classes and was home in time to catch Ellen after school. Annette returned at about six and they ate dinner together. It was a much better situation for the young family.

The furniture the Horiuchis purchased for $99 included a green mattress couch, a lamp and a dresser, which they used for years afterwards. They also bought a sofa bed for Ellen. They used a credit plan, paying only five dollars a month. Russell paid the bill diligently but the idea of owing money and having credit debt wore on his conscience. He remembered seeing his parents dealing with debt and making payments. "I told myself no, not me. No more," shares Russell. After three months he walked into the store and paid off the balance. "I never got a credit card. [I] didn't buy anything if I didn't have it [the money.]"

"[It might be] convenient to have but not necessary," agrees Annette, "When you die you don't keep any of it. Why [do] people hustle after money?" Annette concedes that people do need some money but not as much as many seem to think. She adds that she is comfortable now so maybe it's easier to say.

Russell and Annette never hesitated to acknowledge the many people who helped them along the way. They recalled one Christmas during these early years when there was no money for gifts and they had nothing for Ellen. At the eleventh hour, on Christmas Eve, a godsend in the form of a check arrived from Uncle Nakamoto in Hawaii. Annette believes Uncle Nakamoto was the brother to Shizu who was Uncle Codac's (Kikuyo's brother) wife but admits she can't remember for sure.

Uncle Nakamoto owned a successful jewelry shop in Lahaina and was always very kind to Russell and Annette. A first generation immigrant, Uncle Nakamoto enjoyed speaking Japanese with Annette when she lived in the islands. Annette remembered when she first arrived in Hawaii Uncle Nakamoto told her she could have anything in his store. At his insistence she picked out a simple ring to replace one of Shige's that she had borrowed and lost. Russell later teased Annette that she could have chosen a gold watch or something fancy instead. Annette still has the ring, which was never sent.

Uncle Nakamoto's Christmas Eve check was for twenty dollars, enough for Russell and Annette to hurry out and buy the life-size doll that Ellen had been wishing for. Instantly inseparable from her new toy, Ellen pushed the doll's baby buggy wherever she went.

Between Annette's jobs and Russell working as a teaching assistant they managed to survive. It was a struggle but they always saved their money. From their meager income they paid a full tithe and set aside an additional 10% for spending. The rest was for housing and expenses.

The ten percent they set aside went towards family activities. Every two or three months they went out to dinner, sometimes at Pier 1 down by the wharf below the bridge in Berkeley but usually across the bay at Fisherman's Grotto No. 9 in San Francisco. Ellen would order fried prawns, a favorite to this day, and Russell still raves about the sourdough bread there. On occasion, dinner was followed by a trip to the movies.

Even with pennies being carefully watched, there was time for Sunday afternoon drives up Berkeley Hill to Tilden Park or the Berkeley campus tower. Golden Gate Park in San Francisco was another favorite place, particularly the Japanese Tea Garden.

One of Annette's joys was attending the ballet. Even though it was expensive it meant a great deal for her to take Ellen to the Sadler's Wells Ballet at the San Francisco Opera House. Both women remember Margaret Fonteyn as the principle ballerina. Taking Ellen to the Christmas production of The Nutcracker quickly became a favorite mother/daughter tradition. Russell wasn't particularly interested. The two women would hop on the bus and head into town, often accompanied by Yulia and Francis Motofuji. Yulia was a ballerina and helped introduce Annette to the ballet and other cultural events, including seeing Vincent Van Gogh's first exhibition in the United States. Russell didn't attend, claiming that he couldn't afford to. Annette says that was just an excuse.

On the Fourth of July, the family was usually one of the first to arrive at Lake Merritt in Oakland to watch the spectacular fireworks. A camping trip to the Sierras was another highlight. Christmas was not Christmas without a visit to Santa Claus at Hinck's Department store. After Saturday shopping they treated themselves to a BLT at Woolworth's lunch counter on Shattuck Avenue. Over time Annette was able to buy a few dresses on Shattuck, which she eventually gave to her niece Harumi.

Around this time, Russell's sister, Kay, relocated to San Francisco, getting a job as a beautician at the May Company. It was nice having her nearby. The Horiuchis were also grateful that Uncle Roy and Auntie Ethel were close by. Bay area traffic wasn't very heavy at the time and Russell and Annette often made the two-hour drive up to Lodi to visit. Annette's youngest sister, Kyoko, eventually moved to Tiburon on the north side of the bay but that was years after the Horiuchis had moved to Utah.

Russell made time for fishing. He recalls an outing with Annette and the Motofujis to Berkeley Pier when the smelt were running so heavily that he was catching as fast as he could drop the line. There were four hooks on the line and all four came up with a fish. Everyone had a great time and it wasn't long before they had a bucket full of perch. They deep-fried the bounty at home for a delicious dinner.

The move to Milvia Street placed them in the Berkeley First Ward, under the leadership of Bishop Leland J. Fife. Russ was called as assistant ward clerk working with Emerton Williams, who was also an assistant professor of forestry and botany.

Emerton was a nice, humble man and he and his wife, Margaret, often invited the Horiuchis over to dinner. Years later, when one of their children broke her leg in a skiing accident while attending BYU, the Horiuchis had the chance to return the family's kindness by taking care of Janet for a more than a week while she recuperated.

Russell also got to know Mack Hughes, then serving as counselor in the bishopric. Mack had flown as a bomber pilot in Northern Africa during World War II and was now working as a chemist at Standard Oil. Each summer they invited the ward to use the Chevron employee swimming pools in Richmond. The Hughes won fond laughter when they named their twins Jack and Jill. The burly chemist was a down-to-earth, straightforward man who became very close to Russell.

Another couple the Horiuchis often dined with was Gordon and Helen Rose. Gordon was quiet while Helen was talkative. The Horiuchis also remained close to the Rose's son, Buckley.

Buckley remembers the time they "went backpacking and planned a tough first-day hike with full packs, all uphill, and fully ten miles to the first night's camping site, [Russell] wandered in at dusk and responded to our questions of, "Where have you been?" with, "I went fishing at some of the good spots along the way; this hiking is too much like work.""

Karl Johnson served as the other counselor in the bishopric. Karl worked with the church welfare program, managing the bishop's storehouse. Russell went one or two times to help him. Russell vividly recalls the people who drove up in a new Porsche and came in demanding steak. The bald-faced audacity left Russell feeling disgusted and he never returned to the storehouse again. Russell did, however, enjoy continuing to work with Karl in the bishopric.

Russell and Annette also kept in touch with friends back in Utah. When Professor Carr went on sabbatical with his family to New Zealand Russell met them at the railway station and took them to the airport. Rebecca Carr Lewis remembers Russell telling her father to get a porter to carry their luggage to the car so they wouldn't have to carry it so far. It was a good chance to catch up a bit and Russell was glad to help them out.

Professor Carr attended Berkeley himself when he was a student. One teacher he was fond of was Dr. Eric Cyril Bellquist. So when Russell enrolled at Berkeley Professor Carr wrote to Dr. Bellquist praising Russell.

When Russell attended Dr. Bellquist's class, Dr. Bellquist mentioned a man's name and without warning began to question Russell about him.

"Was this man secretary of agriculture?"

"Yes," answered Russ.

"Was this about the wheat case?"

"Yes," confirmed Russ.

Out of the clear blue sky, Russell was able to give the facts of the situation and the holdings of the case. Dr. Bellquist was impressed and praised, "William Carr said you were a good student. Now I believe him!"

After years of work, the time came for Russ to defend his doctorate work. His chairman on the doctoral committee was Dr. Scalapino who was notoriously hard to visit with, not giving a lot of time to the students. While this was frustrating to Russell, the two men must have had some sort of rapport. Paul Hyer recalls "Scalapino was soon attracted to Russell, who was receiving top grades, had a real grasp of Japanese politics, and still had his free-wheeling manner." Russell worked for Dr. Scalapino and the department first garnering a reputation as an impressive teaching assistant and later as a research assistant.

Disappointingly, when it came time for Russell to defend his oral exams Dr. Scalapino went on sabbatical, somewhat ironically to Tokyo. A temporary chairman, Dr. Henry Mah, was appointed in Scalapino's stead. Dr. Mah suggested to Russell that he should sign up for his class, telling him that he'd make sure Russell "made it through" to his doctorate. What at first sounded like a nice promise turned out to be a veiled threat of what would happen if Russell didn't take his course.

Russell signed up for two of Dr. Mah's classes but was told by one of the advisors that he shouldn't. He found out very few students actually took Mah's classes. Additionally, the Chinese-American descended Mah was rumored to be biased against Japanese. Never having been a politician, Russell followed the advice given him and withdrew from the classes. When Russell took his orals he was failed.

Paul Hyer, in a letter to President Earl C. Crockett, then President of BYU, wrote "Mah raised the question as to whether or not the candidate, Horiuchi, had taken his class. He had not. It was not required and did not necessarily fit into his program. Then on a choice of optional questions presented in the examination Russell chose to answer a question or questions on Japan. Professor Mah indicated that Russell should have treated the question of China. This was a personal preference and not mandatory, but these two things apparently prompted Mah, the chairman, to decline in passing Russell. Mah . . . is known at U.C. to be prejudiced against Japanese and . . . had just previously failed . . . another Japanese of my acquaintance who is now at UCLA. Professors Bellquist and Ike both supported [Russell], but just the two of them could not decide the examination in favor of the candidate and had no recourse." Without Mah's approval, Russell was barred from completing the program.

Dr. Bellquist, also on the committee, adamantly stated that Russell should have passed with flying colors. Russell had fulfilled enough requirements for a PhD in two disciplines, both Political Science and Geography but was denied either. These days this most likely would have fallen under discrimination laws—not that Russell was ever the type to sue—but there wasn't much recourse at the time and years of diligent scholarship came to naught. Once again the words of his patriarchal blessing that he would be reviled because he was Japanese were being fulfilled.

Russell asked Mah if he would be willing to work with him in going over the topic and Mah said no, it would take too much of his time. The only thing Russell was able to walk way with was a resolution to "never be that kind of teacher."

Eventually Dr. Scalapino returned from sabbatical and tried to get Russell to come back but Russell had "had it up to here" and refused.

Russell wasn't the only one having problems. Everything had slowed down at Berkeley. Matriculation from the masters program into the doctoral program was dismal. The backlog of students in the Political Science department numbered in the hundreds with only a handful passing each term. Berkeley simply wasn't getting people through the program.

The problem became so severe that people were quitting and going elsewhere. Richard Wirthlin also failed his defense. His wife, nine months pregnant at the time, stormed up to the campus and persuaded the committee to change their minds. Richard was one of the few who walked away with his doctorate. Annette always felt she should have done the same, but held back because she felt her English was still inadequate.

Lee Farnsworth, who later taught political science at BYU, transferred to Claremont University. Hugh Burleson quit his program and started working at the State Department. Francis Motofuji was required to learn five Asian languages for his Doctorate. Finally a professor advised him to transfer to Stanford. Even Paul Hyer thought about going to Harvard because it would be easier. Russell shares that when Paul was going to take his PhD exam, both he and Paul went into a phone booth to pray for him. Paul was one of the few who made it through and received his PhD in History from Berkeley.

Why was the situation at Berkeley so dismal? They had admitted too many students into the Masters program and needed to cull their numbers. Paul Hyer, by now an active member of the Association of Asian Studies, recalls some professors from the East stating that Berkeley was "making their reputation on the blood of their students." Berkeley was giving itself a bad name.

Regardless of whether Russ had plenty of company or not, to have all those years and financial sacrifice washed down the drain was a grave disappointment. Ever pragmatic and needing to provide for his family he began redirecting his life.

Interviewer: Did you ever argue?

Russell: Oh, we exchanged words frequently. I was quick tempered and she was headstrong but we loved each other. Things
just cooled off.

The first Eagle Scout
in Puukolii, Maui.

US Navy Fleet off Lahaina shore 1938.

Aiko, second from right, in her Aoyama
School uniform circa 1939.

箱根松坂屋旅館の庭先でおにぎりをほばる
グループの益子と.

ko, second from right, enjoying a picnic with her high school friends in
kone, Japan.

NOZOMI HORIUCHI

Military mug shot of Russell
early 1940s.

Aiko, on the right, with sister,
Hisako, on the way to work at
the PX. The tie-dyed kimonos
were made by their sister, Yaeko.

Hawaiian Nisei soldiers in the snow, possibly at Fort Snelling. Russell is top left.

Sgt. Horiuchi in Tokyo on left.

The girls of the PX at GHQ circa 1945. Aiko is second from the right and her sister, Hisako, is second from left.

The girls of the PX with Paul Cockrell. Aiko is on the far right, her sister, Hisako, is third from left.

Russell in his army uniform.

Aiko during a work break at GHQ circa 1945. Aiko was grateful for the clothes that Russell's sister, Kay, would periodically send.

Russell at work in Tokyo circa 1946.

Russell working in the GHQ utility shop. By this time he was working as a civilian in order to remain near Aiko.

Courting Days in Tokyo circa 1946. Taken by Adney Komatsu.

OFFICER'S BILLET
3186TH SIG SV BN

Going to church. Aiko's coat was sewn by Shige who sewed all of the sisters' clothing.

Courting in Hibiya Park circa 1946.

The courting couple at Hibiya Park.

The handsome couple in Toyoeiwa School garden in Roppongi circa 1947.

A Sunday outing near the Tama River 1946.
Picture taken by Fujiya Nara.

The earliest church members to respond to Clissold's ad after the war. Top to Bottom, L to R Brother Shiraishi, Brother Nara, unknown sister, Sister Watanabe, Sister Nara.

Russ and Aiko in front of the American Consulate in Yokohama on their wedding day. Kay sent the dress to Aiko. Russ and Aiko each carried half of the dollar bill until they were finally allowed to marry. Photo taken by Allen Ebesu.

Yoshizo Mori Family 1948. Top Row L to R Aiko and Russ, Tomoya Kikuchi (Hiroko's husband), Shigeko Mori (her husband, Iwakichi, is not pictured), Charles Shibata, Ichiro Mori (brother). Front L to R Hisako Shibata, Hiroko Kikuchi, Hatsu Mori, Hajime Kikuchi (Hiroko's son), Yoshizo Mori, Kazuko Mori (Ichiro's wife), Kyoko Mori. Note that all the sisters in western dress eventually moved to the United States while all the sisters in traditional kimonos remained in Japan.

Leaving Japan 1948.

Modeling for Kay in Hawaii.

Aiko holding Ellen 1948.
Russell's sister, Kay, styled
Aiko's hair.

The family on the back porch in Hawaii 1949. Russ was a journeyman electrician earning a good wage when Aiko said it was time to go to college.

Sketch of Ellen by Aiko. Russell procrastinated shooting a photo of the baby so long that Aiko finally drew a picture.

December 2nd 1948

Aunt Kay with Ellen in Maui.

Aiko with 8 month old
Ellen under a mango tree in
Lahaina.

Ellen playing with the neighbor's dog in Lahaina.

Aiko and
Ellen with
Okie Bennett,
far left, and
Uncle Roy
Koyama,
far right, at
Yosemite
1950.

Ellen's first birthday.

Aiko in front of the
Joseph Smith Building
circa 1951.

Ellen in front of the Horiuchi's first
rental in Provo.

Ellen in the
Pioneer Day
Parade Provo
1951.

Russell's 1953 valedictorian photo used in the
commencement program.

Family in Berkeley, Easter 1956.

Annette returns to Japan for the first time after the war, 1961.

Family photo at Ahlborn's house, Provo, Utah 1963.

Annette's graduation from BYU.

2 New Missions, Stake To Be Created In Japan

Newspaper announcing first mission call, 1970. In ten days they went from sitting in President Eldon Tanner's office to speaking at a conference in Sapporo, Japan.

Two new missions will be created in Japan and the first stake in that country will be organized later this month, the First Presidency announced this week.

The two new missions, tentatively named the Japan East and Japan West missions, will be formed through division of the Japan and Japan-Okinawa Missions. The changes will be effected by Elder Ezra Taft Benson and Elder Gordon B. Hinckley of the Council of Twelve.

Called as a mission president to serve in one of the two new missions in Japan is Russell N. Horiuchi, 1947 S. Main St., Orem, Utah. He will be accompanied to his field of labor by Mrs. Horiuchi.

The new Tokyo Stake will be created March 15. The new missions will be formed during the following week.

An indication of the growth of the Church also is the announcement that a stake will be created in the South African Mission. Elder Marion G. Romney of the Council of the Twelve is scheduled to officiate at that action on the same day as the creation of the Tokyo Stake.

The present Japan Mission is presided over by Pres. Walter R. Bills with headquarters in Tokyo. This mission will retain its present name and headquarters.

The new Japan East Mission will come from a division of the Japan Mission and will be headquartered in either Sapporo or Sendai.

The two missions contain a population of about 50 million persons with almost 6,500 Church members.

The other new mission will be called the Japan West Mission and it will be taken from the Japan-Okinawa Mission, presided over by Pres. Edward Y. Okazaki. The Japan-Okinawa Mission will be renamed the Japan Central Mission.

Japan Central Mission will retain its headquarters in Kobe, while Japan West Mission will operate from the city of Fukuoka. Japan West will contain the Kyushu and Okinawa Districts with a population of 11,251,000 and a Church membership of 1,977, plus about 900 servicemen.

The mission area in the Japan Central Mission includes the Chubu, Kinki and Shikoku districts. There are 3,455 members now living in the mission and among 37,202,000 Japanese.

In addition to Elder Benson and Elder Hinckley, two other General Authorities will be in Japan this month. They are Elder Hugh B. Brown, of the Council of the Twelve, and Elder Bernard P. Brockbank, an Assistant to the Twelve. Elder Brockbank is already in Osaka overseeing completion of the Church Pavilion in Expo '70.

President and Mrs. Russell N. Horiuchi

The pavilion will be dedicated March 13 and the fair will be formally opened March 14.

Elder Benson, who supervises the Far East missions with Elder Bruce R. McConkie of the First Council of the Seventy, said that hundreds of thousands of visitors are expected to visit the Church pavilion at Expo '70.

He foresees many thousands of referrals coming from the visitors and with the missions set up this will accomplish the maximum in proselyting and the prospects for growth of the Church in Japan will be greatly increased because of the fair in Osaka.

A minimum of 2,500 baptisms have been forecast for 1970 in Japan and Okinawa.

A seminar for mission presidents in the Orient already has been set up for Sept. 22 and 23 in Osaka.

Besides Pres. Horiuchi, another president will be named to preside over the other new mission.

Pres. Horiuchi is an assistant professor of geography at Brigham Young University and is a native of Hawaii.

He was born in Lahaina, Maui, Hawaii, Jan. 21, 1923 to the late Mitsutaka Horiuchi and Mrs. Kikuyo Koyanui Horiuchi.

Pres. Horiuchi has been serving in the bishopric of the BYU 14th Ward as well as teaching on the campus. He has been a member of the Church for about 25 years. He has been active in all aspects of Church work.

He met Annette Aiko Mori of Tokyo while he was serving with the U.S. Army on the staff of Gen. Douglas MacArthur. They were married Aug. 6, 1947, after Pres. Horiuchi was discharged from the Army and was working in Tokyo as a civilian translator for the Army.

They have one daughter, Eileen, 21, a school teacher.

Mrs. Horiuchi was born in Tokyo, Dec. 27, 1925 and part of her family still lives there. She was converted and baptized by her husband in 1950. They latter were sealed in the Los Angeles Temple.

Pres. Horiuchi received his bachelor's degree in 1953 from BYU, his masters at the University of California in 1956 and recently received his Ph.D. degree. He was valedictorian of the BYU graduating class in 1953.

He joined the BYU faculty in 1961 after teaching and doing research at the University of California at Berkeley, and also at the College of San Mateo, Calif.

Japan East Mission Conference with Elder James A. Cullimore.

Saying goodbye to Elder Harold B. Lee in Sapporo. Judy Komatsu is on the far left with Russell while Adney Komatsu stands third from the right.

Russell's desk in the mission office. Elder Kimball complimented Russ on the austerity of his makeshift office.

Japan East Mission Conference circa 1971.

A private moment with Apostle Spencer W. Kimball. Camilla Kimball is on the right.

Russell posing with salmon before dinner with Elder and Sister Spencer W. Kimball in Sapporo. A vendor delivered the fish and Russ couldn't resist a photograph.

Russell and
Annette 1981.

Annette preparing for
one of her exhibitions.
She completed a
master's degree in
art with emphasis on
watercolor.

Luncheon with Elder
and Sister Gordon
B. Hinckley. L to R
Russell, Spencer
and Shirley Palmer,
Tammy Palmer (former
daughter-in-law),
Annette, Kyunghae
(Rhee's daughter)
Sister Marjorie Hinckley,
Ho Nam Rhee, Elder
Gordon B. Hinckley,
Paul Hyer, Youn Soon
Rhee, Harriet Hyer.

Russell and Annette
serving as Temple
President and Matron of
the Tokyo Temple
1988-1991.

Russ was a featured speaker at the Washington DC Temple Visitor's Center Asian Pacific Week. He is dressed in Pakistani clothing.

The joy of mission work Japan. Visiting Hokkaido while on their Temple mission.

Mowing the lawn 2000. Russell took pride in his yard, mowing twice a week and growing flowers for Annette.

Gathering of the Hawaii boys and their spouses at the Nishimoto home. From L to R Adney and Judy Komatsu, Russ and Annette Horiuchi, Ralph and Lily Shino, Larry and Misao Wada, Bill and Sadie Tateishi, Roy and Uta Tsuya, unknown sister (second from right), Arthur and Grace Nishimoto.

Russell being honored by the BYU Alumni Association 2001. Russell often used his hands to emphasize a point.

Japan East Mission Reunion 2007.

14

BLESSINGS IN DISGUISE

Professor Bellquist mentioned an opening for a teaching position at San Mateo Junior College on Coyote Point. Russell applied and was hired immediately. The job was enjoyable and Russell soon found himself falling into step with teaching. His colleagues were cordial, his students rated him well and he began refining some of his teaching techniques that would later become well known among his students and peers. The most difficult part of the job was the hour-long commute from Berkeley to San Mateo over the Bay Bridge. Russell took turns driving, carpooling with one other fellow.

Because the position was temporary, the family was hesitant to move the first year. Finally they took the plunge and purchased a house at 1617 Maxine Drive in the shore view area of San Mateo, cutting Russell's commute down to under fifteen minutes. It was a three bedroom tract home built on a landfill but affordable, costing $17,000 dollars. Today the homes in the area are worth a half a million dollars.

The Horiuchis didn't have money for a down payment so Emerton Williams lent them the money without interest. Russell and Annette saved as much as they could to return the money as quickly as possible. The previous owners were smokers so Annette spent the better part of the year trying to rid the house of the lingering odor.

The family's stay in San Mateo was to be a short one. What exactly happened is unknown but one theory is that Russell mentioned something about Catholics (try discussing geo-politics and not mentioning the impact that religion has on a culture and people) and it filtered back that because of his Mormon background that he was severe on Catholics. There are also signs indicating that the college president disliked Mormons.

Other faculty members intimated that there was a certain factor of prejudice involved regarding Russell's status as Japanese-American. Ironically Russell was hired because he was a member of a minority group in an effort to showcase "liberalism and a lack of prejudice," not because of his credentials as a teacher. The fact that he turned out to be a good instructor was simply a bonus. He was being let go for the same reason he was hired, which had little to do with his teaching skill. A Japanese Mormon in an exclusive and strongly Catholic area was seen as a potential liability in public relations.

Some of the faculty and administration, including his division chairman, fought hard to keep Russell. The students, upon learning the news, created an uproar, creating petitions and bombarded the administration with upset visits, letters and phone calls. In spite of it all, after two years of teaching and only one year living in his own house, Russell was not offered a continuing contract. The news was delivered only nine days before he was scheduled for tenure.

Now Russell was truly frustrated. He began searching for a new position. He missed an interview near San Francisco because his car broke down. He still had midterm papers to correct. The typewriter broke. The vacuum quit working. The straws seemed to be piling high on the camel's back.

The trouble at Berkeley, the miscarriage, and now the expulsion from San Mateo placed a tremendous amount of strain on the Horiuchis' relationship, so much so that for a time Russell and Annette even spoke of separation.

Russell wrote "it seems that every time I feel things are finally going to break for us, we have run into roadblocks. I feel so dejected, and defeated—with the goal in sight and never achieving it. Wherever I turn I seem to stumble. My morale is high one day, and it falls into a crevice. I ask if there is any justice to it all—Lord forgive me for having so little faith. Only if I had someone to sit down and talk to . . . I think that in all my living days, I have never felt so alone."

For her part Annette expressed her feeling thus "the thing that makes me so mad is that in the academic field . . . they teach children that America is free country. Teaching them what is constitutional, liberty and democracy and yet they don't act as they preach. If they want to kick me around I don't mind. I was once an alien myself. However, I love this country—how free and challenging, I adopted this country and decided to be loyal to my adopted country and die here. But, Russell was born as citizen and there is no choice. I think of it, I can't hold my tears."

It was a very difficult period but the couple "rediscovered each other" and were able to strengthen their resolve. In a poignant section from a letter to Paul Hyer dated March 9, 1965 Russell relates "the best came out of [Annette] when my spirits were at ebb tide . . . She also said to me that if I am to free myself from the subtleties of racism . . . and unfairness, that there is only one place for me to go . . . She said—Go to the Lord's University—you can only find the inner peace there. She told me to forget the material comforts of California teaching—go and serve. Perhaps this was my apprenticeship. I should now serve.

"I keep fighting it but I know my heart belongs back there. My failures have really been the turning point to better things—not always in the terms of money and materialism, but inner peace. I see much wisdom [in] the words of Annette—I'll go where you want me to—like the song."

At the bottom of the letter Annette chimed in "I am grateful for the gospel I have. Without the understanding of the gospel, how [could we] hold ourselves in this situation?"

Through it all, one lesson was pounded deeply into Russell's mind. He writes, "Wherever I go I will always be physically identified . . . compelled to know my place and to keep it . . . I cannot be just good, I have to be flawless."

It was an upsetting time but another junior college position soon became available. It was not the ideal situation but would have to suffice, so the Horiuchis prepared to make the transfer. Russell also began the enrollment process at Stanford to continue his education in the geography department.

Before they could make the move, however, Russell received a phone call from Dr. Elliot Tuttle at BYU, one of Russell's favorite teachers during his undergraduate studies. Paul Hyer, now living in Provo, had spoken with Dr. Tuttle, now chairman of the Geography Department, and mentioned Russell's situation. Within hours Dr. Tuttle was working on getting Russell to BYU. A job was opening in the department and Russell was able to apply. With his credentials and history Russell was a shoe-in.

At the same time, other job offers suddenly appeared out of the woodwork including a good paying position as an assistant in the dean's office at Berkeley. But for both Russell and Annette Brigham Young was the clear-cut choice. Everything about it felt right and it would be a relief to once again be among good friends.

Only one hurdle remained in the form of his interview by an apostle. No one, including Russell, was particularly worried about this until he was told his interview was to be conducted by Elder Ezra Taft Benson. Former United States Secretary of Agriculture under President Eisenhower, Elder Benson was an intimidating figure to begin with. Of even greater concern to Russell was the fact that he was also father to Mark Benson, the student Russell had a run in with over excessive credit hours during his undergraduate years.

Conveniently, Elder Benson was in San Francisco for some meetings so the interview was conducted there. Russell paced the chapel corridor nervously. Of all the apostles, why did he have to pull the one that he might possibly have a conflict with? Even as he was welcomed into the room by Elder Benson, Russell truly thought he might not receive the appointment.

One of the things Elder Benson asked Russell was what he thought about the United Order. Russell doesn't remember what he answered but it must have been to Elder Benson's liking. Whether he was aware of Russell's and Mark's altercation or not, Elder Benson never made any mention of his son. It was soon apparent that the conversation was mostly a polite formality and that Russell was headed to BYU. Despite the exasperating beginning, leaving San Mateo would prove to be a blessing in disguise.

1961 found the family once more loading all they owned into their car. This was a different car from the maroon Chevrolet, which met an untimely demise in a fender bender in Berkeley wherein, thankfully, no one was hurt. The Horiuchis bought a 1955 Rambler that was, according to Russell's journal, "not very good—breaks [sic] froze but it was okay." Russell always chose his cars carefully and saved ahead so when the time came to buy a new one he could pay for it in full, avoiding payments and interest.

Annette was always very tidy. She wasn't working at the time and there wasn't much furniture so the house was easy to keep clean. One of Russell's colleagues in San Mateo once teased her. "It's so clean! Where do you hide all your trash?" he joked, looking under the sink. When it came time to move, Russ and Annette packed everything up so nicely that the mover asked if it was really all they had.

In Utah, Paul and Harriet Hyer once again played cordial hosts to the Horiuchis, letting the family stay in their basement until housing could be found. Paul had moved to Provo the year before, taking up a position as a history professor. Russell helped Paul and Harriet pack when they left Berkeley and now the Hyers were in Provo to help the Horiuchis land. Russell and Annette joked with the Hyers that they followed them everywhere.

A two-bedroom house for rent was located in Orem at 263 East 1000 South. What the Horiuchis didn't realize at first was that it was located near an active train track. The first time the whistle blew in the dead of night it scared them witless. Annette thought it was an earthquake. The tracks were used only seasonally during harvest to carry fruit from the orchards that covered the valley at the time. It soon became a familiar sound and the Horiuchis learned to sleep through it. When the train tracks were later removed, it was made into a street and first named Orem then Freedom Boulevard.

Ellen had a good friend a few houses down in San Mateo and cried when they left for Utah. They arrived in Orem right at the beginning of the school year and it was with a bit of trepidation that Ellen began 8th grade at Lincoln Junior High School. Looking back, Ellen admits she wound up with better friends in Utah, including Kathy Jackman, whose family lived a block away. Many years later the two best friends became in-laws, marrying a pair of brothers.

The Horiuchis' next-door neighbors directly to the east were Bob and Beth Foutin who were always baking delicious pastries. Bonnie and Wally Allred lived around the corner and proved congenial neighbors. These friendships, like so many others, continued for years. Bob and Russell shared a love of fishing, often rising early in the morning to head to the river together.

Russell was on the staff of the Geography Department in the Heber J. Grant Building. As the newest faculty member on the block, Russell often drew early morning or late night teaching slots. A typical day might find him leaving the house at 7:30 for an 8 am class, with a homemade lunch bag in hand. The whole family usually returned home about four in the afternoon.

Russell wasn't nervous to begin teaching. Passionate about his subject, he was on familiar turf both on campus and in the classroom. Russell also found the university setting was more stimulating compared to junior college. Students seemed more alert and ambitious regarding their education and Russell promoted student participation in his class.

Looking back, Russell was grateful for the training he received in Military Intelligence School. He began to combine his information gathering skills with his natural skills as a teacher to encourage his students to create "interconnecting linkages" for themselves, drawing connections between different pieces of knowledge and data. Instead of memorizing meaningless information from a textbook he challenged them to ask questions—Why? How come?—and to make correlations from knowledge they already possessed.

According to Paul Hyer "students were always amazed if not shocked at his [Russell's] first few lectures in a new class with his racey [sic] unorthodox style . . . Everyone will remember his talents at involving students in the discussion and provoking their thoughtful analyses. He was a master of the Socratic approach to the classroom." Russell wasn't there to show how intelligent he was. He wanted his students to know how intelligent *they* were.

One example Russell liked to use in class was to present a coconut and then ask his students what they knew about it and see if they could figure out where it might have come from. Discussions about tropical climates and geography lead to talking about potential industries in those areas, subsistence farming and fishing, about the people, their sociological structure, what kind of clothes they might wear, what kind of food they might eat, what occupations they might have and what sort of cultures could develop. Russell wanted his students to incorporate what they were learning and think beyond the simple regurgitation of facts and figures.

By chance, the former intelligence officer once had an entire ROTC unit in one of his classes. As part of an exam Russell asked hypothetically if the students were to invade Russia what their top five targets would be. *What cities would you select? Where? What time of year would you attack? Why?*

Caught off guard the students asked what kind of test this was. Russell answered he wanted them to apply the geography lessons they'd studied. What might seem an odd exercise was not about warfare at all, but about analyzing and applying the information discussed in class.

Some of the students took copies of the exam to their officers who then classified it. That's correct. Some of Russell Horiuchi's college exams are now considered classified material by the U.S. government!

Russell liked to practice what he preached, often playing games with kids in his class. He fondly recalls one student who was, for whatever reason, reticent to tell Russell where he was from.

"Fine," he said to the student, ostensibly changing the subject, "Do you like to go fishing?"

"I love it," answered the student.

"What kind of fishing?" Russell continued innocently.

"I like fly fishing."

Russell then inquired what kind of fish specifically the young man liked to go after. Russell then proceeded to floor the student by telling the young man where he was from. How?

"Immediately, what does that tell you?" Russell asked as he related the story, "He's from the Western states. He likes fishing in rivers. If they say they like ocean fishing then they are from Florida and other areas like that. If they like to fish perch then Arizona or Louisiana, certain states. Make the linkages and you can come up with all kinds of information about individuals, even if they don't know it."

Another time he had a student from Maine. Russell told her he'd never been to Maine before but that he wanted to tell about the student's home. "Anytime you feel I am wrong, stop me," Russell challenged before describing her home in great detail, sight un-seen. Finally Russell paused. "Why haven't you stopped me?"

Dumbfounded the student answered, "Because everything you said was accurate!"

"I've never been to Maine," reiterated Russell, "I've never been to your home. How come I'm able to describe it so accurately?" He then continued to explain his line of reasoning. "What's Maine? American right? So in Maine what kind of home do they have? American. I wasn't describing your home, I was describing a typical American home." The students all laughed, a common sound in Russell's classes.

Once he made fun of diamond rings and how senseless such expensive stones were. A female student piped up, "I bet your wife wouldn't agree with what you're saying."

At that point, Russell said, "Mama, stand up." Annette happened to be a student in Russell's class that semester. Annette didn't want to stand. When everyone looked back to see where Russell was looking she looked back too but she was sitting in the back row and there was nothing behind her but a steam heater. So she had to stand up.

Russell later said that all his students listened very well, except for one. "You," he said, pointing at Annette. Both of them laughed at the memory of the time Annette took a 10-question quiz on Japan in class and missed one. "How come you missed this one? You are Japanese!" Russell teased. Annette tells that she had to work very hard for the class. Russell cared for his students but there was no favoritism.

The Horiuchis' focus on their students extended beyond the classroom. Often, the lunch bag Annette prepared for Russell in the morning included an extra sandwich for a struggling student from Berkeley, California who couldn't afford lunch on his own.

Students quickly warmed to Russell's mentally stimulating challenges, thrilled to realize they could develop their own conclusions. His classes were soon brimming to maximum capacity and always the first to fill. Even if the classes were at odd hours, Russell had students knocking at his door trying to gain late entry into a packed classroom. He quickly was nominated professor of the month several times and consistently received the highest student evaluations in the department.

Another hallmark of a Russell Horiuchi class were blue book essay tests. The questions were often situational, asking students to solve them using their common sense and knowledge. Russell operated under the philosophy that anyone could guess a multiple choice question but they really had to understand the information in order to pass a written exam. Sometimes the tests were open book and, on occasion, Russell even sent his students to the library to do their test.

His insistence on hand-written tests often left him with hundreds of tests to correct. Annette remembers him constantly correcting tests in the evenings, taking breaks only to eat. Even though Russell taught the largest number of students he was rarely given any assistants. He requested some but was told that funds weren't available for more assistants.

Russell exhibited a knack for relating to the young men and women who inhabited his classroom and spent a great deal of time counseling those who needed help or were discouraged. Russell was always very candid about his views and opinions, which occasionally drew a complaint or a report to the administration, but most students appreciated his insight and honesty.

Students loved to congregate at his office. If the light was on in Russell's office, it wasn't long before someone would knock on the door. At almost any given time three or four of them could be found there, including the likes of Buckley Rose or Carl Johnson who would come to discuss and debate issues. Other regulars included Mark Wirthlin, Dick Nanto, Ron Inouye and Floyd Mori.

Russell took time to be involved in the lives of his students. Buckley Rose remembers, "When my roommate ran off with my checkbook to pay for a broken window, you skipped church to seek him out and help him quietly correct the things he had done wrong—and thus saved him from being kicked out of school."

One of Russell's friends, a distinguished professor, even sent his son to Russell, recognizing that he could reach the boy in a way the father could not. The son was wandering aimlessly. Russell told him point blank that he wasn't applying himself. *Nobody talks to me that way,* was the reply. *You are far more capable than what you've shown thus far,* said Russell to the young man, encouraging him and mentioning that the boy's father was a professor and his older brother was teaching as well. *Why don't you buckle down and do it?* Russell challenged him. The son later admitted that the talk made him mad enough that he started studying hard, eventually getting his doctorate and going on to be the vice-president of a university.

Russell enjoyed the visits perhaps even more than his students even though it occasionally made it hard to finish his work. He once tried placing a bookshelf across the front of the door but students continued to pour in. Self proclaimed "anti-social" Russ was suddenly the center of attention. Russell could socialize with the best of them and to his surprise he was enjoying it immensely.

One of the greatest compliments to Russell's teaching career was summed up by one of his former students who said simply, "He taught us how to think."

Russell recaps his early years teaching, "We were on modest means. Didn't try to compete with other people. [My] concentration was on developing classes to teach the students. [I didn't] care about accolades. I want to make it worthwhile for the students."

> Dr. Russell Horiuchi of BYU was a mentor teacher, not a data-dump teacher. . . . the questions he posed . . . exercised our mental muscles. . . . Rather than being told how the dots were connected, we had to find those connections ourselves.
>
> —Dr. Gary C. Lawrence in "How Americans view Mormonism, Seven Steps to improve our Image"

My first contact with Pres. Horiuchi was in the summer of 1969, when he taught a summer "Political Geography" class at Brigham Young University. His lectures were always very interesting—and he insisted that as a class we engage in critical thinking to try to understand why certain events occurred in history, why history occurred the way it did, and why certain businesses were successful, and others were not. I remember him asking why Geneva Steel, an industry which was so vital during World War II was located near Orem, Utah, "in the middle of nowhere?" The answer lay in the proximity to a plentiful water supply, and due to the remoteness of the location. I remember he also asked us "why was Kentucky Fried Chicken successful in Provo on the east side of University Avenue, but not on the west side?" (Truthfully, I don't remember the answer to that question!) I also remember he was very good at remembering names because he created a "nickname" for each student. (Mine was: "Mike from Moooab.")

Pres. Horiuchi used to chide us about BYU, saying that when he was on campus he was its biggest critic, but when he was off campus he was its biggest supporter. He used to encourage us not to take ourselves too seriously—a quality which carried over to his service as mission president, and a trait which was very helpful to me during stressful times during my mission.

— Michael Raymond

15

TEACHING

W HEN THEY LEFT SAN MATEO, Russell and Annette received a small severance check. Even though international travel was extremely expensive, they decided to use the little egg nest to send Annette for a visit home to Japan. She wrote to her parents every week but finances hadn't allowed her to return.

The news of her coming was rather sudden and her parents were fearful that she was getting a divorce. She quickly reassured them it wasn't the case.

In the fall of 1961, Annette flew to Hawaii, visiting with Russell's parents before continuing on to Japan. Annette's mother and father greeted her with Shigeko and Kyoko when she landed at Haneda airport (Narita wasn't built yet). Harumi and Hiromi, two of Annette's nieces, made a *senbazuru* necklace of one-thousand *origami* cranes for her. This was Annette's first time home since leaving after the war, thirteen years prior. No longer the devastated wasteland of her memory, Tokyo was growing at a terrific rate, transportation had been re-established and skyscrapers dominated the skyline against Mount Fuji. As testament to the strength of the human will, the entire nation was on the rise again.

Annette was so accustomed to American roads that the once vast streets of her childhood now seemed quite narrow by comparison.

The clothing for women was leaning increasingly western in style except for special occasions like *Obon* or New Years. Although it was uncommon for women of Hatsu's age, she often wore simple western dresses and skirts around the home. However, when she went out, it was always in a properly tied *kimono*, even during the hot summer. Hatsu wore *geta,* traditional wooden slippers, but sometimes at home she would borrow Kyoko's high heel shoes and practice walking around the garden. She told Annette she wanted to visit the states and when she did she wanted to be ready to wear western style shoes.

In terms of clothing Yoshizo was the opposite of his wife, wearing a suit for business but a more relaxed *yukata* or *kimono* at home. This was common for men folk and Annette's brother Ichiro generally dressed in the same manner. Yoshizo proudly displayed his new suits for Annette to see.

Yoshizo was now working as a successful real estate broker. When he was 80 years old he once told Annette that he stayed at home and made money. He admitted it was an easy life, working by telephone or being picked up by clients when they wanted to meet in person.

While she honored tradition, Hatsu always carried a very practical, forward thinking view of life. Once when the family was remodeling the house the issue of toilets came up. Everyone wanted to stick to the conventional "squatter" toilet, essentially a hole in the floor. Hatsu fought for a western sit-down style because it was more comfortable, and less stress on her arthritic knees. She was overruled but much later, when her son built his own home, he installed western style toilets.

Perhaps it was Hatsu's open-mindedness that helped her accept her three sons-in-law, even though none of them were Japanese nationals. If there were reservations, nothing was ever expressed. She never let little things—like language barriers—ever stand in her way. Once, she engaged an American granddaughter's husband in conversation, even though he didn't understand a word of Japanese. He kept nodding at the appropriate moment and Hatsu kept talking, telling about how the table in the house was too high.

The family had purchased a TV by then and it was somewhat of a secret that Hatsu loved watching western wrestling. This was news even to Annette. Hatsu's spunk was most evident when she watched the matches, throwing her body this way and that in sync with the wrestlers, something that Annette does as well. Whether she learned it from watching her mother or it's hereditary is unclear but she gets into any sport she watches, growling and yelling, even punching for intensity during critical plays.

This was also the first time Annette saw the newly rebuilt Mori house. Relatively large compared to other houses at the time it sported two restrooms, versus the usual one; one for the guests at the end of an L-shaped hallway and one off to the side of the kitchen. Constructed on the old foundation, this house would stand until it was rebuilt and modernized in the late 1980s by Shige.

Annette was glad to be with her family. Her elementary classmates even held a reunion for her. Annette and her family went out every day visiting, running errands, and taking care of family business. She said all they did was talk and talk and talk.

Kyoko's husband, Motohiko, had his chauffeur drive them everywhere in his Chrysler. Kyoko met her husband, who they affectionately referred to as Mo-chan, while she was working for the VIPs in the airlines. Considerably older than she, he was the biggest stockholder in the National Cash Register company and could afford a luxurious lifestyle. With money not being an issue, Kyoko and Mo-chan lived in the Hotel New Japan.

After two weeks, Annette's mother confessed to her that she could finally understand her daughter's Japanese again, saying that Annette had a different dialect when she'd arrived. "I think you picked up some Hawaiian," she told her. The same charge of speaking archaic Japanese had been leveled at Russell as well. His Japanese was pre-war and frozen in time while the living language was evolving rapidly in Japan.

Six weeks sped by and the time for Annette to return to the states drew close. Shigeko recounts it was very hard to see Annette off.

Even though they could fly, the trip was still a major undertaking and she didn't know if she would ever see her sister again.

The family held a big farewell dinner. When Annette went to the airport, all of her family went including her aunts, uncles and cousins. It was the first time many of them had seen a commercial airliner. Mo-chan sent several limousines for everyone, sending Annette off like a real celebrity. Annette's mother told her to wear white gloves so they could see her waving as she boarded the plane.

Knowing many students couldn't afford to go home at Thanksgiving, Russell invited everyone who didn't have a place to eat to his house. Most students that came were from Hawaii and Asia but there were others as well. The student body was much smaller then and Russ would simply ask in class, "Who needs a place?" and the word got around.

With Annette visiting her family over the holiday, Russell prepared Thanksgiving dinner by himself, including pumpkin pies for the twenty-two students who crowded into the tiny house. After dinner no one wanted to leave and so everyone pitched in to help clean, even scouring the oven.

Russell served as the Japanese Club Advisor, spending time sponsoring activities. With so many returned missionaries, *Nisei,* and Japanese on campus the club was very active. One of their major activities was presenting a sacrament meeting program, visiting various wards as far away as Spanish Fork. The club provided speakers and music, sponsoring a large choir led by Robert Sonomura, a masters candidate in music. Rehearsals were every Sunday afternoon. Robert was married to Marion Okawa. Many years later Robert served as stake choir director in Ellen's stake in Hawaii. The program was not only good for the wards they visited but for the club members as well, providing them with a chance to get involved and to bear their testimonies. After meetings they were often invited over to a ward member's home to eat.

The students from Hawaii also hosted a party once a month, holding the event at the Horiuchis' house. Everyone felt like a family. Russell also served as an unofficial matchmaker, encouraging Floyd Mori and Irene Mano and also Irene's brother Ken Mano and Carolyn Inouye to tie the knot.

After her return from Japan, Annette planned on working but when told the pay was half of what she earned in California, she hesitated. The interviewer informed her that faculty wives could attend school for free. Ever curious to learn something new, Annette jumped at the opportunity, beginning with an upholstery class. Then she took another class and another, feeling a whole new world open up to her. She did well in all her courses, enjoying everything she studied. She found herself wanting to major in each and every new subject she came across.

Finding a flair for art, Annette finally chose to earn her degree in it. Still not trusting her English skills, she took only one or two classes a semester. In the end it took her eight years but she completed her bachelors degree in 1969 graduating *cum laude*! "Life was," according to Annette, "very smooth."

To make ends meet, Russell taught during summer session, continuing to hone his teaching skill and style. He was getting encouragement from a lot of different people to obtain his doctorate, a necessary step in order for him to remain in academics. Once more, Paul Hyer enabled the transition, speaking with an acquaintance, Professor George Kakiuchi at the University of Washington. (If you're wondering whether Paul Hyer knows everyone, the answer is yes!) Hearing Paul describe the young teacher to him, Professor Kakiuchi told Paul to have Russell call him, which Russell did, receiving an official invitation to join the program. Russell had been interested in UW since graduating from BYU and was thrilled to be able to go.

Arrangements were made for Russell to attend during the summer, in between teaching. Russell's GI Bill was expended but he was able to pay for everything with a scholarship. During the summers of 1962 and 1963, Russell boarded a bus and headed for Seattle by himself seeking a degree in Geo-Politics. Even though a doctorate program is intense, Russell later reflected that as busy as he was at BYU, Washington was like a vacation for him.

Russell used his time at Washington not only for obtaining his degree but also as an opportunity to help develop and improve the academic program at BYU, observing the way their programs were designed and administered.

Annette and Ellen remained in Utah, Annette continuing to take classes. Annette kept a *katana,* samurai sword, and *tanto,* short bayonette, beneath her bed for protection while Russell was gone. She was never trained in sword fighting but having the *katana* made her feel safer.

Though immersed in her own studies and being a mother, Annette accepted an offer to participate in the Utah Valley Opera Associations production of Roger and Hammerstein's "South Pacific." Her role was the assistant to Bloody Mary who was played by Sue Teramoto. Of her theatrical debut Annette joked, "No words were spoken and I just acted dumb. It was not hard after all, that is natural for me."

Although Russell was able to finish most of his coursework during the first two summers, one of the final requirements was a three-year residency, which the couple began in 1964. Annette joined Russell in Washington while Ellen remained in Utah to complete her junior year at Orem High School, living with the Earnest Ahlborn family, who had moved to Provo from Berkeley. It was hard to leave their daughter but the family kept in touch. Phones were still quite expensive so most correspondence was by mail.

In a letter to a friend Annette wrote "we certainly miss Ellen. It is a heartache and pain to go through this separation. However, through this we all grow and develop. To our surprise when we had an opportunity to talk to her on the phone the other night she said that she missed Japanese foods. When we were together, she was quite reluctant and did not care for Japanese food. We are certainly grateful for the Ahlborns in taking care of her while we are here." For her part Ellen did well academically and was very active in her school, participating in cheerleading, sports and student leadership.

Russell and Annette rented a small apartment close to the university. At $109 a month plus $5 for electricity and another $3 for monthly parking, it was quite a bit more than they'd planned on spending but the location was unbeatably convenient since they were able to walk most everywhere.

The couple enjoyed Seattle, with its green hills and tall trees surrounding lakes and rivers. Annette particularly loved the azaleas, which reminded her of Japan and found a new American delicacy in the form of soft pretzels. One thing the couple disliked was the constant drizzle and rain that poured during the winter.

Annette got a job working at the UW testing department from September 1964-June 1965. The job was not very busy which gave her time to work on her knitting, which she put to good use making a sweater for Ellen. One time it started to snow and everyone including her boss got very excited. Coming from the deep powder snows of Utah, the thin snow didn't seem like a big deal but the office closed and everyone was sent home.

Ellen came up to spend Christmas vacation with them. Her flight was almost three hours late arriving. Annette got the scare of her life when the counter clerk mentioned something about engine trouble. The plane arrived safe and sound and the Horiuchis were delighted to see their daughter again after nearly four months. After the holiday was over, it was very difficult to take her to the airport to send her back to Provo.

Russell continued to work hard and excel in his studies. He got along well with his professors who respected Russell since he was already teaching as a professor at BYU. Russell was occasionally asked to substitute teach for his professors and was sometimes told by the students that he did better than the assigned teacher!

Dr. George Kakiuchi served as one of Russell's principal professors, both pushing and encouraging the younger Japanese-American. In class he once challenged Russell on his Mormon "cult" beliefs asking out of the blue, "Do you believe in God?" When Russell answered in the affirmative, Dr. Kakiuchi asked him to prove it.

Russell followed up with, "Do you love your wife? Can you prove it?"

"I married her so I love her."

"Because you married her doesn't prove anything. Can you prove it?" Russell pressed further while the class sat wondering what was going on.

Dr. Kakiuchi hemmed and hawed unable to conclusively prove anything.

"It's the same with me," Russell stated, "I know. I can't prove it to your satisfaction but I know in my heart God exists. Please allow me to believe."

It was mostly a good-natured mental exercise but Russell admitted he was afraid that he might have upset his professor. Instead his straightforward, sincere defense garnered more respect for him in the department. After class, several of his colleagues congratulated him on his response and they wound up talking for several hours. Other professors and fellow students also grew curious about Provo and BYU.

Another doctoral requirement was passing two foreign language exams. Somewhat humorously, Russell, one of the top translators for the entire United States military during WWII "flubbed" his first Japanese exam at UW. With no chance to prepare Russell was asked to translate a historical account of castle towns. Much of the vocabulary and characters were so obscure that the administering professor admitted that he didn't know them himself. The professor felt the exam was unfair and arranged for another more practical one to be given.

With Japanese well under his belt, Russell decided to try his hand at French. He enrolled in a course that met for an hour once a week for six weeks. As always Russell studied intently, supported by Annette who spent hours making thousands of flashcards for him.

When the next round of national qualifying tests came up Russell took them just to see what he was up against. He was able to make calculated guesses on the multiple-choice section of the test. The most difficult portion remained in the form of two essays that needed to be translated from French into English. The first was on Cardinal Richelieu's fiscal policy and the second on the French Railroad. Russell had some familiarity with both issues but with so little French at his disposal he only made it through two-thirds of the test before running out of time.

Nose to the grindstone, Russell continued studying and preparing to take the exam in earnest. He needn't have bothered. Eight weeks later, Russell received a letter from the national examination board congratulating him on passing. The cut off was 75 and he scored an 80. In shock and disbelief Russell showed the letter to Annette and they both began crying.

After only six hours of lessons, Russell's French teacher said it was impossible but after seeing the letter she told him he didn't need to continue and advised him to drop the class. When he reported his results to the department, he was informed it was one of the toughest qualifying French exams ever given.[1]

Russell qualified for his doctoral examinations in less than a year and one semester. When the time came for him to defend his dissertation, Russell said it was more like being in a staff meeting with the entire committee treating him like a colleague. After the defense he was sent out of the room while the committee debated

1. "Is that true?" I ask him. He nods and asks, "Parlez vous Francais?"

his merits. They took an unusually long time with Russell's unease growing every minute. Finally the doors opened and Russell was admitted to the room.

"I bet you were worried why we took so long in there," Dr. Kakiuchi said.

"Yes, I was getting a bit worried," admitted Russell.

Dr. Kakiuchi told him that after he'd left the room the council reached a unanimous decision in a matter of minutes. The rest of the time was spent debating where they felt the promising new doctoral graduate should teach. They wanted him to fill an available position in the East at Cornell University instead of returning to BYU. It was flattering but the new Doctor of Geography politely declined, knowing his place was in Utah.

Russell still had two more years of residency to fulfill but the Assistant Provost told him to buy the remaining credits. There was no need to come back, he said, Russell already qualified.

"I was 27 when I started school but I look back and I am glad. The Lord's hand was in it all the way through. Amazing," Russell credited the Lord for accelerating his abilities and saving him time in completing his degree. He humbly added, "Just because I got the grad degree doesn't make me any smarter but it does give me a certain amount of credential and leverage."

In the meantime, a house came up for sale in the Horiuchis' ward in Orem. Annette and Ellen went to look at the house first. The family contacted a realtor to see what other options there were but in the end they decided on the yellow brick house at 1167 South Main Street. It was only a few houses from Bob and Joan Gallagher's house (who also moved from Berkeley) and the Horiuchi family stayed with them for a few weeks during the transition.

The neighbors were great and, with a price tag of 16 thousand dollars, it was affordable even on a teacher's salary. The family moved into the home in 1965 and has continued to live there for almost fifty years. Russell returned home from Washington and went straight back to teaching. His evenings were spent working on his dissertation, still incomplete due to his residency being cut short.

Even though the second World War was twenty years past, having a Japanese face in Utah still brought occasional discrimination. Once in an elevator at BYU, a student asked Russell when he was planning to return home.

"Home? What do you mean? I am home."

The young man persisted, "You are from Japan, aren't you?"

In retrospect the boy was likely trying to be politely conversational, but if Russell was upset at the question, who could blame him?

"I am of Japanese descent," Russell replied, "but I was born in the United States. Young man, I served in the United States Army. I fought for my country and deserve to be here in the United States more than you! What have you done to defend your country?"

The young man's face reddened and he dashed out of the elevator without an answer.

More often, however, Russell's cultural experience and background was accepted and even celebrated. When Dr. Charles Metten, a member of the theater faculty, directed a stage production *Kagemusha*, Russell was asked to advise for the sword fighting scenes.

Over the winter holidays the Horiuchis again played host to many out-of-state students.

On New Years Eve it's customary for the Japanese to eat noodles, the long strands representing the wish for a long life. They then gather at the local *jinja* shrine to ring in the New Year at midnight, giving thanks for the old year and to ask for blessings on the new. With no family or *jinja* around the Japanese and *Nisei* students phoned the Horiuchis, mentioning they wanted to come over. Russell and Annette agreed.

Newlyweds Dick and Masako Nanto came along with Katsu and Hilda Kajiyama, Tonchan (Brother Toma) and several other singles. No real noodles were available but they made do with Top Ramen. After eating they started playing cards. When the games ran well past midnight Russell and Annette decided to go to bed. It didn't look like anyone was ready to call it quits for the night so the Horiuchis asked who was staying and if they wanted any blankets. Everyone politely refused. Figuring their guests could get themselves home, Russell and Annette turned in for the night, Russell undoubtedly wearing one of the ubiquitous knitted caps he invariably wore when he slept.

The Horiuchis woke the next morning to find students sleeping on the floor, on the couch and chairs—all without blankets. The students stayed all the next day as well, making *ozoni*, the traditional new years soup with pounded rice cakes. After lunch the group decided to go sledding at Sundance. Still not wishing to go home, the students went back to the Horiuchis' where Annette fixed a simple rice dinner while everyone continued talking and laughing and having a great time. After dinner everyone finally returned home.

Russell was called as second counselor in a university student ward where he cherished his time working with Bishop Jae Ballif. Jae's father was Ariel Ballif, head of the Sociology Department who had also served as president of the New Zealand mission from '55-'58. Like his father, Jae was very capable, later earning an appointment as the vice president of BYU. Jae and Russell both approached problems in a sensible and practical manner and worked well together. Of Russell, Jae wrote "I have come to hold [Russell] up as one of the great examples of Christlike character that I know."

In between all of this Russell, managed to squeeze in time to go fishing whenever he had the chance—which was pretty much everyday—polishing his burgeoning reputation as a fisherman. Occasionally Annette got a call at home in the late afternoon from a student looking for Professor Horiuchi. When Annette told them he was out they knowingly asked if he was fishing. When Annette admitted yes they would say they knew where he parked his car and go find him on the Provo River, often bringing their own pole and tackle with them.

Russell also spent time developing his skill at tying his own flies and lures, which became popular and treasured gifts among his sportsman friends.

The fish Russell caught helped feed more than his own family. His copious catch was often shared with neighbors and students. One student, Linda, from Hong Kong, depressed and wanting to quit school and go home, came to talk to Russell one late summer. She mentioned that one of the things she missed from home was good fish to eat. With hardly a better excuse available, Russell grabbed his tackle and headed up the river even though it was almost dark. That evening he dropped off a haul of fresh fish to Linda. The next day she had perked up, excitedly explaining to Russell how she steamed the fish, seasoning it with salt and pepper, ginger and green onions. His gift had given her the boost she needed. Linda and her husband still visit the Horiuchis when they are in town.

Around this time an incident unbeknown to most occurred on campus. Ernest Wilkinson, then president of the university, decided to run for state senator. He was disgruntled to learn that his bid was opposed by several of the faculty, many of who were considered part of the more liberal element at the university. Wilkinson was so upset that he planted students equipped with hidden tape recorders in the classes of these professors, attempting to catch them saying anything that might be held against them. Particularly targeted were people in the Political Science department. Because of his close connection to many of the people in that department, Russell's lectures were taped as well.

When the taping was discovered Wilkinson resigned. His senatorial bid ultimately failed. Later referred to as the Black Box incident, the event was chronicled by Ray Hillam, whose manuscript is now reposited in the L. Tom Perry special collections at BYU. Ray received a lot of persecution for his work.

Russell was never "called onto the carpet" for anything but some of his friends were, several who left the university for positions elsewhere as a direct result of the affair. One such friend was Richard Wirthlin who left to start Wirthlin Worldwide, ultimately a more rewarding endeavor for a man of his abilities.

In the fall of 1969 Annette began teaching Japanese language and conversation part-time. After their first mission, she began teaching calligraphy as well. She enjoyed working with students so much that she says she almost felt guilty receiving a paycheck. Teaching also gave Annette the opportunity to meet many of the returned missionaries from Japan, which now had two missions.

The years the Horiuchis spent establishing themselves were peaceful ones. The promise that Russell would "have joy in [his] labors" was being fulfilled. He loved his interactions with bright young minds immensely. The aloha spirit of his Hawaiian upbring-ing manifested itself in the frequent gatherings and dinners that earned him the reputation as a caring professor. It was never about making a name for himself and he was obviously not concerned about the money. He was there because he genuinely loved his work and his students.

After nine years at BYU, Russell and Annette thought they were settling into the routine. Annette said things were working out so well that she didn't think it could last. "We were enjoying life a bit too much." She was right. In the spring of 1970 a phone call changed everything again.

16

CALLED TO SERVE

IT WAS THURSDAY THE 26TH of February 1970. Shortly after Russell walked into his office his secretary informed him that President N. Eldon Tanner's office was trying to reach him. He tried to return the call several times but the line was busy. It was the end of the day so Russell went home.

Moments after he walked in the door the phone rang. A pleasant woman's voice asked, "Is this Brother Horiuchi?"

"Yes, this is Brother Horiuchi."[1]

"President Tanner would like to talk to you," the lady continued, "Please wait a moment." Russell wasn't sure if he heard correctly—a call from N. Eldon Tanner, the first counselor in the First Presidency of the church.

A familiar voice came on the line. "Russ, this is President Tanner. I'd like to see you tomorrow."

---

1. This is interesting for at least two reasons:

It is evidence that Grandpa actually used to answer the phone! He was notorious for never answering it. The few time he did his extended phone conversations went something as follows:

"Hi, Grandpa."

"Hello. Here's Grandma." He didn't care much for phones.

During the interview I asked, "Did they call you at work or at home?" Grandpa and Grandma's answers are simultaneous and directly contradictory. "Home," says Grandma. "At work," says Grandpa. Then Grandma laughs, "He's creating answers! I'm the right one!"

"Are you coming down to BYU campus?" Russell asked. As part of the First Presidency, Elder Tanner was also part of the board of directors for BYU and a visit in this capacity was not uncommon.

"Oh, no. You'll need to come to my office in Salt Lake."

President Tanner indicated he could meet at either 8 a.m. or 4 p.m. Russell chose four so he wouldn't have to get a substitute.

"After hanging up the phone I felt some degree of apprehension," Russell understates. His mind began racing through a list of every possible thing President Tanner might want to speak to him about and what he might have said or done to warrant a call from a member of the First Presidency. His foremost thought was that he was going to be reprimanded for something he'd said in class. This wasn't long after the black box incident. It could be fallout from that. It had happened before. As popular as he was as a teacher, not everyone enjoyed his candidly stated opinions and the occasional student complaint—though extremely rare—was not unheard of.

Despite a "gnawing feeling inside" Russell says, "I slept well and enjoyed my food." Reviewing the event he wrote "I prepared my mind—come what may if I was going to be reprimanded and get dismissed—well, so be it."

After an uneasy drive to Salt Lake, Russell described walking into the gray church offices on 47 East South Temple Street as "frightening." He didn't know what to expect. Russell was directed to an elevator and ushered into the well-furbished office of President Tanner, who greeted him warmly, alleviating some of the teacher's anxiety. President Tanner sat behind a large executive desk. Russell was about to take a seat across the desk when President Tanner motioned for him to take the easy chair next to him instead. In Russell's words President Tanner "was warm and personable and evinced a kind demeanor."

Russell always remembered President Tanner's next words. "What I will tell you will shock you." Here it comes, thought Russell. President Tanner then launched into a series of questions. *How are you feeling? Are you in good health? How are your finances? Do you owe any money or have any debts?* Russell couldn't figure out what any of this had to do with being chewed out. Finally, President Tanner cut to the heart of the matter.

"What do you think of presiding over a mission in Japan?" he beamed.

Russell could hardly fathom what he was hearing, "You're asking me?"

"Yes, I am asking you," replied President Tanner.

Shifting his weight, Russell blurted out, "I personally don't think too much of it."

President Tanner's eyes widened, incredulous at such a frank answer, "You don't mean that do you?"

"You asked me a question, and I am not going to lie to you," Russell pursed his lips as he habitually did when he was adamant about something.

President Tanner eyed Russell again, "By golly you mean it, don't you?"

Russell did. "Yes, I don't think much of it. I don't feel I measure up to it and besides, I just don't want to."

Taken aback but wise, President Tanner smiled, "Well, let me tell you this. I am not asking you. I am calling you."

Being called versus being asked was a different matter altogether. What could Russell say if the Lord was asking him through President Tanner?

"Well, I sustained you as a member of the First Presidency and I sustain you in your position." Russell maintains that he never actually said yes to the mission call in the first place.

President Tanner grew more solemn as he informed Russell that he needed to be ready in ten days. With more bravado than he felt Russell answered that if they wanted him to go tomorrow he'd be ready. Russell inquired as to what was going on and mentioned he'd need to talk to BYU. President Tanner informed him they were splitting the two existing Japanese missions into four but that Russell wasn't to discuss it with anyone. As for BYU, said President Tanner, "We'll take care of everything."

"What about my wife?" Russell asked. He didn't have a clue how to break the news to Annette.

"Don't worry about her," said President Tanner, "We know her. She will support and sustain you all the way down the line."

As a last word President Tanner shared with Russell, "I have the distinct feeling that you have a mission within a mission. I don't know what it is, but you will find it out."

President Tanner stood up and shook Russell's hand. Russell managed to walk out of the office despite the weakness in his knees. President Tanner called out as an after thought, "If you have any problem, call me up anytime!"

The drive home was a blur as Russell, "somewhat in a trance," tried gathering his thoughts. Certainly he was fluent in the language. He had served in a few bishoprics, but never really held an important position of leadership in the church. How on earth had the brethren ever thought to call him, a peasant farmer from Hawaii?

The family theory is that Arthur Haycock, then serving as secretary to the president, was in attendance at the funeral of George Haraguchi, a teenager who had a seizure in a swimming pool and drowned. Russell was one of the speakers, catching everyone's attention with his fiery oratory on the plan of salvation.

However it came to pass, the First Presidency had been thorough long before ever speaking to Russell in person, inquiring among his colleagues and co-workers. One of the people the First Presidency spoke with was Jae Ballif. Jae told them that Russell "won't mince any words and will be level with you." Jae also mentioned that Annette was a nice lady who would support Russell.

It was dark by the time Russell returned from Salt Lake to find Annette, Ellen and her fiancée Michael Hurst waiting anxiously in the living room.

"You all sit down on the couch," Russell told them as he slumped into a chair, "We've been called to preside over a mission in Japan."

Both women gasped. Annette blurted, "No. I am not going. If you want to go you go yourself."

Usually both husband and wife are interviewed together. Annette isn't sure why she wasn't called to Salt Lake with Russell. "If they call[ed] me to be there, I wonder if I'd say no," she laughs looking back decades later.

"Woman, you go where I go," Russell stated flatly. Knowing what they had to do they both "had a good cry." It was going to be a very busy ten days.

Both Russ and Annette dug out their patriarchal blessings and were surprised to read passages pointing to this calling. Russ was told "you shall be an influence for the advancement of truth among your people" and Annette was blessed "to become a missionary to all men." The words had always been there, but the sentences jumped out at them like never before. Both felt humbled that the Lord had been preparing them for this day.

The days that followed drove home what commitment to the service of the Lord meant. "To say that we were bewildered and demoralized is a gross understatement," confesses Russell. The only one excited was Ellen, who was very proud of her parents.

Russell and Annette began by figuring out their finances. Typically those who were called on missions were better financially established and able to support themselves. He knew their friends

Adney and Judy Komatsu were using their own money and that a mission was long and expensive.

After going over their savings and making some calculations Russell realized that if they were careful they could manage for exactly three years. They didn't have a lot of liquid cash but they were not in debt. They would come home with nothing left but they could do it. It wasn't until later they learned that they would receive a small allowance. Russell and Annette had gone prepared to spend everything they had.

On top of it all, Ellen had postponed a marriage earlier in the fall and signed a contract with the Alpine School District to start teaching. Annette thought to take her with them to Japan but Ellen preferred to fulfill her contract. With Annette insistent that Ellen either marry or join them in Tokyo, the young couple decided it was better to marry and arrangements were made for the very next week in the Salt Lake Temple. It was short notice but after explaining the situation to President Stone (who coincidentally was the stake president in the Bay Area while the Horiuchis were living there, although they didn't know him very well) a time was made available. It added to the chaos of getting ready but, according to Annette, "At least we felt good that Ellen wasn't going to be alone."

Annette had been traveling so her passport was ready, but Russell's was not. He applied at the county courthouse explaining their problem and the clerk called the passport office explaining the situation. She got an envelope and filling out all the forms, told Russell to get to the post office and mail everything that day. Russell's passport was back from San Francisco in three days, a miracle in the days before overnight express.

Immunizations were also required. After a hectic day Russell went to the BYU dispensary where the medic argued with him to go to his regular physician since it was near closing time. When Russell said that the family doctor had referred them to the clinic in the first place the medic told them the clinic was out of serum and that he and Annette should "make other arrangements."

Frustrated with the lack of cooperation, Russell quietly but firmly insisted, "Look doctor, I am going home and calling President Tanner. I am going to tell him that I was refused vaccinations to prepare for this mission call. Let me tell you, President Tanner will then call President Wilkinson. President Wilkinson will call you out." The medic knew Russell was not bluffing and all the shots were administered within minutes.

February seemed an odd time to be calling a mission president but teaching at a church school made the mid-semester departure less worrisome. Annette talked to J. Reuben Clark, Jr., her department chair. Although Annette was in the middle of her second semester teaching, he told her to forget about class, releasing her right then and there to get ready.

But Russell, by choice, taught class up until the very last minute, including administering midterms, ensuring a thick stack of essays for him to correct. He had always corrected all of the books himself and this was to be no exception. In between packing, whenever he stopped or took a break he was correcting. This continued right until the day before their departure with Russell managing to get them all finished and turned into the department at the eleventh hour.

The timing of the call also placed both Russell and Annette's degrees in jeopardy. Annette was about to take her qualifying examination for her master's. She had been studying diligently and knew if she postponed the exam for three years that she would forget everything. Roman Andrus, her art advisor, reassured her that he would make arrangements for the exam to be taken within the week, calling each professor on her committee. Annette was able to pass the four hours of qualifying examinations for her master's degree. "With Brother Andrus's help," she adds.

Russell was still in the middle of writing his dissertation. To finish it before leaving was impossible and by the time they returned his allotted time for completion would run out. Russell contacted the University of Washington and was told ambiguously by Dr. Kakiuchi that they would see when he got back. It wasn't clear whether the university would allow him to keep his eligibility or not. Still Russell remained determined to go, even if it cost him his degree.

The mortgage on their house in Orem was another issue. Ellen and Michael were willing to stay and care for the home but, on a student budget, were not able to cover the cost. Lee Farnsworth heard that Russell had gone to Salt Lake and came over that evening to ask what happened. Lee solved the dilemma of the house when he mentioned a new faculty member was looking for a place to stay. The Horiuchis charged the family exactly what their mortgage payments were, forgetting to add in the property taxes, which Russ and Annette wound up paying out of pocket.

Packing dominated much of the week prior to leaving for Japan. According to Annette, they didn't really pack so much as throw things in boxes and put them in the basement. The packing was so fast that they weren't even sure what was in each box. A lot of items were donated to Deseret Industries, Russell making at least one trip a day.

The Horiuchis left the piano, dining set and other large furniture for the new family. The Wrights, who moved into the home, had three boys. Annette worried about leaving the piano with three small boys but says that, "they took care of it well."

According to Annette when they left for Japan, "the house was a mess." They didn't have any more time to deal with it. With her master's exam only two weeks away, the normally fastidious Annette let the housekeeping slide to focus on her studies, thinking to clean up afterwards. Annette felt bad because she left the house a clutter for Ellen and Michael, who finished cleaning up after they'd left.

On March 6th, Ellen was married to Michael Hurst at the Salt Lake Temple (the closest in the area at the time) with a brunch held afterwards at the Hotel Utah. Russell and Annette were so busy they couldn't even stay the whole meal. Halfway through they had to go to Murdock travel to pick up their tickets and visas.

Ellen and Michael's reception wasn't held until after the Horiuichi's departure for Japan. Family friends including the Allreds, Foutins, Shaws and Gallaghers, pitched in holding the reception at the Gallagher's house. With copious generosity they helped prepare everything for the event including refreshments and Bonnie Allred created the wedding cake.

Brother and Sister Tuttle, the former chair of the Geography Department that hired Russell, stood as surrogates in the line. Russell and Annette's departure was so hasty that many of the friends in attendance were surprised to find they were already gone. With so many friends coming from university settings it seemed like every other guest was introduced as doctor so and so. Michael's father, Riley, joked that he'd never seen so many doctors in one night.

The Sunday before departing, Russell and Annette were asked to speak at Sacrament meeting. Annette remembers looking out and, to her great surprise, seeing Margaret and Ernie Ahlborn sitting in the congregation. They drove all the way from Tridell, roughly 150 miles east of Orem, to hear them speak, a gesture so thoughtful it almost made Annette cry. They didn't have much time to talk to each other as Russell and Annette had to excuse themselves early from the meeting to go home and pack.

Meanwhile, a constant stream of people stopped by wishing the couple well. The flow of traffic was so steady at the house that the family went out to eat when they wanted to discuss things with Ellen and Michael. The suggestion of holding an open house was raised but quickly nixed due to lack of time. They did attend an open house held by the university for the social sciences department at the Maeser building, hosted by President Wilkinson.

In the midst of the rush, the couple went to the office of the First Presidency to be set apart as mission president and wife. President Tanner set Russ apart giving him counsel and blessed him to be protected from any dangers. He reminded Russell that "in a sense you are the president of the church in this mission" and that he should act accordingly.

Annette was set apart by President Harold B. Lee. On the way to Salt Lake, Annette confided to Russell that she didn't know anything about a mission and felt she wasn't qualified. Elder Lee, unaware of the earlier conversation, took Annette's hand and reminded her, "Trust in the Lord." The blessing admonished her that the Lord knew she was worried about many things, but to have confidence. He told her to dress properly as a mission wife and comforted her in all things.

Annette remembers the tremendous fatigue from trying to complete everything. With little time to sit down and eat or even sleep both she and Russell lost weight. They didn't have time to go shopping for clothes they needed, leaving instead with suitcases filled with old clothing, hoping they did the job. They didn't even know if they were going to a warm or cold climate yet. They wouldn't find that out until two days after arriving in Tokyo.

In all the excitement Russell forgot they still needed to pay their income taxes. The trouble was everything—receipts, forms, files— was already packed away. They would have to search through the mountain of boxes one-by-one for the information needed. This was the last straw and the exhausted Russell sat on the floor and cried. Out of time and with no choice but to begin, Russell said a prayer and grabbed the first box. All the files he needed were sitting right on top and he was able to quickly get everything in order.

It was usual for mission presidents to attend a seminar before embarking but, having been called out of the normal rotation, the Horiuchis were given their own private two-day briefing by the general authorities. Sister LaVern Parmley of the Primary and Sister Barbara Winder of the Relief Society met with them. Every one of the apostles they met, including Spencer W. Kimball, Gordon B. Hinckley, and Mark E. Peterson, consistently told them "Stay close to your missionaries, stay close to your missionaries." It sounded like an echo. Had the Horiuchis not been so shell-shocked they might have picked up the subtle message that things were not running smoothly on the other side of the Pacific.

The Horiuchis' visas required a valid passport and a stamp from the consulate, which they hadn't received yet. They boarded the plane in Salt Lake, hoping their visas would be ready for them when they transferred in San Francisco. As they deplaned at SFO they heard Russell's name over the intercom paging them to a counter where they were handed their passports and visas, enabling them to continue their journey.

In ten short days the Horiuchis were able to check everything off their list including marrying their daughter, passing a master's exam, packing their entire household and obtaining passports and visas. In their own words, "There were many miracles. The Lord really wanted us in Japan."

17

THE JAPAN EAST MISSION

The Horiuchis arrived at Haneda airport in Tokyo on the 14th of March 1970. They were met by several old friends, including Brother and Sister Nara and Sister Matsumoto. Shigeko was there too, having been informed of the arrival time over the phone by Sister Nara. The current Tokyo mission president and his wife, escorted by a couple of missionaries, were there to pick them up, and Annette didn't have much time to visit. She told Shigeko she would call when they got to their hotel.

Annette would have a few chances to visit with her family while on her mission, but not often. When the occasional church business or meetings brought her and Russell to the Tokyo area she might see them for an evening or so. Sometimes she stayed a day or two longer while Russell returned to Sapporo.

It had been almost 30 years since Russell was in Japan. When he left it was little more than rubble. Now it was considered the second greatest economic power in the world. He was happy to see the country had made good progress and recovery.

At this time Japan was divided into two missions: Japan Tokyo, which included the entire northern half of the country, and Japan Kobe, which included the entire south.

1970 was the year the World Expo was being held in Osaka. In anticipation of the increased number of investigator referrals the Expo would bring, the missions were now being split into four.

The man in charge of the church exhibition was the Japan Kobe mission president, Eddie Okazaki and his wife, Chieko, both old friends of Russell's from Hawaii. Eddie had participated in scouts with Russell in Maui and served in the 442nd division during the war. Chieko was a swimmer for the University of Hawaii and would later serve in the General Presidency of the Relief Society. It was a real treat to be able to catch up with them, even if briefly.

That evening Elder Gordon B. Hinckley, who was already in Japan on church business, called Kan Watanabe as the fourth mission president. The two newly called mission presidents met with Elder Hinckley that night for further instructions and information. Annette, exhausted from the previous ten days and jet lag, slept the entire three hours.

The one detail that hadn't been determined yet was who was to preside over which mission. The next day during a phone conversation between Elder Hinckley and Ezra Taft Benson, who was in Guam, it was decided that Brother Watanabe would preside over the newly formed Japan West Mission, splitting off from the Kobe Mission. The Horiuchis were to preside over the new Japan East Mission, splitting off from the Tokyo Mission. Their headquarters would be located in the city of Sapporo on Hokkaido, the northernmost main island. Hokkaido, according to Paul Hyer, "was kind of an undeveloped frontier at the time" making Russell and Annette, in his estimation, pioneers in the area.

During a recess, Elder Hinckley asked Russ how he felt about working with a pair of missionaries who had been earmarked for an early return because of run-ins with their mission president. Neither wanted to perform regardless of who they were put with. Russell said he'd be willing to work with them, and so the young men were sent north.

Russell decided to put the two together as companions. For a while they played around, going golfing and so forth. Then, out of the blue, on their own initiative they decided to get back to work. It turns out they had both struggled to learn the lessons in Japanese so the previous president pigeonholed them as lazy. Discouraged, they eventually adopted the labels given them. Under Russell's care they shrugged off the label and both finished honorable missions, serving the entire length of their calls.

Before heading north, the Horiuchis were able to witness a milestone as the Tokyo Stake was established. Russell was asked to speak. The event was momentous for the Horiuchis because of their personal involvement in gathering the saints after the war and help in nursing the branch along in its infancy. Kenji Tanaka was called as stake president with Yoshihiko Kikuchi and Sagara Kenichi serving as first and second counselor, respectively. It was an emotional moment for these men as well and Russell remembers tears in the usually stoic Brother Kikuchi's eyes.

The next day at 8 a.m. Russell and Annette drove to the airport with President Benson and his wife, President Hinckley and his wife and Elder Harding of the Church Building Committee.

The plan was to fly to Sapporo to formally establish the Japan East Mission, however a midwinter snowstorm forced the cancellation of all flights, so the party wound up staying in the airport VIP room all day, which was crowded with other stranded passengers.

With nothing else to do but sit around and "talk story" it was a perfect time for everyone to get better acquainted. Annette remembers Sister Benson showing pictures and talking about their family to pass the time. President Benson confided that he knew Flo would become his wife the first time he met her.

When someone mentioned that one Japanese member closed the coffee shop he owned when he joined the church Sister Benson said that it wasn't right, because that was his living. She felt he should continue doing business as long as he didn't drink the coffee himself.

It also gave time for the Tokyo mission president to talk to Russell. The exact geographical boundaries for the two missions hadn't been set and the president asked if he could keep Hitachi City and Misawa Air Force Base. It seemed a little odd since the base was located far to the north in Aomori Prefecture but, after the president persisted, Russell taciturnly agreed, "Whatever you think is right is okay."

It was only later they found out how much the boundaries were being gerrymandered and why. Hitachi in Ibaragi Prefecture was a good place for baptisms at that time. And Misawa was an American base, which meant it was a good source of tithing. Eventually, both districts were returned to the Japan East Mission.

The president also suggested that Russell should send all of his monthly reports to the mission home in Tokyo instead of directly to Salt Lake. This notion also struck Russell as funny, but he kept quiet. The president further challenged Russell to have a competition to see how many baptisms he could have versus the Tokyo mission. Not particularly keen on the idea, Russell politely shrugged it off.

What Russell and Annette didn't realize was that they were walking into a living nightmare. The "lazy" missionaries that Elder Hinckley placed with Russell weren't the only ones having issues with their former president. All was not as well in the mission.

The church in Japan was growing and the event of the Expo was legitimately a timely opportunity to split the missions but the general authorities must have had an inkling that something odd was going on in Tokyo.[1] How much they knew is left to speculation, but it's clear that the full extent of what was transpiring remained hidden from them or they would have acted much more quickly and decisively. None of this was shared with Russell and Annette, nor in truth did it need to be. For now the Horiuchis remained focused on the more immediate issue of setting up a new mission.

---

1. One missionary wrote home telling how the missionaries were being mistreated. Outraged, his mother shared the letter with their next-door neighbor, who happened to be Spencer W. Kimball. This was certainly one of the first, if not *the* first reports to reach Salt Lake about the situation in Tokyo.

The delegation finally arrived in Sapporo late in the evening during the heaviest snowstorm in fifty years. Only the gift of a small break in the clouds allowed them to land at Chitose Airport. It was the only flight to make it through all day. Sapporo's population in 1970 bested 800,000 people making it smaller than Dallas, Texas and slightly larger than Washington, DC. Despite this, it was still considered a rural town by Tokyo standards, whose own population of 16.5 million more than doubled America's largest city, New York, with its comparatively small 7.8 million people. The church there was only a few hundred members strong. There were no wards, only five or so branches in Hokkaido and several more in Aomori, Sendai and other areas. The Japan East Mission started with roughly 75 missionaries who were split off from Tokyo, a number that would double over the next few months.

The small airport was filled with Japanese saints who had been waiting all day, carrying welcome signs and banners. From the airport the entire group, saints and all, traveled directly to the chapel. The melt from the storm flooded the roads making travel by normal cars difficult enough that everyone had to take a bus. To Annette it looked like they were driving in a river. The normally hour-long ride took two and a half hours.

At the Sapporo chapel they were greeted by the remainder of the northern saints, who filled the building. They too had been waiting all day. The Sapporo building was the only actual chapel in the entire mission. Other branches met in member's homes or in missionaries' apartments.

The dedicatory meeting for the Japan East Mission began as soon as the delegation arrived, with Elder Hinckley conducting. Not knowing what to expect upon their arrival in Hokkaido, neither Russell nor Annette had prepared any comments when they were asked to speak at that first meeting.

The Tokyo Mission president and his wife spoke first, saying how hard it was to let these missionaries go because it was like dividing a family. They loved all the missionaries like their own children.

They also invited the Horiuchis to share the same goal of placing copies of *The Book of Mormon*.

When it was Annette's turn she related their past ten days of getting everything packed, marrying their daughter off, taking her master's examinations and generally just being exhausted.

The saints and missionaries in attendance were given their first hint of what they were in for when Russell stepped to the pulpit and announced, "I didn't want to come here!" He went on explaining that he was there because he had been called, that he and the missionaries were in the same boat so they would work through it together.

According to Elder Durrant, one of the missionaries in attendance that first conference, President Horiuchi went on to say "that he only had one daughter, and that he would never love any of us as much as he did her, so not to plan on it. Then he said that it was going to get cold and that placing the *Book of Mormon* would be tougher than if we were in Tokyo, so not to worry about it. We were not in competition with the Tokyo mission in any way, shape, or form. And no comparisons would ever be made (none were to my knowledge). He expressed appreciation to [the Tokyo president] for hand-picking the right missionaries for the new mission (it had been obvious by some last minute transfers that the talent wasn't equally shared)."

Russell also added, "I think our biggest goal will be to keep warm this winter, so if you want to come in early, if you're feeling a little under the weather and have a runny nose, come in and take care of it. No sense killing yourself for a couple of *Book of Mormons*."

Though the full impact may not have been entirely understood by the missionaries at the time, or even intentional on Russell's part, his words were the opening salvo of a revolution. It was a declaration that things were going to be very different in the new mission than they had been in the old.

With no mission office, budget or even an apartment to speak of yet, the entire entourage spent the first three nights in a hotel. The next morning, President Benson invited everyone to breakfast at the hotel restaurant. After eating, the search for suitable quarters began in earnest.

Annette couldn't figure out why an apostle was performing a task like searching for living quarters but he was. Tokyo and other big cities had nice, new apartments at the time but Sapporo was still remote country. The best apartments, not fancy by city standards, were in an eight-story structure called the *Sky Koporasu*. Facing Ishiyama Road and close to the middle of downtown it was one of the earliest high rise buildings in the city.

A short taxi ride later found the group inspecting a typical Japanese apartment of the time. There was linoleum in the kitchen (called the "dining kitchen") and the rest was traditional *tatami*. Instead of central heating the building was steam heated in the mornings but the heat was turned off from 8 a.m. until 4 p.m. in the afternoon. The apartment they found was on one of the upper floors (fourth or sixth depending on who you speak with) and remained comfortably warm. It was small but it did have an extra bedroom, which would often be occupied if a missionary fell ill. Annette confesses with a laugh that it was the sight of the Japanese *ofuro* bath, which she hadn't seen in a long time, that made her choose the apartment.

Returning from the apartment to the hotel, Elder Benson wanted to stop at the American Consulate. Never afraid to throw his weight around—he once delayed a commercial flight because he wanted to catch the plane—Benson told the taxi to wait while he walked up to the door and knocked, bringing a staff member to the door despite the early hour.

"I am Ezra Taft Benson, former Secretary of Agriculture in President Eisenhower's cabinet and I want to see the Consulate General," Elder Benson announced himself and they were invited in. Introducing himself and his party to the Consul General, Elder

Benson explained that they were a church opening a mission in the area and asked the consulate to take care of them.

It was towards the end of March when the Horiuchis moved into their new residence. Annette dashed to the local department store and begged them to deliver beds that same day. It was late afternoon on Saturday and Annette was told they couldn't deliver until next week. Annette explained the situation, that they had just come from the states and didn't have anything. Taking compassion on her the saleslady spoke with the manager who agreed to deliver the *futons* himself in his own car.

Dinner that night proved another challenge. The apartment was located in a residential neighborhood and all the small shops and restaurants closed early in midwinter. Every restaurant they found was shuttered, making the prospect of them going to bed hungry a real possibility. Finally they stumbled across a small store on the corner selling sushi. There was only one *bento* box left on the shelf, which they quickly purchased. It wasn't until they got home that they realized there was only one pair of chopsticks in the box. They each broke one in half and sat on the otherwise barren kitchen floor to share their first dinner using Russell's briefcase for a table. There were no glasses so they cupped their hands together and drank from the faucet. They had no dishes and no furniture except a *futon* but they had a warm roof over their heads. It was an inauspicious but somehow appropriate beginning to the newest chapter in their lives.

Having never served a mission, not having an office or budget or official residence the first month was particularly difficult for Russell. Nothing was in place. He had no chair, no desk, no telephone, not even a pencil. The mission never owned a car until the third year when the mission home was finally built. Everything was starting from scratch. Church headquarters shared the basic organizational structure but gave no instructions on how to actually run a mission.

Seeing the need for a mission office the branch president, Bin Ki-kuchi (who coincidentally later served as a mission president him-self to the Horiuchis' grandson, and first president of the Sapporo Temple) offered his office in the branch building as an interim solution. It was a small room, barely big enough to hold two desks and a handful of chairs but it did the job.

It was an incredibly stressful time, not knowing quite what to do, but knowing something needed to be done. Russ was tense and irritable. Annette was often the recipient of his frustration, always reminding him that he was on the Lord's errand and that the Lord would open the way. After a few weeks, the pressure abated and Russell knew he could stick it out. After all he'd promised Presi-dent Tanner, and, in Russell's mind, that was as good as promising the Lord.

Annette worked on piecing together their apartment. Taking taxis, she went to the department store and purchased basic utensils, pots and pans, silverware, cups, and toilet paper. There was no washing machine so she purchased laundry soap and began do-ing the wash by hand. Her hands became so red that she visited the dermatologist who happened to live on the first floor of their building. When asked what she did to get such chapped hands Annette was embarrassed to admit she was washing their clothes by hand.

The Horiuchis made sure all the missionaries had their own washing machines first before buying their own. They felt that the young men and women were working hard and needed them more. This act did not go unnoticed by the missionaries. It was over five months (or more by some accounts) before the Horiuchis finally got a machine for their apartment. It was actually the elders that found it in a pawnshop. Elder Roger Harris, serving as assis-tant to the president at the time, carried it to the apartment.

Elder Harris was towering, about six and a half feet tall. While most Japanese washers are smaller than most American washers, the sight of the giant American missionary dressed in a suit carrying a washing machine on his back must have been a great spectacle. Annette was touched that the elders were so concerned for them.

Simple things taken for granted in the States became major obstacles in Japan. To receive phone service a large down payment was required and installation could take up to three months. Needing to keep in touch with the missionaries, particularly if any emergencies should arise (which they invariably would), the Horiuchis couldn't wait for three months. Annette visited the condo manager and asked if he could help with their dilemma. The manager personally visited each family in the building asking if anyone was willing to share their phone line to create a party line until the Horiuchis could get their own line. A pair of sisters (actual sisters, not missionary sisters) said they would share since they had taken lessons from the missionaries before.

For the three weeks before they got a refrigerator, Annette used the small shelf wedged in between the storm window and the regular window pane, which provided enough space to keep a few items such as milk and eggs. The Hokkaido winter kept the items more than cold enough.

For most of the first month the Horiuchis subsisted on *satsuma-age* for dinner, a deep-fried *tempura* made from ground fish patty and vegetables that the local store sold four for ¥100. Luckily it tasted so good they didn't grow tired of it. It turns out this particular store happened to be home of the best *satsuma-age* maker in Sapporo.

When one of the members, Brother Takasugi, an electrician originally from Asahikawa, found out the Horiuchis didn't even have a stove in their place he brought over a little electric oven with four compact burners and an oven so tiny that a small American sized baking sheet wouldn't fit inside.

The Horiuchis were grateful for the generous gift, which enabled them to prepare their own meals. Thin slices of lamb (at ¥100 for 100 grams it was cheaper than beef) cooked with green peppers became another common meal, stir-fried together to kill the strong lamb smell.

Japan is a very vertical country, running from the tropics in the south to sub-arctic temperatures in the far north. Hokkaido, being the northernmost main island, is extremely cold country. The severity of it caught even Annette off guard. Growing up in the much milder Tokyo climate hadn't prepared her for anything like this. She remembers being cold all the time during the first year. The first time Annette went shopping, she waited for 15 minutes on the street for a taxi. When she went to the *ofuro* that night she couldn't figure out why she was burned until she finally realized she was windburned.

When local members came to visit the Horiuchis' apartment, they often complained about being too hot. Annette couldn't figure out why until the members explained they wore wool undershirts, sometimes two or three layers thick. They recommended she buy some when they went on sale in late summer, advising her to do her shopping early since they often sold out quickly. The following summer Annette bought thick clothing for her and Russell to prepare for the winter.

One night a set of sister missionaries came to the apartment so chilled their lips were purple. Annette realized the missionaries were making the same mistake she had, wearing only nylons under their dresses. Annette instructed them to wear leotards and helped prepare them for the cold by buying woolen underwear like the members showed her. She began to encourage all the missionaries to dress more appropriately for the subzero temperatures.

Another important but difficult task was selecting counselors from men they didn't know. After prayerful consideration Russell called Professor Kunihiko Samejima, a professor of dairy science at Rakuno Gakuen University and Toshio Yanagizawa, who worked for the telephone company, as first and second counselors respectively. Both men were steady, provided good advice and together forged a strong presidency.

18

THE FROZEN CHOSEN

ELDERS GREGG TAGGART, TREVE STEPHENSON and Glenn Monson arrived overnight by train the evening before the Horiuchis landed. They had been given little more than a day's notice that they were going. Once in Sapporo they joined Elder Daniel Heiner, affectionately nicknamed Hokkaido Bear,[1] who was already serving as a traveling zone leader. Knowing their day had been hectic, Russell asked them when they last ate. When they didn't have an answer he said, "Let's eat!" The group found a nearby ramen shop and Russell ordered eight bowls of ramen, paying for all of their meals.

People in snow country often wear shoes with spikes on them to prevent slipping but these city slickers, Russell and Annette included, wore ordinary dress shoes and had to hang onto each other to avoid sliding in the foot of ice and snow left by the blizzard.

One of Annette's first impressions was that all the missionaries' trousers were wrinkled because of getting wet from the snow and stuffed in snow boots. It was snow country so nobody paid attention but it was still strange to a Tokyo girl.

With no mission home or proper apartment, the elders slept on *futons* crammed into a single classroom in the chapel building. Being assigned as mission office staff should have been an honor. However the missionaries felt their former president was using the

---

1. At the time of the Horiuchis' arrival, Elder Heiner had spent most of his mission in Hokkaido, which earned him the nickname. He never ended up being transferred south to warmer climates.

split of the mission to get rid of everyone he didn't care for. Any one he liked or felt he could utilize he kept. The rest were essentially discarded to the north. Missionaries from the Tokyo mission continued to trickle in, some well past the regular transfer time.

In the case of Elder Glenn Monson, he had actually been serving as office recorder in Tokyo. His attempt to explain an abacus to the president, who was unfamiliar with them, was taken as "talkback" and he suddenly found himself on the wrong side of the president's favor.

Complicating matters, Elder Monson's father was the Assistant Academic Vice-President at BYU, in charge of learning resources including, among other things, electronic media and the BYU Motion Picture Studios. His responsibilities involved the church pavilion at the Osaka World's Fair, business that naturally brought him to Japan. Elder Monson's father wrote to the Tokyo president requesting to stop by the mission home to meet him and say hello to his son when he passed through. The president seemed paranoid to meet, vehemently avoiding the meeting request, perhaps fearing that Elder Monson was leaking what was going on.

The president quickly made Elder Monson's mission life miserable, including daily attempts to humiliate him in front of other missionaries.

Elder Monson writes "It was actually dear Elder Hinckley (Gordon B.), who rescued me from that purgatory, I'm sure without fully realizing . . . what had been transpiring! We were having a friendly chat, and he so casually said . . . 'Elder Monson, at this time of Church growth in Japan, we're finding ourselves needing to staff certain positions. I feel inspired to ask you how you'd feel about going up North with this newly appointed President Horiuchi and help him establish the new mission up there?' I can't describe my thoughts at that instant! I gave him the biggest YES he's ever heard in his life! From THAT VERY MOMENT, until 10 months later when I boarded the plane to come home, EVERY DAY was a golden day for me!"

Elder Monson wasn't alone in his response. Many missionaries who felt like cast offs were willing, if not eager, to get away from their current situation without even knowing what the alternative was. As one elder recalled, "I didn't care if the new mission president was the devil himself, it would have been better."

According to Russell, the overall tone of the mission when they arrived was "strict. The missionaries were uptight. They didn't trust one another. They didn't trust the president. [There were] too many orders, told what to do so much."

During his personal interviews, Russell began to sense how truly low the morale was among the missionaries. Every one of the sister missionaries cried. They felt they had been rejected for not being pretty enough while all of the attractive sisters were kept in Tokyo. Russell told them to not talk about being pushed aside and Annette encouraged them as much as she could as well.

Like Elder Monson, many of the missionaries were there because they'd had run-ins with their former president. They dared voice an opinion or tried to defend another missionary. Elder Stephen Peterson (often Pete Choro for short) recalls Russell's response to this sentiment in conference. "One man's trash is another man's treasure, and I'm just tickled pink to have you all. I don't care how you got here. That's immaterial. I'm glad you're mine."

During one personal interview, Elder Walters, a cousin to Jae Ballif, stood at attention. Russell motioned for the young man to sit down and reminded him, "You are an elder not a soldier." As he sat down Russ noticed his suit lining was shredded and his elbows and knees were patched. This contradicted what he was about to ask the young man. "Elder Walters, I've been looking at your monthly spending records and you have spent more than the average missionary. Please tell me about it."

The young man looked up at Russell and then down at his feet as he explained that he was district leader in Hakodate. His requests for bedding and pots and pans were rejected. Feeling his missionaries were in dire need of the items he paid for them himself. The biggest expense was replacing an *ofuro* bathtub the missionaries melted accidentally when they turned on the heater before filling it with water.

Russell took off his glasses and stared. "Young man, you have an extraordinary sense of obligation and caring. What you did, you did in the best interest of your elders. You are to be commended." Tears streamed down the elder's cheeks because someone recognized his sacrifices. Russell did his best to make sure Elder Walters' remaining four months of his mission were memorable, even taking him out to dinner. The things Elder Walters mentioned were the very things Russell himself was addressing. Russell had to check his anger at the bureaucracy that was making the lives of the missionaries unnecessarily difficult.

Elder Walters wasn't the only missionary in these circumstances. During interviews Russell could sense when a missionary had no money. Some were converts with little or no family support. As always Russell gathered his information subtly, asking simple questions. How are you doing? What do you hear from home? When one missionary answered that he hadn't heard anything in four or five months Russell knew the elder hadn't received any support from home, so Russell gave him some small change to help him out.

Humorously, word spread early on that the new mission president had been an interrogator in the war, making the missionaries a little nervous about their first interviews. Their concerns were quickly laid to rest as they grew familiar with President Horiuchi but Russell's keen intuition continued to serve him—and his missionaries—well.

Russell made sure that the missionaries, like Elder Walters, were compensated for their expenses. Russell began to naturally bond with his missionaries, like he had with his college students. "Every chance I had, whatever I could afford I bought them lunch when I went to visit them. Aw, drop everything, let's go eat. Noodles and what not. Just give them encouragement. Help them to be happy. Just encouragement. Not spiritual way."

One elder couldn't sit during his interview because he'd had an operation on his rectum before coming on the mission. He was told there was nothing that could be done about the discomfort and to tough it out. Russell told him to relax and take care of his health first, then he could get to work.

He wasn't the only missionary with health problems. For the first month in Hokkaido, Annette spent almost every day taking missionaries to the hospital, sometimes five or more at a time, for different ailments—heat rash, ulcers, spitting blood, pneumonia, colds, and on and on. They found a Catholic run *Tenshi Byouin* hospital nearby that was clean with a kind staff. There was no mission car so the missionaries rode the bus to the hospital with the Horiuchis footing the bill. Annette was able to get the missionaries enrolled in the government health program, but the Horiuchis paid for the medications out of their own pocket since there was no fund for medical expenses. A governmental health insurance existed that could have defrayed the cost, but Russell and Annette didn't find out about it until twenty years later on their temple mission. They were never reimbursed for these expenditures. Then again, they never asked to be.

Interviews with the previous president were often held in a grand hotel suite he stayed in, with the elders kept waiting outside. In the interviews the missionaries were often berated for not selling enough copies of the *Book of Mormon*, not proselyting enough, etc. By contrast Russell's interviews were very informal and more focused on the missionary. Annette distinctly remembers one elder coming out from an early interview with the new president announcing excitedly, "He said I'm a good missionary!"

Annette was privileged to witness many such reactions. She would bring her sewing kit and sit in the hallway mending clothes for the missionaries while Russell conducted his interviews. If the repair was a big one or required a sewing machine Annette had to find someone in the branch who could sew it but the small things, holes and buttons, she could do by hand. It didn't seem extravagant to her but it was really appreciated by the missionaries. She remembers Elder Brent Ludlow saying repeatedly, "Golly. By golly. Oh, my gosh." When Annette asked him what happened he said, "I never thought the mission mother would help missionaries like that."

One other story about Elder Ludlow poignantly sticks out in Annette's memory. It was at the mission office the night before he was going home. Choking up as she relates the story nearly forty years later, Annette tells how Elder Ludlow shared how he was so disgusted with his early mission experience that he had no intention of going back to church once he got home but his time working with the Horiuchis helped change his mind.

Another elder's story Annette remembers vividly is Elder Brian Galbraith who wanted to go home. He'd told the previous mission president that he was not feeling well but the president told him he was being lazy. Not surprisingly Elder Galbraith ended up in the Horiuchis' mission. When Annette took him to the doctor they found out he had an ulcer. He received treatment and was able to finish his mission.

At the end of his mission Elder Galbraith shared how thrilled his family, especially his grandparents, were for his return: they were converts and he was the first one in his family to fulfill a mission. Elder Galbraith later served as a bishop at BYU Idaho.

Annette realized that the individual missionaries weren't the only ones affected by a mission, that entire families and friends and neighbors were involved as well. "Like ripples in a pond. You never know how far reaching your influence is." The Horiuchis felt strongly that the responsibility of all mission presidents is to help the young men and women serving to complete their callings. The sense of accomplishment says Annette, "makes a difference, truly."

The Horiuchis understood how Elder Galbraith felt. "[There were] so many dirty things going on," Annette tells.

THE FROZEN CHOSEN

The heart of the matter was that the former mission president was running the mission as a personal base of power. He made no bones about playing favorites with his missionaries, treating those in his favor well and castigating the rest. It was a mission filled with vicious politicking, an unhealthy environment that encouraged backstabbing and contention among the missionaries, especially those vying for leadership positions.

It is almost unimaginable that any mission president could behave in this manner, but it was happening.

Initially, the Horiuchis, like their missionaries, were thoroughly disillusioned. The mission was being treated like a grand competition for glorification, and missionaries were being neglected and abused. The Horiuchis felt "a mission shouldn't be like this. If it's like this then we're going home." Both converts, with no previous mission experience of their own, to the Horiuchis the idea of a mission was a dignified one. Landing on the ground now the reality of the situation was a shock. Annette felt they should quit and return to BYU. Russell knew if they quit there would be no going back. In the end the decision came down to this: what would happen to the missionaries if they left? And so they stayed.

Russell was aware he was facing an uphill battle to reverse the practices and mentality that had developed. Instead of proselyting and baptisms he placed his emphasis on the wellbeing of the missionaries. "I got the feeling," says Russell, "that a lot of these leaders go around (he pounds his fist into his hand repeatedly) like that you see. I said, no, no, relax, relax. So when they have conferences, they have meeting after meeting after meeting. I said forget it, forget it. Let's go eat. Take it easy. In fact I told them, 4 o'clock we have dinner. Until then go out, go see the town." Still it would take time to shift from the pre-existing condition to the Horiuchi state of mind.

Local leadership also had to learn to keep stride with President Horiuchi. In April, shortly after their arrival, Russell was informed by the district president of an upcoming district meeting. A few weeks later the district president approached Russell again to inform him about the meeting. Upon another reminder a short time later Russell asked, "This is the third time you've informed me. What are you trying to tell me?"

The district president replied, "We need you to give us the instructions of what songs to sing, who says the prayer and who will speak."

"You're the district president," Russell said kindly, "You plan it."

The district president was surprised. "Really? We can do that?"

At the conference the leaders talks ran over time into the lunch period. When they announced that they would now hear from the mission president, Russell walked to the pulpit and said, "Brothers and sisters, it is past lunch time and you don't want to listen to me. Let's dismiss the meeting." That was the last time a meeting ran overtime with Russell in attendance.

After another church dinner function, the brethren stood around the room while the sisters broke down the tables, put away the chairs and washed the dishes. Observing this Russell said to Annette, "Guess we had better teach them!" He took off his coat jacket, rolled up his sleeves and began washing dishes. The saints learned fast. At the next dinner when Russell went into the kitchen, he was told there wasn't any room for him because the men were already cleaning.

True to his aloha spirit, leadership meetings were often held over plates of food. District leaders, branch presidents and local leadership gathered to eat and discuss matters affecting their area. Involving the missionaries in planning and solving issues helped empower them and allowed them to grow.

One of the earliest tasks President and Sister Horiuchi assigned themselves was to inspect the living conditions of the missionaries. Russell depended heavily on his two well-grounded assistants, Elders Daniel Heiner and Gregg Taggart, asking them what needed to be done. They began first in the Sapporo area, completing their initial rounds in three weeks.

The first stop outside of the city was Iwamizawa. Annette cried when she saw the conditions. Snow piled up against the eaves of the inexcusably old house and freezing wind whistled through every crack and notch in the joints of the walls and windows. Without even *zabuton* cushions available the elders sat directly on the cold floor, the room so chilly that everyone kept their overcoats on to stay warm. The missionaries kept their milk and vegetables in the refrigerator not to keep cold but to prevent them from freezing. "Even the poor among the Japanese weren't living like that," says Annette who felt that if the missionary's parents ever saw the circumstances their children were living in they would demand their return.

Russell asked, "Where is your heater?" The elders explained it was upstairs but they were short on fuel so they only used it at night when they slept.

"How come?" asked Russell, "Did you turn in requests for heaters and what not?" District leader's requests for pots and pans, fuel and futons had all been dismissed.

Russell told them to buy fuel and a second heater whether the mission had the money or not. There was no budget in place for this but the Horiuchis made sure there was a heater in each *dendosho*, missionary area. The priority was to keep the missionaries healthy. From this point on in their travels, if the APs came across an apartment without a heater they were instructed to purchase one. The Horiuchis also reminded the missionaries to keep adequate ventilation since one apartment nearly asphyxiated themselves with the fuel burning heaters.

Annette was impressed that the missionaries still seemed bright-eyed and happy even with the horrible conditions. To her it was a marvel and a testimony to the spirit of these young men and women.

The elders in Iwamizawa were not alone. Conditions everywhere in the mission were "terrible" according to Russell. He remembers finding the elders in Akita very discouraged as he spoke with them over breakfast. Russell told them to cancel their appointments for the day then joined them in *jan, ken, po,* rock, paper, scissors, to see who had to wash the dishes. The young men clapped as the chore fell to Russell, who would have not have had it any other way.

Russell also treated the missionaries to lunch. This was again from the Horiuchis' personal funds but they knew the missionaries needed support and love. After lunch Russell hugged each of them adding a personal word of confidence to each of them before he left.

Next on the Horiuchis' list were *futon* beds. The beds were not made for westerners and the average missionary's feet stuck out over the end forcing the elders to curl up like a shrimp to keep their toes warm. Special *futon*, larger and thicker than usual, were ordered with the money again coming out of the Horiuchis' pockets. Annette also contacted a member who was a *futonyasan*, futon maker, asking how to properly care for the new *futon*. He mentioned most people perspire about one rice bowl's worth of sweat when they sleep and that the *futon* needed to be aired out.

Both to save money and to get better acquainted with the missionaries when he traveled Russell stayed at the missionaries' quarters rather than at hotels. Elder Genji Ichikawa remembers how surprised he and the other elders were when President Horiuchi announced he was staying with them. There weren't enough *futon* for everyone so the elders offered him one of theirs but Russell refused, insisting instead on sleeping on a pile of *zabuton*, small cushions made for sitting on the floor.

Elder Ichikawa said he couldn't sleep that night he was so moved by the presidents actions.

When Annette went along, they asked the missionaries to rent a *futon* and blankets for both of them to share. The Horiuchis would fix breakfast for the missionaries and "chew the fat," often treating the missionaries to lunch, usually *ramen* or something inexpensive but delicious.

In Japanese the term for mission president is *dendo bucho*. Missionaries often refer to the president endearingly as the *Buch,* pronounced "booch." Other common *senkyoshi-go* missionary slang included words such as "dode" short for *doryo* companion or "triff," a common term for Japanese schoolgirls who often developed crushes on the elders. The term "triff" doesn't come from any Japanese word but is derived from the word "triffid" from the 1956 movie *Invasion of the Body Snatchers*.

News that the new *Buch* had chosen to stay in missionaries' apartments instead of a hotel spread like wildfire. While much of the decision was practical and provided Russell with a good chance to assess the missionaries living quarters it also provided both the *Buch* and the missionaries a chance to become better acquainted, an experience cherished by both parties. Elder Gary George remembers the *Buch* once curling up in the drapes to sleep when there was no other bedding available. Before long, letters began coming in from missionaries asking how soon the *Buch* was going to visit their area. Russell claims it was because he fed them but the elders will tell a different story.

By simply being himself—warm and caring—the new mission president began sending an unspoken message throughout the mission that the ministers of the Lord were valued. The elders sensed it. The tone of the mission was shifting.

Hard work and discipline were emphasized but Russell also encouraged and maintained a good sense of humor. Elder Monson was known for falling asleep at his typewriter after lunch. Elder Raymond Swenson remembers "one afternoon [President Horiuchi] motioned for all of us to hide behind the countertop while [he] turned out the lights. [He] made a sharp sound to wake up

Monson Choro, who started when he thought we had all gone home and closed up the office without him."

Russell took time to read the missionaries' weekly reports. He treated them with the same scrutiny and personal care as he had his blue books at BYU. The reports mentioned the number of contacts, the hours spent tracting, etc. Even though he was new to the mission experience some of the numbers coming in seemed impossibly high, some as high as 120 hours a week. With the help of his assistants he calculated out roughly how much time a missionary could possibly spend proselyting, factoring in wake up time, personal study, meals and even time spent to go to the bathroom. The numbers to time ratio didn't add up; no one could possibly put in so many hours in one week.

Russell didn't blame the elders. Feeling that stats and unreasonable expectations were making liars out of the missionaries Russell quickly instructed them to forget about weekly stat reports and instead write a letter to him once a month telling him how they were doing. Russell did his best to foster an environment of trust so the missionaries weren't afraid to be honest with him. A great deal of his time each day was spent reading and answering every letter by hand, a personal touch the missionaries enjoyed. Some of the missionaries have kept and treasured all of their correspondence with the *Buch* to this day.

Sister Kazuko Kimura remembers how aware the Horiuchis were of their needs. Sister Kimura carried an old shoulder bag so used and worn that it needed to be patched several times to keep it together. One day she walked into the mission home and Sister Horiuchi handed her a brand new bag telling her, "My daughter is expecting a baby so I went to buy a bag for her and I bought one for you too."

Before a district conference in Sendai, complaints from some church members came into the mission home that the missionaries in Hachinohe were sitting around all day drinking Coca-Cola. Prior to the Horiuchis' arrival, Hachinohe was considered a *batsu,* punishment branch, a place where missionaries out of favor with the former president were sent.

Though a somewhat laughable offense now, the strictures around not drinking Coke were much stronger at the time, especially in Japan, and it was a real concern for some of the members. When Russell and the APs arrived, they found the apartment decorated with a pile of Coke bottles and reinforcements in the fridge. The collection apparently belonged to Elder Greg Ludlow.

As Elder Durrant tells it, when Russell asked if it was his Coke in the fridge "Ludlow blew up and stomped up the stairs. 'I can't take another one [meaning an overly strict, authoritative president]. I'm out of here.' He'd had a pretty bad time with the former president."

Initially, Elder Ludlow was banished to Hachinohe after arriving at the Tokyo mission home, after traveling for 23 hours straight, with the whisper of a mustache on his lip. Feeling this was clearly out of regulation the former president took it as reason enough not to like him. Not surprisingly, Ludlow felt that if the president didn't care then he had no reason to care himself.

Instead of chastising the elders, Russell empathized with them. With the welfare of the missionaries foremost in his mind, Russell told them it was okay but to make sure and clean up after themselves because the members were complaining.

As was his custom, Russell spent the night at the elder's apartment instead of a hotel. The next morning the elders showed up for study sharply at 5:30, dressed in their shirts and ties and were surprised to find Russell in his sweats.

"What are you guys doing?" Russell asked, "Where are you going?" When the elders answered they were only having study time it was Russell's turn to be surprised.

"In your clothes like that? You'll wrinkle them. Why don't you loosen up a bit?" Not needing any more incentive than that, the elders quickly dressed in more comfortable attire for study.

Elder Cyril Figuerres says one of Russell's gifts was the ability to discern people's circumstances and really develop a good feel for where they were coming from.

The next transfer, Russell placed Elder Ludlow together with Elder Figuerres. Figuerres, genially called "Fig" by those who know him well, happened to be from a town very familiar to President Horiuchi—Lahaina, Maui.

Like other missionaries, Elder Figuerres ran afoul of the Tokyo president early on in his mission. Once when the president was drilling into the missionaries how fanatically they were going to sell the *Book of Mormon,* in sincere surprise the young Hawaiian asked, "Oh, I didn't think we were book salesmen." The president didn't take the comment well and the young man from the tropics found himself sent to serve among "the frozen chosen" in the north.

Russell knew Figuerres and Ludlow were a study in contrasting personalities. Elder Ludlow wasn't a so-called "golden missionary" but had a good heart. Possessed with a strong sense of self-expression and frustrated by the excessively rigid environment, Elder Ludlow acted out. In addition to his wisp of a mustache and Coke drinking he often wore his hair longer than regulation and was known to carry a guitar around town on his back.

With all this in mind, Russell called Elder Ludlow as District Leader. Figuerres said this was not only a boost of confidence for Elder Ludlow but it also allowed him to do things he was good at. Though he wasn't the type to admit it, Elder Ludlow paid careful attention to the needs of the missionaries around him. Often, just to make Elder Figuerres happy, Ludlow often said he wanted to do or see something or eat something special, not because he really wanted it but because he knew that his companion or another missionary did; it was really for the benefit of the other person. Figuerres describes Ludlow as "a wonderful companion."

The two elders were transferred into Akita and began producing results different than either of them had ever seen before: in the Horiuchis' words they "burned the city," finding lots of investigators and seeing baptisms. Annette says the difference was "because they were happy. [Russell] encouraged them, didn't scold them." The elders found out that President Horiuchi trusted them to do their work on their terms.

Elder Figuerres later served in the mission office as Assistant to the President. He remembers working at his desk in the office shared by all of the mission staff, including Russell, whose desk occupied the back of the room. Elder Figuerres describes Horiuchi *dendobucho* as always striving to make the missionaries think. As Elder Figuerres describes it, to "enlarge their vision."

After dealing with administrative minutiae at his desk, Russell would grow fidgety. Elder Figuerres recalls the time the *Buch* rolled up a newspaper, wielding it like a *samurai*. With a "hup!" he playfully tapped the AP on the shoulder.

"Wow," thought Figuerres, "He sure is a different kind of mission president!"

Russell knew Figuerres was from Lahaina. He also knew the young man had graduated top of his class from Lahainaluna. Even so, very few islanders ever left for the mainland and Russell surmised, accurately Figuerres confesses, that the young Hawaiian was going to stay in Lahaina, perhaps work a plantation job. Russell knew he was capable of more.

"So," Russell said, "Do you want to be a big fish in a small *lua*, reservoir?"

Then Russell wandered off. It was a pattern Russell followed often: pose a question, planting a seed to make you ponder, then walk away. He could be "very mysterious," tells Figuerres.

After a bit Russell wandered back towards Figuerres' desk, and much to the Lahaina boy's surprise, began singing the Lahainaluna school song.

O La-haina, La-hai-nalu-na na-ni,
Ka hoku hele ho-i o ka Pa-ki-pi-ka
I-pu ku-ku-i a-a mau (Pio o-le)
I ka ma-ka-ni Kau-wa-u-la

Figuerres didn't know Russell could sing the alma mater. The *Buch* didn't come straight out and say it, but Figuerres finally figured out what Russell was telling him. Russell knew that Figuerres saw him as a venerable mission president, as a respected university professor. Both high positions, especially from a small town point of view. But Russell was saying that they were both from the same small town, they were both from the same school. Russell was telling him, "No, I'm just like you."

"He made me feel like I could become like him," Figuerres says, "His counseling repertoire was amazingly broad. He used humor, suspense, teasing, and debate. He raised tough questions and the intent was to make paradigm-shifting changes in our mindset and dreams."

Russell discerned the missionaries who were sent to him as "problems" weren't that at all. They just needed love and support. While Russell was very understanding of his missionaries, he also expected them to be their best. The nicest apartment in the mission was located next to the chapel in Sapporo. From their initial tour, the Horiuchis were well aware of the difficult living conditions of the missionaries in other areas and were upset to find that the four elders living in the chapel apartment had left it a mess. Russell and Annette cleaned the place themselves, washing dishes, etc. There was a blackboard in the apartment and Russell wrote "We didn't enjoy cleaning your quarters," signed "President."

When the elders returned they couldn't believe it. They asked some members who were at the chapel if it really was the new president and his wife that cleaned the apartment. The members said that it was. The elders hurried over to the office where President Horiuchi told them they had it lucky compared to missionaries living in other places but since they didn't take care of it they were all getting transferred out.

Happily, not all of Russell's interventions were to solve problems. He is proud that he played matchmaker for several of his missionaries. Sister Holly Johnson, from California, in the field only two months and frustrated with the language, questioned why she had been sent to Japan. Russell saw her coming out of the furnace room closet where she went to pray and asked her what was happening.

Later that day, Elder Kevin Hopkins from Ogden, Utah, admitted to Russell that he couldn't keep his eyes off Sister Johnson. Instead of discouraging the young man President Horiuchi suggested, "Go talk to her." It was not what the elder expected to hear but he quickly followed the counsel. Afterwards the young elder asked, "What should I do now? Should I write to her?" Russell gave his blessing provided that the letters weren't "mushy" and pertained solely to missionary work. Of course, the president made sure they never proselyted in the same area. After their missions, the two were married and Elder Hopkins went on to work in the Air Force.

The Horiuchis made sure to avoid favoritism. Even when the children of friends, such as the Komatsus, or Teramotos, or general authorities showed up in their mission they were treated on an equal basis as everyone else. The missionaries seemed to sense this and, after what they had been through, highly appreciated it.

Annette relates that much later, after returning to teach at BYU, she had President Kimball's grandson in one of her classes. He had served in the Sapporo mission and was assigned to Sapporo city itself for his entire stay because the mission president thought he should stay in a nice clean town because his grandfather was a General Authority. Annette said it was too bad because he didn't get to see any other areas or meet new people. The grandson agreed. So Annette was doubly happy that they never played favorites.

The Horiuchis' philosophy was simple. The most important thing was how the individual missionary felt. Baptisms and *The Book of Mormon* were secondary. "I didn't care what they accomplished or what they didn't accomplish," said Russell, "[I wanted to] make sure that they were happy in what they were doing."

Annette says the idea was that if the missionaries were happy then they would work and baptisms would follow. Missionaries worked hard because they didn't want to disappoint the mission president, not because they were afraid of him. It was a direct result of Russell placing his trust in the missionaries to realize what they were capable of.

Russell felt the very characteristics the previous president disliked in these missionaries were the ones that made them great. Like he did with his students at BYU Russell gave the missionaries a lot of room for growth and creativity, allowing them to figure things out and develop themselves from within.

Elder Figuerres remembers President Horiuchi saying the reason he liked his missionaries was that when a leader says jump most missionaries jump. But his missionaries asked "How come?" and "Why?" Russell called it intelligent, thinking obedience. He felt it made their service more meaningful since they knew the purpose behind what they were doing.

Elder Quentin Steele took the *Buch's* advice to "use your head, use your talent" to heart. Discouraged with the language and feeling like he was making no progress in his proselyting he came up with the idea of putting his shoes, which were an impressive size 14, on the sidewalk outside his apartment with a sign that read "If you can fill these shoes, you'll get a free bowl of ramen." It turned out to be a great icebreaker in introducing the gospel and Elder Steele was excited to report making a lot of new contacts, all from finding a way to serve that was uniquely his own.

Another prime example of the trust Russell placed in his missionaries is the time when Elders Randy Johnson and Ernest Durrant were called to open up Kushiro, a new area remotely located about 8–9 hours from Sapporo. Elder Durrant writes "As we met at the mission office prior to leaving, I asked Pres. Horiuchi what process he wanted us to follow as we began there. I was thinking that he would tell us to dedicate the city and how. What he said was "I don't know, I've never been in that situation. I don't know what the Spirit will tell you to do, but do it. You'll be fine. Let me know how it goes! *Gambatte* . . . He wasn't into micro-management."

Elder Dudley, who served as one of Russell's APs adds "President Horiuchi's philosophy of missionary work has always been to have few, if any, rules. He allows us to use our own ideas and programs, within the framework of the church's standards. So, true to form, he has said little, if anything to me concerning my duties and responsibilities other than a basic outline."

When the first all mission conference was held in Sapporo, the Horiuchis found themselves picking up missionaries who'd traveled in from Sendai.

One of the first things Russ did was to pro-rate travel expenses for meetings so that conferences were no longer an onus to the missionaries living farthest away. He also counseled the missionaries to be frugal so those taking overnight trips packed sandwiches, candy and fruit with them instead of stopping at vendors. Every care to avoid unnecessary expenses was considered.

In total, seventy-seven missionaries, all split from the Tokyo mission, attended the first conference. There was much wonder among the missionaries as to what the new president would be like. Considering how many of them had been (mis)treated up to this point, the intensity of their interest ran beyond mere curiosity. For some it was literally a matter of life changing significance.

The Horiuchis started out by introducing themselves. Russell's message was to "just relax, do your best. And hang the rest." The missionaries were surprised when the new *Buch* stopped the testimony meeting by saying, "It's lunch time. Let's close the meeting and go eat." Russell didn't understand why meetings were often dragged out for hours on end at times. After half a dozen testimonies were shared, he excused everyone to lunch. What was the missionaries' reaction? "Oh, they were happy!" laughs Russell.

The Relief Society sisters generously offered to fix the meal for the missionaries. They prepared Japanese dishes, *donburi, gohan, gyudon, oyakodon,* etc. with typically small Japanese portions. The food was delicious but Annette, figuring that the missionaries ate Japanese food all the time, decided it would be nice for them to have some American style food for a change.

Through his experience as a professor of animal husbandry at the Raku no Daigaku Brother Samejima knew how to make his own salami. He also knew where to buy meats and was able to provide whole boxes of chicken very inexpensively.

Russell requested a commercial stove through Salt Lake but was turned down. He was able to locate a used one in Sendai with six burners and a nice oven, finding parts to rebuild it himself. He also found a very large commercial rice cooker as well.

From then on, meals at conference time consisted of large quantities of fried or roasted chicken, salmon or hamburgers with sides of salad, mashed potatoes, cakes and unlimited peanut butter and jelly sandwiches, a real treat since peanut butter and jelly were both difficult to obtain in Sapporo at the time. Annette asked the sister missionaries to make pie. Bananas were fairly easy to come by so they made banana cream pies. Last but not least, Annette also made jello. American jello was nowhere to be found so she used Japanese brand jello, adding fruit to make a tasty dish.

Whenever he felt it was needed, Russell told the missionaries they'd had enough for one day and that they should go downtown and look around for a camera or souvenir items.

Whatever Russell said at the conference, apparently it was the right thing. After the meeting, several of the missionaries rushed to the phone, calling former companions still in the old mission, telling them how excited they were and how different the new president was. Learning that such phone calls were being made, and worried they might cause trouble, Russell kindly asked the missionaries to stop.

The conference was very successful. The missionaries had a good time. Annette remembered them laughing, slapping each other on the back and genuinely enjoying each other's company. No longer a marathon of drudgery and reprimand, conferences quickly became anticipated events.

The Horiuchis once toured part of the mission with Elder Dahle and Elder Harris, who stood close to 6'4" and 6'6" respectively. The two men dwarfed the 5'6" *Buch* and his 5'1" wife. People wondered who the Horiuchis were and how they'd hired such large bodyguards.

19

THE LORD'S MONEY

THREE WEEKS AFTER THE HORIUCHIS' arrival in Japan a Servicemen's Conference, the *Fuji Taikai*, was held in Hakone for all LDS military personnel and mission presidents throughout all of Asia. The Horiuchis were pleased to run into J. Roman Andrus, Annette's art professor from BYU. Roman and his wife Irva were visiting their son, who was in the services.

The mission presidents, including the Horiuchis, served as speakers at the conference. The Tokyo president was in charge of organizing the conference and arranged the speaking assignments to marginalize the other Japanese mission presidents while ensuring himself a prominent speaking position right before the General Authorities during the main meeting.

Seeing the program for the first time Russell and Eddie Okazaki realized they were scheduled to address only the priesthood session and Annette was scheduled to address the Relief Society. Russell and Eddie resolved to give the best talks they could anyhow. Afterwards Russell was approached by Harold B. Lee (who presided over the conference) who told him he'd expressed his feelings very well. Several of the mission presidents wives heard the talks were excellent and expressed disappointment at not getting to hear them.

A few months later the Horiuchis received their first official visitors, Elder Bruce R. McConkie and his wife Becky.

Annette stayed in Sapporo to prepare for Elder and Sister McConkie's eventual arrival while Russell and his assistants traveled first by ferry from Hakodate then by train to meet the McConkies in Sendai.

"We should roll out the red carpet for you, but I don't know how to," Russell greeted them at the airport, "First of all, we don't have a red carpet." Elder McConkie laughed.

Elder McConkie attended the Sendai district mission conference. The elders who were in Tokyo the last time Elder McConkie visited commented that he seemed like a changed person. He had been very stern before but now he seemed much more relaxed and treated the missionaries really tenderly. Annette believes Elder McConkie's demeanor reflected the mission president he was working with. Russell was a relaxed person so Elder McConkie was able to relax as well and the two men hit it off well.

After the conference the McConkies, Russell and the APs returned north to Sapporo. While Elder McConkie and Russell conducted interviews, Annette was left to entertain Sister McConkie. At a loss of what to do she asked Russell if he thought it was okay if she took their guest shopping at the Mitsukoshi Department Store. Russ shrugged, "If there's any complaints they can send me home." The two women had a wonderful time.

After shopping Annette and Sister McConkie waited in the small branch president's office Russell was using as an office. The plan was for the two couples to go to dinner at the Grand Hotel but the interviews were running behind, and the restaurant closed before they were done. It was well past dinnertime and the two women began eating from a *bento* box of vegetable *tempura* some members bought earlier in the afternoon.

Finally finished with their interviews, the two men joined their wives in the office. Elder McConkie asked what they were eating and Annette explained that it was deep fried vegetables. Interested in trying some, the tall Elder McConkie knelt on the floor bringing his head close to level with Annette's. Holding open his mouth he said, "Okay, feed me!" Everyone laughed as Annette fed him by hand like an infant saying, "This is a carrot. And this is a sweet potato."

"Oh, that's good," he said as he tried each one.

With the restaurants closed, Russell and Annette brought the McConkies to their apartment. Annette hadn't prepared anything, apologizing for having only bread and milk. The McConkies said it was fine.

Entering the apartment, Elder McConkie removed his shoes, sat on the *tatami* and propped his feet up on the coffee table revealing a large hole in his sock. Elder McConkie knew Russell was under a great deal of pressure and the apostle's informal—often joking—attitude really helped him unwind as well.

The couples shared Donq bread with butter and milk, which was still being kept in the windowsill in lieu of a refrigerator. The Horiuchis didn't own a pitcher either so the milk was served straight from the container. Elder McConkie gazed at the milk carton studying the *kanji,* Japanese characters, intently before asking with mock seriousness, "What percent of manure is in this?"

The Horiuchis received a letter from Ellen and Michael asking if they could come and visit but they were a little hesitant because of mission visiting rules.

At dinner Annette brought it up, explaining that their newlywed daughter and her husband wanted to visit. Would that be allowed? Russell explains: "Of course, when you ask something like that to a General Authority they can't directly say yes or no. [They learned the reason for this was because it wasn't a matter pertaining to official church policy.] . . . "Well, [Elder McConkie] said and then he started writing on a napkin or something—I wish I would have kept it. But he wrote something, and in a very nice way said, well, of course the family can visit. He didn't write that directly but in nice way he did it. So grandma [Annette] told Ellen and Michael that you can come and stay with us, not too long but you can come."

Gordon B. Hinckley gave a similar answer to Elder McConkie's when Russell asked him if the missionaries were allowed to visit the new World Expo in Osaka or not. The Horiuchis thought it would be a good experience for their missionaries while they were in Japan. However the Expo was located in Osaka, far to the south. Elder Hinckley didn't answer yes or no. Instead he replied, "If I am in the same country, why not go see it?" So the Horiuchis understood that it was all right and the missionaries that were serving in Tohoku, the southern end of the mission, were able to go visit. Annette heard that President Sakamaki of the Fukuoka mission had a similar question and was able to send his missionaries even though they were about two days south from Osaka (there was no bullet train at the time). It was a good break for the missionaries.

Another mission president asked if it was all right for parents to come and pick up their missionaries and tour together before they were released. Elder Hinckley answered, "Well, the parents have been supporting their children all these years, it's hard to tell them no." That was the end of the conversation. The answer sounded pretty good to Russell and Annette.

The Horiuchis and the McConkies passed an enjoyable evening chatting and laughing. Elder McConkie, who was a big rock hound, invited Russell to go rock hunting together when he was through with his mission. Elder McConkie made stone bracelets for the mission wives and he also fashioned a stone bolo tie for Russell, which Russell still wears nearly forty years later. The McConkie's daughter, Becky, was in Russell's ward while he was in a Bishopric at BYU.

The two couples did make it to the hotel restaurant the next day, before the McConkies left. Annette remembers one scoop of ice cream was about ¥250, pretty expensive at the time, but it was such a treat they couldn't resist.

The Horiuchis really enjoyed the McConkie's visit. They were doing their best to bolster the missionaries and it was nice to have someone hearten them as well.

After the baptism by fire that was the Horiuchis' first year in the mission, things began to settle down and their attention could be turned to fine tuning the details.

One thing Annette noticed was that many of the young missionaries didn't know how to cook and weren't eating enough. One elder mentioned the only thing he knew how to cook was *ramen* noodles. For variety he put mayonnaise on one day then *soyu*, soy sauce, the next. It was the only thing he ate for the entire first month of his mission.

From some of their missionaries the Horiuchis learned that they could purchase *mugi*, cracked wheat, in bulk. Cracked wheat is not a staple of the Japanese diet and the elders were actually purchasing the *mugi* from a chicken feed company. It seemed like an odd idea at first but the missionaries insisted that the wheat was good. Russell began providing it to the missionaries for free to bolster their often meager food supplies.

Realizing the need to teach her missionaries rudimentary cooking skills, Annette set about preparing a cookbook beginning with how to cook rice. Russell, in his humorous wry manner, penned the preface to the volume entitled simply the *JAPAN EAST MISSION COOKBOOK*:

"You are on a limited budget. You do not have too much time to prepare and cook your meals. Your facilities are limited. Your cooking experiences are limited, and it may be that you cannot even boil water satisfactorily. Then on top of all that you have to contend with unfamiliar local products. But you have to eat, even if it means going native — reduced to octopus, raw fish, boiled rice, eels and other *oishii monos*.

"The prospects may look rather dismal for the duration of your mission, and CARE packages may have to be sent to you from home. Yet a closer look at the situation would indicate that things were not as bleak as once thought. Indeed, you may find things rather palatable and nice. It is only a matter of adjusting and knowing how. Rather than finding things difficult and problematical, it may be that you will have an exciting gourmet type of experience on a shoestring budget. If not, at least you will be able to keep yourself well fed and healthy."

Annette worked diligently on the project but, still worrying about her English, the going was slow. The cookbook wasn't finished by the time the Horiuchis left Japan but Sister Kikue Izumizaki, an older sister from Hawaii, finished the project for her. Forty-five pages long, featuring hand drawn illustrations, the cookbook helped the missionaries to identify Japanese ingredients and prepare simple meals including *gyoza* and other staples.

Russell depended heavily on his mission assistants and was careful which elders he selected. Nothing turned him off more than a "brown-noser, someone who kissed up for a position." Instead he watched the elders interact during meetings and conferences identifying those that the others naturally flocked around, usually laughing and joking, as natural leaders. It was important that they were "out-oriented" rather than "in-oriented" as Russell puts it.

One unexpected challenge the Horiuchis faced was the sense of isolation associated with being a mission president in Japan. Russell writes "Our personal private life is rather lonely. We really do no[t] have anyone to really talk to. The missionaries maintain their formality, and the members hold me in awe and reverence. This makes it rough for us—since we are so acclimated to chewing the fat in an informal manner with our friends." One thing the experience taught him was a great empathy for the General Authorities who "are treated similarly" but "they must play the role all the time."

Mission president's conferences were a welcomed respite, a good opportunity to "chew the fat" and be treated as peers. Meetings ran morning to evening but the conferences gave the Horiuchis a good chance to get acquainted or re-acquainted with other mission presidents, including Bob Slover from Korea, Kan Watanabe and Ed Okazaki.

Presided over by President Ezra Taft Benson with Elder McConkie serving as assistant, this year's conference was held in Hong Kong.[1] Bill Bradshaw, as president of the mission, was in charge of planning, and the Horiuchis enjoyed a pleasant visit with the Bradshaws in their mission home.

It was also in Taiwan where they first met Carlos Smith, who was presiding in Singapore. Carlos previously served as president of the Central States Mission and worked on the Young Men's Board of the Church for many years. Coincidentally, Carlos happened to be the uncle of Emery Smith, one of Ellen's good friends from college. Emery himself served as mission president in Nagoya from 1988–1991, the same time the Horiuchis were serving in the Tokyo temple. Emery remembers them bringing him and his wife a turkey for Thanksgiving one year in Nagoya, a hard-to-find treat in Japan.

Taiwan held another treat in the form of the Hyers. Paul was on sabbatical doing research and the Horiuchis were able to visit for two nights after the conference. Together the two couples visited Urai, a popular tourist attraction near Taipei. The area, with its abundance of hibiscus and other flowers, reminded Annette of Hawaii.

The presidents brought each other gifts from their respective missions, all in all about six or seven each. The Slovers brought fabric pouches and bags from Korea while the Horiuchis brought Ainu carved dolls and bears. Kan Watanabe brought elaborate dolls for everyone. Annette wasn't sure how he managed to carry all of them.

During a break in the meetings, several of the wives headed to the restroom. There was only one western toilet, the rest were squatters, and none of the women knew how to use them. Several

---

1. The previous year was held at Osaka during the Expo and the next year it was in Taiwan. The Horiuchis were able to travel to Taiwan with Tomo and Lorraine Abo.

RUSS AND AIKO: THE HORIUCHI STORY

attempts were made, all incorrectly, and the results were, in Annette's words, "messy." Annette acknowledges that cultural challenges come in all shapes and sizes and are often equally baffling to both sides. The first time she ever saw a western style toilet was when she was still a young girl visiting the house of a friend whose father was a foreign correspondent. Their family built a western style house, something quite unique at the time. Having no idea how to use it or even which way to sit, she made a polite excuse and went home to use her own restroom.

One thing Annette particularly enjoyed about the conference was staying in the Hilton Hotel, a real treat compared to the tiny Sapporo apartment. The fact that the food at the hotel restaurant was above par was a bonus as well. When she had time, Annette did a lot shopping. Everything was still inexpensive at the time. She bought several sweaters for herself and tablecloths for the mission home in Sapporo, even though it wouldn't be built for another year.

It was interesting to note that while the other presidents got together and "let their hair down" having a good time, the Tokyo president never joined them, instead spending most of his time schmoozing the general authorities. His son held a military office and the president wanted to get him promoted to some position or another in church leadership.

It was just as well he didn't associate with the other presidents. Over the course of the year, Russell had faced increasing difficulties with him. Something seemed a little off to Russell but he hadn't been able to put his finger on it. Speaking with Eddie Okazaki at the president's conference, Russell was able to compare notes and confirm his feelings. Okazaki shared that he and the Tokyo president often got into arguments over things. The Tokyo president felt that the other presidents should be running their missions his way. To no surprise, the other presidents, including Russell, didn't agree. Russell knew from experience that the man was willing to deny his missionaries many of their basic necessities while surrounding himself with the best furnishings. Once over a phone conversation the president got upset telling Russell that the mission was "not a classroom situation!"

Ignoring the actions of the former president, Russell simply went about tending to the needs of his missionaries. However when letters of complaint regarding incorrect billings began flooding his office, Russell had to intervene.

Local members and missionaries were being billed for copies of *The Book of Mormon* that were being sent by the box load from the distribution center in Tokyo. It was impossible to sell the quantity of books being sent. The Horiuchis remember visiting the Otaru Branch and seeing a large stack of them piled in the room. When they asked why there were so many books it was explained to them that the distribution center kept sending more regardless of whether the first books were sold or not. Some saints, such as Brother Samejima, paid out of their own pockets to appease Tokyo. Some elders admitted that they left books on trains or benches just to get rid of them. The unrealistic expectations served only to encourage, in the missionaries' words, "cheating and lying."

It was all part of the Tokyo president's ambition to make a name for himself by having "*Book of Mormons* piled higher than Mount Fuji." In fact, in one issue of the Church News they printed a picture of Mt. Fuji next to a stack of *Book of Mormons*. The president was very proud of the amount of *Book of Mormons* being sold but it was built upon the sacrifice of the missionaries and the local members, who sarcastically referred to the picture of piled books as "the Tokyo tower."

Upset, Russell got on the phone. "I really let them have it with both barrels." The excess books were returned and the distribution center was told not to send any more until they were requested.

Even more disturbing were letters Russell received from members regarding a proposed trip to the Salt Lake Temple that had fallen through. Members in several areas paid deposits that went unreturned and no one knew who to contact for refunds. It was the first Russell heard about it and, although he didn't realize it, the earliest real clue that something deviant was going on.

Russell and his counselors began attempting to track down the funds, talking to members, trying to follow the trail. Russell didn't believe anyone was pocketing the money but it was a large sum of money that needed to be accounted for and returned.

"That excursion was a little funny," shares Annette, "I heard that when [the Tokyo mission president] favored members then they came to Salt Lake free. I don't know how he did that. They had a *nihonjin* man handling it. Sounds like it should be a local function but the mission president still had his fingers in it."

In a letter to the First Presidency, Russell mentioned that something odd was going on with the handling of funds. Auditors were sent to investigate but they reported nothing unusual. The funds were being kept in a private account and didn't appear on any regular accounting documents.

For the next year and a half Russell and his counselors carefully amassed evidence, including records and letters from members. Some people refused to give their statements, afraid of either damaging themselves or the Tokyo president. Slowly Russell began to uncover who paid what and to whom. There were many who paid that never went and there were some that never paid who did. The further Russell and his counselors probed the more irregularities they found. The final stack of papers was a frightening confirmation of abuse, waste and negligence by the Tokyo mission president and several key members of the church in Japan.

Russell debated heavily whether or not to send the evidence to Salt Lake. He knew it would be hard on the Tokyo president and many of the members involved once the church learned what was going on. Annette counseled Russell to send everything in. The Tokyo president grasped ambitions to climb within the ranks of the church. If Russell didn't send it, she reasoned, how much more trouble would he cause the church before he was stopped?

The papers were organized in great part through the help of Elder Glenn Monson, serving as mission secretary at the time, and sent to Elder Ezra Taft Benson, who was in charge of Asia. Once the documents were out of his hands Russell said he felt like "a ton of weight lifted from my shoulders."

Shortly after the investigation a check for 750,000 Yen (roughly several thousand dollars) came to the mission office from the financial department in Tokyo. Russell made sure the money was returned to the proper members. The check might have been a last minute attempt to avert further investigation but it was too late.

A letter was sent back to Sapporo informing Russell that President Benson took the letter to President Harold B. Lee and auditors had once again been dispatched to Japan. Armed with new information the second audit was meticulous and in the end confirmed Russell's findings. The Tokyo president was abusing church funds for personal gains.

In a quiet moment, with great humanity, the prophet assured Russell that he had done the right thing. "It's in our hands now. I want you to sleep well," said President Lee, showing clear understanding of how stressful the whole undertaking must have been.

No one can say what the president's motives were but they were clearly not for the benefit of the church and its members. In most cases he would have been sent home early but, since only a few months of his tenure remained, he was allowed the dignity of finishing his call. Eventually he was brought before a church tribunal and suffered the consequences of his choices.

The Tokyo president's ambitions were not limited to the church. He planned to return to Japan after his mission and set himself up as a business mogul. If he was able to demonstrate a large pool of funds in the bank then it would be easier for him to obtain loans. Though never in his personal checking, the monies existed outside of regular church accounting and were being amassed for personal use.

Regarding audits, it was church policy for every mission to be reviewed each year. Accountants from Salt Lake set aside four days to go through the mission records in Sapporo. In two hours they finished all the inventory, supplies, books, and expenditures. "We are done and going back," the head auditor told Russ. "I wished others would keep such clean books." Not only were his books clean, Russell actually returned about one-third of his budget allocation to the general funds.

"Come again?" an astonished President Marion G. Romney asked during a mission presidents conference. Russell repeated that he was returning funds.

"Unbelievable. How did you do it?"

When he traveled, Russell continued to stay with missionaries in their apartments. If Annette went together, they lodged in a businessman hotel, which cost about one third of a regular hotel. For food, they avoided restaurants and instead bought *bento* boxes from department stores, another delicious yet cost effective solution. When they needed to go somewhere, they usually traveled by bus or taxi. When the time came to furnish the mission home the budget was limited. Although guidelines allowed it, the Horiuchis never had a gardener, cook or chauffer. They did hire a part-time housekeeper once the new mission home was finished, so that someone was there to answer the door when they were traveling on mission business. They could have hired a maid full time but neither of them saw the need.

In fact, of the over one hundred missions in the world, Russell's was one of the few to operate entirely in the black during his tenure. When it was mentioned that his next year's budget would be adjusted to fit his expenditures, meaning reduced, Russell requested that it be left where it was. That way he could continue to run the mission as he was but maintain some breathing room and not have to risk running over budget or need to ask for more the next year. His request was granted. Russell's philosophy was that he was handling the Lord's money, so he was extremely careful.

As a result both Russell and Annette claim the Lord has blessed them tenfold since their return from their mission in the form of friends, health and financial stability.

20

MISSION HOME SWEET HOME

While preaching the Gosspel [sic] of Jesus Christ is one of our most important assignments, we are nevertheless most concerned with the well-being and development of the individual missionary. We want our missionaries to be happy and healthy in their work, and we need the help of each of you in achieving that end.

— Excerpt from Christmas letter to parents from the Horiuchis.

1972 was a big year for Japan as it hosted the Winter Olympics. In a volume entitled *The Japan East Mission, the Horiuchi Jidai* written by missionaries commemorating the 25th anniversary of the mission, it speaks of the international event thus: "The winter of 1972 brought great excitement as the winter Olympics were held in Sapporo. English classes seemed to quickly grow in size as so many Japanese wanted to perfect their English skills in advance of the arrival of many foreigners to their country. Missionaries in Japan and especially in the Sapporo area found that the Olympics brought a great interest in foreigners and opened many doors to missionary service."

In a letter to Emerton Williams dated Christmas 1971, Russell wrote of the Olympics saying only "since I am not particularly interested in skiing or skating—all the preparation and ballyhoo does not excite me a bit. What does excite me is that after the Olympics we will have just a little over a year to go."

While the world cheered on its best and brightest athletes, for the Horiuchis the major event of 1972, their third and final year in Sapporo, was the completion of a new mission home.

Located near the west side of Maruyama Park, the building took nearly a year to complete. The property was the former site of a church owned chapel that burned down when Brother Nara was still young. Someone forgot to put out a fire or stove and the building was destroyed. The property remained vacant until the decision to locate the mission home there was made. Brother Hardy, who was a realtor for the Church and in charge of the buildings in Japan, came up occasionally from Tokyo to check on the progress of the construction.

The mission home was a large, square building with white walls. Annette never saw the new building until towards the end of her mission, when she was asked to help coordinate colors and decide what carpet to lay. To Annette it felt a lot like a hospital. When the Horiuchis first moved in there was nothing inside, not even drapes. Working in the kitchen one evening, Annette was startled to see people outside staring in through the windows. Curious to know what kind of building it was, they wandered in from the street to peek inside. After operating for two years from a small stark office in their apartment it was nice to have real rooms and office space for everything.

Furnishing an entire mission home from scratch was costly and took the better part of the year. There wasn't a specific budget for it but they did have a little extra money set aside that they could use. By approaching the task carefully, they were able to afford everything without going over budget.

The mission home needed drapes but it also needed the entrance paved. The front was only dirt and became very muddy when it rained. The Horiuchis both agreed that paving was necessary and decided to put the money into cement instead of drapes. For the curtains Annette asked around for seamstresses and was able to find two sisters, Sister Asaka and Sister Muroya. The sisters knew the best place to buy cloth. The mission paid for the materials but three women provided all the labor. The biggest challenge was they couldn't get the drapes to pleat properly. The answer to this dilemma came in the form of Elder Michael Dudley. It turned out he'd worked for a drapery store as a student and was able to show them how to properly tie the ends in order create the pleats.

Buying furniture proved challenging as well. The Horiuchis realized they couldn't simply purchase regular Japanese furniture. The American missionaries were large by Japanese standards and could quickly break most sofas or chairs by sitting in them. They needed sturdy, western style furniture, which was very expensive and much harder to find. Annette searched all the stores in the area but none of them sold what she was looking for.

The missionary quarters in Sapporo had a good sofa about the size of a love seat but the elders didn't know where it came from since it was there before any of them. And so the Horiuchis were left wondering how and where to get the furnishings they needed. The Horiuchis could have ordered everything through Brother Harding and the Church Building Committee in Tokyo, saving them a lot of hassle, but they weren't aware of this at the time.

Perhaps it was to renew her passport, Annette doesn't remember exactly but some business brought her to the *Kencho* prefecture offices. She noticed the furniture in the waiting room of the red brick building was very nice with good leather over a solid wooden frame. It fit the bill exactly. Upon inquiry with the secretary Annette was told the furnishings were made in Asahikawa, a town in the center of Hokkaido two to three hours away by train.

Annette asked if there were a store in Sapporo and was disappointed to learn there wasn't. However, the secretary continued, the company did have a storage facility in town. That was good enough for Annette. She got the salesman's name and contacted him as soon as she could.

The salesman told her they didn't have any furniture he could show her but they did have a catalog if she'd like to see it. The photos looked good but Annette was concerned about buying furniture solely from pictures. After debating and talking with the salesman she decided to go ahead and order. The furniture turned out nice enough that she ordered a dining table as well. It was slightly smaller than she hoped for since they would be entertaining guests, but it was the largest the company offered.

All of the furniture was purchased from Asahikawa except for the beds for the mission home's five rooms. In order to find the larger American sized beds the Horiuchis wound up going through Brother Harding in Tokyo. Brother Harding's office sent sheets that fit the larger beds but no blankets so Annette had to track those down. Some of the local stores sold American sized bedcovers but they cost about ten thousand Yen more apiece. They weren't much larger than regular Japanese bedspreads so Annette opted to purchase the Japanese ones instead. Even though they were slightly short the good woolen comforters fit the beds well. "At least they were decent looking," says Annette.

Another detail was finding dinnerware. *Settomonoya* was the only store in the area that carried anything but they didn't sell full sets, only individual dishes. Annette hunted through everything in the store until she managed to find enough similar white plates to make a full set to serve twelve, including salad bowls and an assortment of medium and large dishes. It took some effort but at 150 yen apiece, the price was right.

After more than two years in Japan, the Horiuchis finally got a real oven. It was smaller than American style ovens but it worked well enough.

Annette went to Mitsukoshi, the only department store in Sapporo at the time, in search of a pie pan. Not only did Mitsukoshi not carry them but the salespeople weren't even familiar with what one was. It wasn't until after the Winter Olympics came to Sapporo that western goods became more common.

Once when a nearby garden center held a plant sale, Russell was there at five in the morning to purchase everything he needed. Having arrived by bus, Russell realized he hadn't thought about how he was going to transport all the plants and trees home. Russell spoke with the owners who said they could deliver everything for him.

The yard wasn't big but Russell did all the landscaping around the office and in the center of the home himself. This was partly to save money but Russell honestly enjoyed the work as well. He found sweeping the sidewalk and shoveling the snow a welcome break from his deskwork. Neighbors who saw him assumed he was the gardener or custodian until some business brought one of them to the mission office. The neighbor was taken aback that the man presiding behind the desk was the same man he saw sweeping each morning.

With less than a year to live in the mission home, the Horiuchis knew they were basically furnishing it for the next president. With this in mind, they did their best to provide all of the necessities so the next president wouldn't have to worry about it and could focus on his missionaries. The one thing the Horiuchis didn't provide was any decoration or artwork. Annette shopped around but found the prices prohibitive, in the 120,000 Yen range. In the end they decided to leave decorating to the next mission president's wife. The Horiuchis visited Sapporo again seven years later and were surprised to find the walls were still bare. The furniture was still arranged essentially the same way and not much had been added. Looking back, Annette says, "[I guess] I didn't do that bad."

Following gracious Japanese tradition, Annette made sure she and Russell took small *omiyage* gifts to the three or four neighbors living around the mission home. Even though their stay was temporary, they felt it was important to introduce themselves. With a *yoroshiku onegaishimasu,* polite greeting, they took the opportunity to explain that the new building was a mission home and there would be young Americans coming in and out occasionally, apologizing if they ever made too much noise; "*Urusai kamo shiremasen keredomo.*"

Across the street was a small kindergarten. Next to that was an *ikebana* flower arrangement teachers studio. In reciprocation the *ikebana* teacher brought over a beautiful bouquet of flowers to the mission home.

The Horiuchis were approached by a car salesman when they were still living in the apartment building but had declined. They knew they needed a car eventually but parking in the city was expensive and they opted to travel by bus instead. After moving into the new home, they finally purchased a vehicle. The vehicle was mostly used by the APs and the Horiuchis continued to ride the bus or streetcar around the city most of the time.

When the car was needed, the assistants usually did the driving with the Horiuchis seated in back. Elder Figuerres tells the story of his companion, Elder Don Sessions, who purchased a pair of white gloves so he looked like a chauffer when he drove. Anyone who saw them drive by must have wondered who this Japanese couple was to have a Caucasian driver.

Most visits from general authorities happened early during the Horiuchis' mission but they continued to entertain visitors from Salt Lake on a regular basis even after moving into the new building. Today there are area presidencies and other callings that help handle the expansive elements of church business, but this was a time when the general authorities still handled such business themselves. The average visit was only a day or two, their schedules so filled with meetings and church business that they rarely found time to visit any of the local attractions, such as the ice festival, before moving on to other missions.

Conferences were especially busy. With both general authorities and local authorities visiting, it was common to have four or five people staying at the mission home. Annette prepared breakfast for everyone on top of preparing her own talks and getting ready for the meetings.

Despite the hectic schedule, the Horiuchis were blessed to be able to spend time with some amazing people, including Harold B. Lee, Ezra Taft Benson, Gordon B. Hinckley, Bruce R. McConkie, James A. Cullimore, Adney Komatsu, Boyd K. Packer and L. Tom Perry. By the end nine out of twelve apostles visited the Japan East Mission during the Horiuchis' tenure.

The Horiuchis, of course, met Ezra Taft Benson when they first came to Japan. Elder Benson was a staunch Republican and proponent of the John Birch Society. Politically, this brought him directly opposite to Russell's more moderate Democratic beliefs. Russell wasn't "a dues paying member" of any political party but leaned towards the Democratic Party, part of which stemmed from a negative reaction to being raised on a plantation where all the bosses were Republicans. The first presidential election Russell voted in was 1948 between Harry S. Truman and Thomas E. Dewey. Russell was a Truman man all the way.

At one testimony meeting, Russell mentioned how they had practically nothing when they first arrived in the mission. It was a very emotional gathering and Russell came to tears at one point. Elder Benson was very moved as well and called the Horiuchis after the meeting. "I'm going to stop by," he said, "I want to give you some candy." And he brought them some See's chocolates. It was a small but very kind gesture. "He liked us I guess," says Annette.

Despite political differences, Russell enjoyed talking with Elder Benson and summed up working with him thus, "Elder Benson has simply been very super. He gets things done. He will back you up fully, and we have gotten along very well, much better than my politics would normally permit. He is a good man to supervise a mission—and the support he gives you is all out."

The Horiuchis heard that Elder Packer was an avid birdwatcher. Russell learned he used binoculars when birdwatching so they bought him a pair of Nikon lenses. Still relatively inexpensive at the time, the lenses were good quality and Elder Packer was quite excited. Annette guesses, "I'll bet he's still using that."

Once, Annette went to deliver something to Elder Packer. She laughs of the memory of him answering the door wearing Japanese style pajamas. Her image of Elder Packer was such a conservative one that she didn't expect to see him wearing them.

According to Paul Hyer, after meeting Russell, Elder McConkie said, "That President Horiuchi is a different kind of mission president." It was a compliment of the highest praise.

Another visit indelibly etched in both Russell and Annette's memories was President Tanner. He came and told Russell: "You're extended."

"Just a minute!" Russell protested, "I was called for three years."

President Tanner looked at him and said, "You're extended. Period."

That was the end of the discussion. He didn't mention how long the Horiuchis were extended for. It turned out to be only three and a half months, until a new rotation schedule could be implemented.

One of the final visitors the Horiuchis hosted before returning home was Elder Spencer W. Kimball. Russell says he felt close to the apostle because Elder Kimball was always so straightforward with him.

Elder and Sister Kimball stayed in the visitors quarters in the new mission home, the largest of the five upstairs bedrooms. Elder Kimball arrived dressed in an old coat, very similar to the heavy military coat Russell wore. Like most buildings in Japan, the mission home was quite vertical with about eight steps going up to the entry way, then another eight steps up from there. Russell offered to carry Elder Kimball's briefcase but the modest man said he could manage.

Russell bought salmon at the wholesale fish market for dinner. Before slicing the fish Russell cried, "Wait!" He rushed into his room and emerged with his fishing pole in hand and wearing boots. He put the salmon in the snow on the ground and posed for a picture, as if he had caught them himself.

Regarding Russell's reputation as a fisherman, which followed him into the field, Elder John Edmunds shares: We always knew how to get on the other side of [President Horiuchi]. If we ever mentioned what were his plans about fishing, he'd get extremely anxious to get home." Russell never went fishing during his mission, though he did peek into the fishing supply stores a few times and purchased a rod for future use. To the amusement of the elders he was prone to wander around the mission office practicing his casting.

The Horiuchis served the salmon with mashed potatoes, vegetables and pie. Sister Kimball marveled that the same meal at home in the Hotel Utah would be very expensive. This was the last formal dinner the Horiuchis held before returning home.

When the mission home was built Annette asked a local seamstress to sew extra large *yukatas*, informal kimonos, for visitors to relax in. *Yukata* are usually made from roughly one *ittan* of cloth for the average Japanese. These were made from about one and half *ittan* to accommodate the taller Americans.

A meeting with the members was scheduled for that night but there was enough time that Annette suggested the Kimballs should rest before hand. When time for the meetings drew close it was quiet upstairs. Annette wasn't sure whether she should wake the Kimballs or not. Finally she went and knocked on the door. Elder Kimball came out wearing the *yukata*. He was not a very tall man, and the tail of the one and a half *ittan* robe dragged behind him. It reminded Annette of a woman's ceremonial *kimono* with a long tail flowing on the ground behind it. Annette though he looked "so cute." He thanked her for letting them know it was time.

RUSS AND AIKO: THE HORIUCHI STORY

The next morning other regional authorities came in for the meetings. Russell invited the various district presidents as well. The branch president from Sendai brought a gift of strawberries. Sapporo was still too cold for them to grow so they were a real treat. Annette and Sister Kimball, who asked if she could help, served them up with cream. For breakfast they served oatmeal and eggs with a slice of ham, which was also hard to find as well. The only place Annette knew that sold ham was the Mitsukoshi department store. Elder Kimball was amazed by the breakfast as well. He admitted he and Sister Kimball usually alternated what they ate for breakfast, one morning would be cereal the next would be something such as ham and eggs. Elder Kimball ate one bowl of strawberries then humbly asked, "Sister, may I have some more strawberries?" He really enjoyed them and ended up eating all the rest.

Russell and Elder Kimball spent some time chatting with each other before the meetings started. In his down to earth manner, Elder Kimball spoke of his childhood in Arizona and about the work and dealing with people. Elder Kimball also opened his shirt and showed Russell his surgery scar. Of the future prophet Russell says, "I got the feeling that he didn't want to take advantage of anybody. He played it straight."

Again letting the missionaries handle themselves Russell didn't bother them about cutting their hair. Some wore theirs longer than uniform, something which Annette worried about but Russell said not to worry about it. On the day of the meeting Annette noticed one elder who usually wore his hair longer had trimmed it short. "You cut your hair," she observed.

"Yes, I didn't want to get President Horiuchi in trouble," was his reply.

Still Elder Kimball couldn't help notice that many of the haircuts were longer than regulation. "President," he mentioned, "Some of your missionaries have longer hair than usual." Russell explained that it was snow country and if they were to cut it short it was cold and he didn't want them to catch a cold. Also there was an American military base near the airport in Chitose and Russell didn't want the Japanese girls to mix up the missionaries with the servicemen who wore their hair cropped high and tight. Elder Kimball shrugged, saying he guessed he was old fashioned, preferring whitewall haircuts, then didn't mention it again.

The Kimball's visit was in March, about three months before the Horiuchis were to return home, and it was still winter in Hokkaido. Russell drove the Kimballs to the airport himself, which was a rarity. Usually the church members gathered to send the general authorities off but Russell discouraged them this time because of the heavy snow, so only Russell and Annette were at the airport to send the Kimballs on their way.

The Horiuchis received and kept many letters of thanks from their distinguished visitors. Russell says he was too busy being concerned about missionaries and doesn't remember all the letters, but Annette kept the letters dutifully filed and cared for.

Here are a few excerpts:

Never have I met missionaries more enthused [sic] nor work better organized and going forward with the result apparent in organization, leadership training, and in the increase of real converts as contrasted with mere baptismal records.

— Harold B. Lee, April 26, 1971

I am so grateful. In fact, my feelings are a bit tender as I contemplate your love and support . . .

— Ezra Taft Benson, May 7, 1971

I want to express my sincere appreciation for the wonderful hospitality you showed me while I was there. You were so very kind in so many ways, I do not know how I'll ever repay you.

— Boyd K. Packer, April 21, 1972

> "We were pleased with your missionaries and felt that there was a sweet bond of understanding and affection between you.
>
> — Spencer W. Kimball, March 27, 1973
>
> We are pleased to inform you that the First Presidency has directed that tickets be made available to you to attend the sessions of the first General Conference following your release from your mission.
>
> — John H. Vandenberg, September 18, 1973

Even more challenging than the mission home but infinitely more rewarding was the Horiuchis' continuing work with the missionaries. Each new set of missionaries brought new challenges and the Horiuchis had to listen closely to the spirit.

"You are led by the Spirit all the time," tells Russell, "You just don't realize it. The thing is this: you did not worry about you[rself], you worried about the missionaries."

Like most missions, the Horiuchis had a photograph of every missionary with their name on it pinned to a board in the office. The pictures came in before the missionaries arrived and the Horiuchis did their best to memorize everyone so they could greet them by name when they landed.

It was a long journey for the new missionaries. They were often delayed in Tokyo by the northern weather and the "greenies" would arrive in Hokkaido very late, sometimes even at midnight. Knowing they were tired from their travels, the Horiuchis fed them a simple meal, often bread and jam with a drink and then put them to sleep right away.

This is why Annette remembers meeting one missionary, Elder John Edmunds, because he couldn't eat bread because it contained eggs. At first Annette thought he was joking, she had never seen anyone who couldn't eat bread. But he was sincere. As a young boy Elder Edmunds had swallowed gasoline and his father, a doctor, made him drink a dozen eggs. The action saved his life but he developed a severe allergy to them. Annette was able to find something for him to eat that didn't contain eggs.

For his part Elder Edmunds remembers meeting the Horiuchis, particularly the *Buch*, for the first time as well. His group arrived in-country mid-December, having been told very little about their president. What they did know was the rather intimidating detail that he had worked as a military interrogator during the war.

One by one the missionaries were brought into a small, cold office to be interviewed. Elder Edmunds remembers President Horiuchi sitting behind a battered desk with single, stark light hanging above it. His expression was severe. In his hands was a file with Elder Edmunds name and photo on the outside. It was precisely how he imagined a real interrogation would look. Elder Edmunds admits he was "scared to death."

Without looking up, the president told him to take a seat across the desk. Then, and only then, did the president bother to peer over the top of the file. His face stern, his voice gruff he spoke, "Well, Edmunds *Choro*, I see here you are a troublemaker. Are we going to have problems with you?"

The now terrified green bean could barely reply, "Well, sir. I will try very hard to behave."

The grim face of the president remained unmoved. Then, when Elder Edmunds figured all was lost, the *Buch* put down the file and with a big smile said, "Well, Edmunds *Choro* I'm a troublemaker too. So you should do just fine in this mission."

Elder Dean Johns remembers the first time he sat down with the *Buch* as well. President Horiuchi "leaned forward in [his] chair and asked, "Elder Johns, are you dumb enough to believe that a 14 year old boy saw God and Jesus Christ?" I remember saying, "Yes, I guess I am." [His] reply was, "So am I Elder Johns, So am I." After hearing that reply from [him], I knew that we were going to have a good working relationship."

Another missionary, Elder Lee Groberg, after only two months in Japan, developed acute appendicitis while he was in Hachinohe, a small town in Aomori Prefecture. It was critical enough that by the time his companion called the office in Sapporo, Groberg *Choro* was already on the operating table.

With no departing flights remaining out of Sapporo, an upset Russell was forced to wait until the following morning to leave. Mercifully, he found Elder Groberg in good condition and recuperating well. The Horiuchis were alarmed to learn that the surgery was performed right in the office of the small town doctor, who neglected to close the windows or even wear gloves. Groberg Choro's companion was allowed in the room and took pictures during the surgery. They even failed to administer enough anesthetic. When Elder Groberg said, "Ouch" the doctor told him, "Shut up."

Naturally upset to hear the news, Elder Groberg's sister wrote "a bit of a scathing letter," chastising the Horiuchis for not taking her brother to a bigger, more sanitary hospital. But there was nothing they could have done. "We are so grateful we can look back and laugh at this story and that he survived. And no after effects," says Annette. For his part Elder Groberg states that he was "touched . . . to see President Horiuchi walk into my hospital room . . . that act alone spoke volumes about his role as a mission president."

I was in the first group of greenies to arrive in the new Japan East Mission, May, 1970. I really didn't know what to think about the Horiuchis other than I thought President Horiuchi had a very brief but thorough way of interviewing. He didn't say much, but I guess he didn't have to. I remember he was very down to earth. He went shopping with us greenies to buy a shoulder bag for *dendo*-ing [proselyting]. He showed us how to use the *benjo* [squatter toilet]. (not literally, but he showed us the porcelain and explained how to crouch).

Sister Horiuchi was the perfect mission mother. Very warm, very lovely, and very friendly. Aside from my own mother, she was the perfect role model for a wife and mother.

I loved them both then and I love them both now. My mission experience and the relationship with a loving and personable young couple was life changing. The memories are as indelible today as they were the day they were made.

Thank you both for your great service and the fabulous role models you have been then and still today.

— Elder Lee Groberg

Shortly after moving into the new home, Russell woke up with pain in his back severe enough that it sent him to the ground while he was changing his clothes. Sitting on the floor, he told Annette to have the elders give him a blessing. Annette called for Elder Ronald Gabrielson (who usually went by the name Joe), and Elder Grant Walker to come. And then they waited. Annette hoped they would hurry because Russell was in so much pain but the elders were very slow in arriving. Finally the elders appeared, administered the blessing then disappeared back to the office.

It was about eight in the morning. Other missionaries gathered in the office asking how the *Buch* was doing. From hearing how bad it looked they were all surprised when Russell appeared in the office a few minutes later dressed and ready to work.

Annette found out later why the missionaries took so long. They admitted they were so scared to give a blessing to the president that they stopped to pray as hard as they could. Annette smiles fondly as she recalled the sweet sincerity of the young men. Russell has never experienced any back pain problems since.

Once, on a flight returning from Akita to Sapporo, they ran across some extremely rough weather crossing over the Sugaru Straight "It was so scary," Annette remembered. The mountains were visible right below the plane, which was being tossed about on the wind, almost flipping completely on its side at one point. Everybody inside screamed. Russell said for them not to worry, that he'd been promised by President Tanner that he would be "protected from any danger in the mission" so they would be all right. Ultimately, the plane arrived safely at its destination but it was a frightening experience they never forgot.

It was around this time that the Horiuchis had a profound experience when one elder, struggling with his faith, ran away from his companion. Concern grew as the young man went missing for several days. There was some fear of him leaving the country but Russell knew his passport was in the office safe and that eventually the young man would come seeking it.

When the missionary turned up at the mission home ten days later he was accompanied by a minister, an Englishman from a local evangelical church. The three of them met in Russell's office. Russell asked the minister not to bother his missionaries to which the minister rebutted that the young man had come to him.

The conversation evolved into a discussion about Christ. Russell maintained a calm demeanor but was "screaming in his heart" because the minister was trained and very fluent with his knowledge of the Bible. Russell's only thought was, "I have to save this missionary." Reaching out to the Lord he pleaded, "You put me in this position, I need your help!"

The minister mentioned that Christ was crucified and resurrected. "On this," he said, "the Bible is clear and effervescent." For some reason the word "effervescent" reminded Russell of when he was a professor conducting oral exams for master's candidates. He suddenly found himself on ground he knew well.

Russell asked the minister where Christ was during the three days between his crucifixion and resurrection.

The minister said, "Oh, he went to heaven."

Russell said, "Okay, then you testify that Christ is alive and with Father in Heaven."

The minister replied that that was what he'd been saying the whole time.

"So tell me that," challenged Russell, "Bear your testimony."

The minister protested again that he'd been saying that very thing the whole time. Again Russell challenged him to bear his testimony of Christ and Heavenly Father and again the minister faltered.

"I can bear testimony," said Russell and he did, again challenging the minister, "Now you say it exactly like I said it."

The minister started shaking and couldn't say anything. Then he started crying.

Suddenly the runaway missionary came to life, "President! President! I can bear testimony! Let me bear testimony." And he bore his testimony.

There was nothing else to be said. The minister left and the missionary asked Russell if he could stay. The Horiuchis had already received two or three letters from Salt Lake instructing them to send the missionary home. Russell was troubled. He really wanted to assist the boy. In the meantime, they received a phone call from the elder's father begging Russell to aid his son. Russell didn't want to go against Salt Lake's orders but staked everything on his instinct to keep the young man in the field.

A month or so later, the Horiuchis found themselves in Hong Kong at the mission president's seminar presided over by Lawrence E. Dunn. The presidents were each assigned a theme. Russell was assigned "save the troubled missionaries." After Russell finished speaking, President Dunn approached him and commended him for doing the right thing saying, "You saved the missionary." That was a huge relief to Russell who worried if he'd made the right decision by going against the letters from Salt Lake.

Very few have any idea how scared Russell was at the time and how relieved he was that everything turned out well in the end.

The elder not only fulfilled an honorable mission, he remained active after, eventually marrying in the temple.

Nearly forty years later, before Christmas of 2010, the Horiuchis answered their doorbell to find this elder and his wife and children caroling on their porch. Seeing the family singing, Annette was struck once again by how many generations are influenced by the actions of a single person.

This elder's companion recalls the experience:

I remember clearly an experience with Pres. Horiuchi helping my companion stay true to his mission and priesthood covenants during a time in Sapporo as we were tested by a minister of another faith who challenged our beliefs. My companion was convinced of the truthfulness of the gospel when Pres. Horiuchi bore fervent and powerful testimony of the reality of our Savior, Jesus Christ and His role in the gospel as restored by the prophet Joseph. I have reflected on this experience in a far-off land on many occasions, and will always appreciate the wisdom and guidance of an inspired mission president.

—Elder Michael Raymond

President, I vividly remember the day when you convinced me to stay on my mission. That one single event has meant more to me over the years than you can imagine. I am grateful for a Mission President who never gave up and had faith in me. I have been able to draw from that experience many times in my life. It has strengthen[ed] me in so many ways and I know, had I returned home, I would not be where I am now. So Thanks again for your leadership, love, confidence and faith that you had in myself and all of the other Sisters and Elders you served with.

—excerpt from personal letter dated March 10, 1996

Thankfully, not every experience was a harrowing one. There were plenty of good times with missionaries as well.

A particularly fond memory was "entertainment day." Once or twice a year at mission conferences the program consisted of funny skits the missionaries put together. They played crazy games and generally "let loose" providing a good outlet for everyone.

One of the main events each year in Hokkaido is the Sapporo *Yuki Matsuri,* the snow festival. Since its beginnings in the nineteen-fifties, the festival has grown into a major cultural celebration. Featuring intricate and skilled ice carvings from small to massive, the festival attracts millions of visitors from all over the globe. There is food and activities for the entire family, including snow slides, snow "rafting" and even concerts and other attractions.

With the Horiuchis' blessing, the missionaries not only attended the festival but got to participate as well, working with members from the Sapporo branches to design and create their own ice sculptures. One year they did a large carving of Snoopy and the next they made a 12' tall sculpture of a family of bears riding a bobsled, showing family unity. They passed out flyers and put up a sign that read "Foreigners made this" and even had a chance to appear on TV, radio and in the newspaper, helping to strengthen the positive image of the church in the area. In 1971, the missionaries were one of seven groups to receive special awards for participation in the festival. The activity was enjoyed by the missionaries and was a positive experience for everyone involved.

Annette laughs at the memory of Elder Roger Brown who rigged his alarm clock to automatically uncover his *futon* blanket in the morning leaving him no choice but to get up.

Many missionaries will always remember (and be glad for) the *Buch*'s advice to them as they prepared to leave for home. Knowing they would be looking for suitable marriage partners he advised them, "You have been in a desert a long time. When you see a mud puddle you might think it is an oasis. Make sure you find a real oasis."

The advice stuck so well that for years after returning home, missionaries often introduced their spouses to the Horiuchis excitedly reporting that they had found their oasis.

"As a mission president," concludes Elder Figuerres, "he constantly counseled us on missionary work but additionally about educational attainment, establishing a career, and marrying well. Succeeding as a missionary was not enough. He wanted us to succeed scholastically, in our future careers, and especially in our marriages and family life."

> Elder Hanvey will never forget one time the *Buch* passed him in the hall.
>
> "Hanvey Choro," asked President Horiuchi, "what are you doing?"
>
> "Nothing, President."
>
> Anyone who knows Russell can't help but imagine the mischievous twinkle in his eye as he replied, "You're not having a very good time here then, are you?"

In true Horiuchi style, when the time came for them to return home Russell didn't want any kind of big farewell. They didn't mention when they were departing and considered a district conference, held a few weeks prior, as their farewell. The missionaries knew they were leaving but the general membership did not. Part of the reason for this was that the Horiuchis knew many of them would feel obligated to come if they knew. When word leaked out anyhow, the Horiuchis told the members not to bring gifts, as was Japanese tradition, but if they felt the need to bring something they should bring pictures instead. The stack of photos they ended up with still resides in their albums to this day.

There wasn't any fanfare from the official Church side either. The Horiuchis were simply notified that their replacement was coming. President Kotaro Koizumi and his wife Grace, the Horiuchis' replacement, arrived on the first of July 1973. Russell and Annette moved out of the main room and stayed the night in the guest room. The next morning Russell went to the office early, then, after conferring less than an hour with President Koizumi, Russell's assistants drove the Horiuchis to the airport. Elder Edmunds remembers the last thing Russell did before walking out of the office was put on his fishing hat.

The Japanese office secretary sneaked along for the ride as well. Annette thought it was so cute that she didn't want to upset the president but came along anyways to see them off.

A fitting summary of the Horiuchis' tenure in the Japan East Mission can be found in an excerpt from a young editor of the mission newsletter during the last year of their mission:

"The Japan East [M]ission started its infant status in March of 1970 with a new mission president and a set of problems all its own. In the 2.5 years of operation the Japan East Mission has or is being functioned by roughly 140 missionaries. Since its beginning, about 870 people have entered the waters of baptism and many have gained the oppurpunity [sic] of receiving the priesthood.

"The Mission has seen its expanding regions. From the basic 7 branches and 9 prosyliting [sic] areas. New chpels [sic] and sparkled Sendai and Otaru, with luxurious Hakodate, Morioka, etc., have passed the growing pain days and changed areas. Akita and Ishinomaki are looking in the near future for their expansion.

"The climate in our region, adds another enhancing factor. The weather may range from the Iwamizawa blizzard the Asahikawa-Kitama cold, to the sultry bathe of the Koriyama-Sendai sun. Many various city lay-outs can be observed, in that Sapporo supports a population of over 1,000,000 whereas Iwamizawa can be found the scant population of about 80,000.

"As the varying degrees of climates and people have been shown, the "featured product" of our individual areas also lend variable content. Akita can be known for its "bijin" (beauty, more specifically beautiful women) while Tomakomai has its Oji [a famous paper company]. Hachinohe and Ishinomaki have been known for its peculiar smells, where Otaru has the "parfait" [strawberry]. And you can't forget the Fukushima "triffid" [young girls], or the ever famous Yamagata "byoin" [abandoned hospitals].

"Yes, with the contrasting nature and the individual character 23 cities are molded into the "The Japan East Mission" where their best can't match our rest."

Once asked what it was like serving as a mission president Russell responded that it was like supervising scout camp for three years. In a letter to Emerton Williams Russell wrote of being a mission president "I am expected to be a realtor, a business agent, banker, father, confessor and such all at once. It is of little wonder that I often find myself fondly looking at the more tranquil life with a fishing rod in my hand with a nice trout on the other end of the line." In the same letter Russell adds "I find my greatest satisfaction in dealing directly with the missionaries themselves."

Looking back years later Russell reflects, "Come to think about it, the mission experience wasn't that bad. I didn't do too badly." If the reactions of the missionaries who served with the Horiuchis are any indication then Russ and Annette did very well indeed.

Russell expounds on the experience: "When you start looking at it, I know for a fact that I survived in the mission field because of the quality of the missionaries that they sent me. That's the thing that kept me going. I wanted to quit and come home. But the missionaries were really good. When I came home from the mission I didn't think 'Oh, it was a wonderful experience!' I never said a wonderful experience. I was glad I went. But I'm home now."

Home they were, and mighty happy of it.[1]

> Interviewer: It seems that when you first went you were kind of overwhelmed.
>
> Russell: Not overwhelmed. Devastated.
>
> Interviewer: Why Devastated?
>
> Russell: I never had any experience in the mission field. Never been on a mission. I just didn't know anything.

---

1. One of Dad's (Stephen Williams) favorite Russell quotes regarding missions is, "It's not the best two years of your life but two of the hardest."

Interviewer: Did you ever get to the point where you felt comfortable?

Russell shakes his head no.

Russell: I was so glad to come home.

Interviewer: Did you ever get to the point where you felt that you could survive this?

Russell: No, I was always riding by the seat of my pants.

21

FROM PRESIDENT TO PROFESSOR

From Hokkaido, the Horiuchis traveled to Tokyo to visit Annette's family for a few days before continuing south to Kyushu, Russell's ancestral home. There they visited his extended family including his cousin Mitsuya in Kumamoto. Afterwards, they returned to Tokyo for a few days more with Annette's family before heading back to the states.

On their return trip to Utah, the couple stopped in Hawaii, staying with Misao in Honolulu before Russell's mother called anxiously asking when they were coming to Lahaina. Russell told her they would go the very next day.

When Russell and Annette opened the door to the homestead, they saw a young couple sitting on the couch. Annette said her first thought was, "Oh, she looks just like Ellen!" It took her a second to realize it *was* Ellen. Ellen wanted to come to Japan to pick them up but Annette said it cost too much and not to worry since they were coming home shortly anyways. So Ellen decided to surprise them in Hawaii instead with their new grandson, Scott, who was three months old. Annette and Ellen both yelled with excitement, startling the (*ahem* dashingly handsome) baby, who started crying.

Annette wanted to be there when the baby was born but didn't think she was allowed to go. Even if she received permission she and Russell didn't have money to spare for a ticket. Ellen re-assured Annette that they had taken pre-natal classes and that the Relief Society was able to help out as well.

The whole family flew back to Utah together. Ellen put the baby under the seat in front of her where he slept the entire way home. He was so quiet that on arrival one of the stewardesses was astonished, "Oh! I didn't know you had a baby there!"

Russell and Annette were excited to come home. Tears streamed down Annette's face as they flew over the familiar mountains of the Wasatch front.

Ellen and Michael moved into the house at 1167 South Main for about a month, to do some cleaning. Michael fixed a gate that had broken and planted petunias, which were blossoming. The home seemed more beautiful to Annette than when they left it. Ellen and Michael moved into the nearby brown house, as Ellen calls it.

Shortly after returning to Utah, the Horiuchis met with President Tanner and Elders Bruce R. McConkie and Hartman Rector at the church offices to report their mission before being officially released. Annette remembers Elder Thomas S. Monson, then still a junior authority, walking by while they were sitting in the waiting room. Elder Monson, with exemplary aplomb and graciousness, made it a point to stop and thank them for their service.

Russell recounts meeting with the First Presidency: "They said, "Well, what did you think of your mission? Don't you think it was one of the most happy times of your lives?" I said, "Perhaps," I told President Tanner, "but we are glad to be home. And [Elder Bruce R.] McConkie was doing this [covering his mouth to hide a laugh]. But it was rough, and thanks to her [Annette] we made it."

The first challenge the Horiuchis faced was unpacking everything. When she first opened the boxes Annette was taken aback by how hasty their packing had truly been. Half sewn clothes, pins still set in the cloth, lay piled on top of dishes haphazardly tossed into the boxes. There was no organization of any kind. It took them several months to get settled in again.

Beatrice and Max Pyne threw a neighborhood welcome home party. It was a wonderful event and Russell and Annette enjoyed seeing their friends and neighbors again, including the Rohbocks and Allreds, but Annette remembers feeling a bit out of place. On the mission, she and Russell had been so focused on spiritual things that the conversations at the party about day-to-day concerns felt somehow immaterial.

After three years of neglect, the yard was in need of weeding and pruning. Russell spent a lot of time every day fighting the entropy that had overtaken his yard, so much so that he wound up injuring his elbow.

One of the Horiuchis' main concerns before leaving for Japan was how their finances would be when they returned. By being careful with their money and with the help of the small allowance from the church they were able to retain a small reserve for when they came home. This was providential, as they had no income until school resumed.

From an income point of view, the fact that it was only a month until school began was a blessing. From a teaching point of view, however, one month was a direly short time to get ready for classes after so long an absence. Annette had a small window to unpack and settle in but Russell hit the ground running, hurriedly preparing lessons and coursework.

Despite being assigned a heavy teaching load, Russell was glad to be home and found that there were many similarities between the mission home and the classroom. Russell was dealing with young people, something he really enjoyed. A double pleasure was when his missionaries, returning home, enrolled in his classes.

For Russell, the biggest challenge lay in his yet unfinished doctoral work. The short time to prepare for his classes left him with no time to begin writing until halfway through the year. It took nearly another year and a half but in 1975, Russell finished his writing and prepared to defend his dissertation entitled "Chiseigaku: Japanese Geopolitics."

His writings were based on the relatively new concept of how geography influences politics. At the time there was not much written in English, most studies done were in Japanese and German. Russell, with Annette assisting, did a lot of original translation for his thesis.

When Russell flew to Washington Professor Kakiuchi personally came and picked him up from the airport. They found the professor's attitude very different than before. It was unclear how leaving on a mission with his doctorate work unfinished would be received by the faculty. Now, however, Dr. Kakiuchi was cordial and clearly supportive of the candidate. Russell's tenacity and anomolous choice earned a great deal of curiosity and respect among his collegiate peers. Russell passed with flying colors officially earning his PhD in Political Geography.

Years later, after Professor Kakiuchi retired, he and his wife drove to BYU to visit with the Horiuchis and to see for himself why one of his star pupils was willing to risk his doctoral work to serve the church.

Meanwhile Annette spent time finishing her thesis as well. Her paper discussed the art and design of the Ainu, the aboriginal people of Hokkaido who were particularly noted for their woodcarving, focusing on the bold designs conveyed in their family crests. She completed her work in 1976, graduating with a Masters in Art emphasizing watercolor. Annette, a curious and devoted student, would have gone on to complete a PhD herself but Russell said "enough." Still, degree or not, studying a vast array of topics and interests is something Annette has continued, almost daily, her whole life.

Annette resumed teaching Japanese language courses and began teaching Japanese calligraphy classes as well. Calligraphy was something she had always enjoyed, taking calligraphy lessons while still in high school as an optional portion of the curriculum. Her teacher was Toyota Sensei, who counted members of noble families among his students. At one time, while teaching at BYU,

Annette returned to Japan for a month to polish up her skills with Matsumoto Sensei, another instructor of note. Even after she and Russell retired, Annette continued to train, this time through a correspondence course over several years with a Zen priest in Los Angeles.

When the *Ensign* magazine ran an article on Japan, Annette was asked to do some calligraphy for it, which she happily produced. Her work was published, and the four beautifully rendered characters prominently appeared—to her initial horror and later amusement—upside down.

Back in full swing, Russell's teaching continued to garner the attention of students and fellow faculty alike. In 1986, he was recognized with the Karl G. Maeser Award for Teaching, the highest teaching honor at the university. Named after the founder and first president of the Brigham Young Academy, the recipients for the not quite yearly awards are chosen by the faculty itself, honoring the most outstanding teachers among them. In a manner that surely matched the way Russell would have preferred, the award was given without much fanfare. He was simply notified one day that he had received it. As of this writing his picture still hangs in the Harold B. Lee Library. Many years later Russell's grandson was attending a study group at BYU and was surprised (and proud!) to look up and see his grandfather's name and picture on the wall.

Russell was also honored with professor of the month. Russell must have known about it, but such honors, while appreciated, weren't high on his priorities and he never mentioned anything, even to Annette. She knew nothing about it until Brother Seiji Katanuma, who was now teaching in the Japanese department as well, chanced to see it one day and told her about it. In 2001, Russell received the Alumni distinguished service award.

When the time came to appoint a new department chairman Russell was picked by Martin Hickman, the dean of the college.

Applying the skills developed over the years handling money and keeping his operations lean, Russell balanced his budget every year of his tenure, like he'd done with his mission in Japan.

He also evened out the course loads for the faculty members, scheduling classes as uniformly as he could. From experience Russell scheduled which classes needed bigger classrooms and so on. Russell kept a heavy load himself so he didn't overburden his faculty. He taught some of the biggest classes, some with over 90 students. As his reputation as a teacher grew, faculty in other departments often encouraged their students to attend Russell's classes.

There were several times when Russell went to bat for other teachers, in some instances saving their jobs. One professor received a letter while he was on sabbatical saying that he needn't bother returning to BYU. Russell went to Robert Thomas, the vice president of the university and said that if this professor wasn't rehired then Russell's resignation would be on the vice-president's desk in the morning, further explaining that it was illegal to fire a professor in such a manner. He added that there would be newspaper reporters with him. Long story short, the professor enjoyed a distinguished career at BYU.

Russell became well acquainted with the Political Science department, in many instances feeling closer to that department than his own. Through this connection he began teaching political geography classes in addition to his regular geography courses.

The Horiuchis' church service continued as well. Not long after coming home Russell was called as second counselor to Bishop Melvin Petersen, working with Reed Payne as first counselor. The three men got along extremely well. A religion professor at the university, Bishop Petersen was known for his kindness and his humility. Many years later Mel, as his friends called him, and his wife Jeneal were called as Russ and Annette's home teachers and the two couples enjoyed visiting for hours on end.

Next, Russell was called to serve as a branch president in the Missionary Training Center for young missionaries going to Japan. Later, he served as branch president for senior couples getting ready to serve on missions. Russell claims there was little work in the couples branches since these were mature, dedicated adults. Annette tells a slightly different version of the story, saying that sometimes Russell was at the MTC every evening. She recalls one couple going to a Spanish speaking mission. The husband was a PhD but his wife, who had no advanced education, learned the language more quickly than her husband, which upset him. They would fight over it, and Russell had to go calm them down. Annette says she never thought senior missionaries behaved like that.

Jeffery R. Holland's mother-in-law was in the branch at one point. Elder Holland was president of BYU at the time and Russell asked if she visited her son and his family since they were so close. "No," she replied, "I'm a missionary, I can't." Russell told her of course she could and that it would do a world of good for her to go visit and be an example to her grandchildren.

Russell's next calling was as Bishop to the Asian Ward, a multi-ethnic ward consisting mostly of Japanese, Koreans, Chinese and Polynesians attending BYU.

In a letter to Emerton Williams, Russell wrote, "I had an assignment at the Missionary Training Center for a little more than 3 years as a Branch President and got released. A few weeks later I was asked to be a Bishop on campus. I refused–indicating that I needed to get re-acquainted with people in my home ward. I thought it was the end of it. Then a General Authority friend gave me the needle and they were back—so I am now Bishop of the Asian Ward on campus. I don't know why I deserve all the blessings. My suggestion that others should share in the blessing went unheeded. Well, such is life."

Russell chose counselors much like he'd chosen APs on his mission, observing how people interacted and with whom, calling Alan McCarter as first counselor and Larry Lew as second. Glenn

Monson, who had served in the mission office as a missionary in Hokkaido, was called as clerk. While serving in the ward, Glenn met, baptized and married Naoko Dan from Fukuoka Japan. It was Russell who married them, performing the ceremony in Japanese. Russell and Annette also served as witnesses for their temple sealing a year later.

As always, Russell's approach was to involve everyone and keep things as balanced as possible, not focusing on any one group but developing leadership among all the different nationalities. He felt it was good for the different ethnicities to serve one another.

When Russell was called, Annette was asked to give a talk in church. She was studying Chinese at the time (she enjoyed it so much that she took the same class three different times to polish her skills) and, in the spirit of a multi-ethnic audience, she gave part of her talk in Chinese. She did well enough that some of the Chinese members debated whether she was Chinese or not. Later, Annette came across a group of Chinese girls including one from the Asian ward who teased, "Watch out! She can understand everything you say!"

The branch started with 60 students attending. It was church policy at the time that budgets for every ward came solely from its own members. At the beginning of the year each member was to contribute five dollars but not everyone paid so the reserve was quite low. Despite having almost no budget (nothing new for the Horiuchis) they began holding monthly activities, which Russell described as "activities through the stomach."

After church, the sisters made sandwiches and everyone gathered to eat and socialize. Ward members watched for sales and stocked up, allowing the ward to feed everyone inexpensively. It was a hit and word spread quickly. The simple sandwiches soon evolved into full-blown ward dinners. Everyone pitched in to help prepare the meals, even the children. Annette remembers them making *gyoza* potstickers. There was flour everywhere, all over the table and especially all over the children. Ward members attended the meals for free since they paid the annual budget. Guests paid one dollar each. For Thanksgiving they were able to serve turkey (eleven of them!) and ham, a great treat for struggling students. Within a years' time the ward blossomed to 350 members with an operating budget of $3,000.

Russell says it went beyond church work. As part of developing the ward community, he also spent time helping students with classes, their writing and composition and other academic matters.

According to Annette, one of the highlights of Russell's time as bishop was how well the members bonded with each other. Laughter was a constant soundtrack after church when, instead of going home, everyone stayed and socialized until the Horiuchis had to kick them out to close the building. Even though they were from so many different nationalities, everyone got along well. Most of these students returned to their native countries after graduating, where they remain active in the church, many of them serving in leadership positions of their own.

Erin Kwong[1] shared that Russell was never one for titles and didn't like to be called Horiuchi *Sensei* or Horiuchi *Dendobucho* but bishop was okay and so was Horiuchi *Ojichan*, Uncle, if it was one of the children who said it.

Russell served as bishop in the Asian ward for five years. The stake president wanted to keep him because he was doing well, but it was time. Somewhere along the line, Gordon B. Hinckley mentioned that the Horiuchis were doing a good job with the ward. He was definitely on Salt Lake's radar.

"I don't know if I really accomplished anything," demurs Russell but praises Annette as a major contributor to the welfare and well being of the ward. "The key to it," according to Russell, "was you

---

1. I once made the mistake of calling Erin "Sister Kwong" and was quickly brought into line. "Call me Auntie!" she insisted, her deeply rooted aloha shining through.

gave of yourself." Russell teases Annette that she always volunteered *his* service when somebody needed something.

Part of Russell's success stemmed from the fact that he treated people as people, not as nationalities. Russell and Annette first became acquainted with Honam Rhee at the World Religion Conference at BYU. They were impressed with the dignified and respectful teacher and hit it off well.

Honam was Korean but spent part of his youth living in Shimonoseki, at the southern end of Honshu, Japan and spoke beautiful Japanese in addition to Korean and English.

In 1978, the Horiuchis took Honam up on an invitation to visit Korea during the summer break. Honam met Russell and Annette at the airport, along with his friend Chabon Kim, who also worked at the LDS Institute. Itaewon was famous for tailored suits at the time. It wasn't far from the airport so the group made it their first stop, so that the tailors could finish the suits before the Horiuchis returned to the states.

Russell told the tailor to take measurements for Honam and Kim as well, buying a new suit for each of them as a gift. Russell says it was the best $50 he ever spent. While he and Annette weren't wealthy they believed in spreading their blessings, which always came back around, even in small ways, such as the persimmons that Chabon Kim sent them every year.

The Horiuchis stayed at the LDS mission president's residence, and Honam was their tour guide around Seoul. They took in the sights including a visit to the 38th Parallel, the philosophical and imaginary line that separates North and South Korea. They also visited the Institute library. There were few English church books so Russell and Annette donated several after they went home. Honam invited them to dinner at his home where they met his lovely wife, Yon Soon, for the first time.

Both Honam Rhee and Kim Chabon were later called as mission presidents in their homeland, helping to build the church there.

BYU began a new education PhD program for students to study only during the summer. Russell encouraged both men to matriculate into the program. The men took his advice, both receiving their PhDs in education, which in turn earned them teaching jobs in the Korean Department at BYU.[2]

Another Korean, Dong Su Choi, joined the church in Korea and came to school at BYU. Dong Su's father, a minister of another denomination, objected to his son studying at BYU. As a result the family had little resources when they started school. They arrived in Utah in the middle of winter, unprepared for the cold of the Rocky Mountains. Russell took the children to purchase winter coats and also build bookshelves for their apartment. Dong Su took Russell's class, and Russell urged him to earn his PhD. Dong Su struggled with a few of his classes but Russell continued to encourage him until he'd earned his degree. Dong Su also got a position at BYU teaching comparative religion until he retired. In gratitude, Sister Choi always brought the Horiuchis the best home-made kim chee, even when she was gravely ill with cancer.

Because of the long and tenuous history of their countries, it is said that Koreans and Japanese cannot get along. The Horiuchis, Rhees, Kims and Chois disproved that fallacy, showing that kindness and gratitude can overcome political boundaries.

One of the things Russell eagerly returned to was fishing. Asserting that the solitude was important, Russell pondered all manner of things while staring into the flowing water of the Provo River. His reputation as *THE* fisherman was wide and justly earned. It was common for Russell to return home with his limit even when others returned empty handed from the same spot. One of the larger trout he caught was mistaken for a salmon because it was

---

2. Both men passed away within several years of each other, shortly before retirement. Brother Chabon's wife cried and cried after her husband passed away. She had a dream where Kim appeared to her and told her that he could not do the work on the other side while she was so distraught. His words in the dream helped her to move on.

so pink and meaty. Annette said that Russell usually went fishing on the weekends to which Russell added, "And then after work." Basically Russell was fishing all the time.

The outlet, besides preventing ulcers (as Russell claimed) also provided food for the table, not only for the Horiuchis but for others as well. Russell took great satisfaction in sharing his catch with neighbors, friends and students. The Horiuchis' next door neighbor, George Rohbock, claimed that the fresh fish, free of any additives often found in store bought fish, helped their daughter Joyce as she recovered from health issues.

Auntie Erin, from the Asian ward, remembers watching Russell catching fish over and over. Erin, a fishing fan herself, kept asking him what his secret was. Russell told her to watch. And he pulled in another fish. She couldn't see him do anything different. He told her to watch again. She still couldn't see anything. Finally he let her in on the secret: keep your finger on the line. Just like in life, he told her, stay observant of what's going on.

Almost as numerous as the fish Russell caught were the visitors who graced their door. The Horiuchis usually sent their guests home with fish. A good thing, says Russell, because he and Annette didn't have much storage in their refrigerator. Everyone enjoyed the fish, especially their Asian visitors. There weren't many markets in the area at the time so they particularly relished the taste of fresh trout.

Russell also took a foray into politics, serving three years on the Utah County Planning Commission. The position was voluntary but you had to be appointed. With his background in geography and urban planning Russell was an ideal candidate. Russell adamantly maintained the importance of keeping all development to the east of I-15, away from the expanding and receding shoreline of Utah Lake.[3] Both the Horiuchis were surprised by how nasty people could get when decisions weren't made to their preference, occasionally receiving spiteful letters in the mail. Eventually the floods of 1984 proved Russell's foresight as everything west of the interstate was inundated with water.

It was after he'd returned to teaching that Russell developed a cough that wouldn't go away. He didn't feel sick but the cough persisted long enough that he decided to see an allergist. Much to his surprise he found out he was allergic to almost everything, including rice! He quit eating the worst offenders—peanuts, barley and parsley—but continued eating the rest, particularly rice. He reasoned he'd been eating it all his whole life, so why stop now?

A tradition that developed in the family was waking everyone up early on Christmas morning with a musical serenade. Scott, the Horiuchis' grandson, began waking the family before dawn when he was very young, sneaking downstairs and getting out Russell's old army bugle which he tooted as loudly as possible. In junior high Scott even smuggled a few of his friends over to play carols on a trumpet, saxophone and French horn. Russell turned the tables when his grandson was in high school, rising even earlier and blaring a full reveille. Russell played bugle in the army but when and in exactly what capacity is unknown. One year, Annette's nephew was visiting from Japan and literally fell out of bed from the shock of Russell's morning salutation.

Despite claiming no musical talent, Russell also played the *shakuhachi,* a traditional Japanese bamboo flute, a difficult instrument to play. Most people are unable to make even a sound on it but Russell could evoke haunting melodies. He never mastered the

---

3. The Hanveys personally benefitted from this foresight. They moved to Utah in 1982 and visited with Russell. Upon learning they were going to buy a house in Lehi, he strongly directed them to purchase a house on the east side of I-15, above the low water table areas. Two years later the Lehi/Saratoga residential areas on the west side of the freeway were inundated with several feet of flood water.

piano but on occasion would pick out a tune, the most familiar being the first line of his most beloved hymn *Oh, What Songs of the Heart.*

Church hymns were much treasured by Russell. Whenever Ellen was around he'd request she play from the hymnbook on the piano. Later when hymns became available on CD, he listened to them constantly while he read the morning newspaper or thumbed through a magazine. Among his favorites were *High on the Mountain Top, Oh, My Father,* both versions of *Abide With Me, Come, Come Ye Saints, God Be With You Till We Meet Again, The Spirit of God,* and *We Thank Thee O God for a Prophet.*

For Russell his crowning musical achievement was the harmonica and he could accompany most any familiar tune. In Japanese the word for nose is *hana,* and Russell brought down the house at a ward talent show with his *hana*-monica—playing the instrument with his nose. Annette remembers everyone laughing and laughing.

In 1979, the Horiuchis' son-in-law, Michael T. Hurst, passed away of colon cancer, leaving their only daughter a widow with a young son.

The Horiuchis were relieved when Ellen moved to Salt Lake City for a year, only to be concerned all over again when she moved to teach school in Tegucigalpa, Honduras for a year. After that, Ellen moved back to Utah, accepting a principalship at Dugway Elementary School. There she met and married Dr. Stephen Bushnell Williams, an Army dentist from Kansas City, Missouri. Russell and Annette were thoroughly pleased with their new son-in-law.

Almost weekly wedding announcements from missionaries arrived one after another in the Horiuchis' mailbox. Averaging about four a month, it was safe to say that the missionaries of the Japan East Mission were diligently finding their oases. The Horiuchis attended whenever they were able. Once, when Charlie and Hisa Shibata were visiting, Russell and Annette went out every single evening.

An astounded Hisa could only ask, "How come you have so many wedding receptions?" Over the years the wedding announcements have been replaced with birth announcements and, eventually coming full circle, children's mission calls and weddings.

The missionaries of the Japan East Mission have continued to hold reunions for over forty years. This is in no small part due to the efforts of the missionaries themselves, particularly Jeff Shields, who held the reunion in his ward chapel, Paul King and Jerry Okabe.

Visits from their missionaries are still common. John Edmunds stops by regularly, bringing Green River watermelon or cantaloupes. Mark Jacob delivered trees at Christmas. Cyril Figuerres and his wife, Eileen, often drop off goodies from Hawaii, also announcing that they were called as mission president and wife of Fukuoka, Japan. Reid Robinson went on to become a dentist with a practice in Provo and has given them excellent dental work with little cost. Reid also shows up every Christmas with a gigantic poinsettia. One evening presented the Horiuchis with Forrest B. Christiansen, from Idaho, who asked with a grin if they ate venison. When the Horiuchis answered yes he asked if they had a place to hang an entire deer—antlers, hooves and all. Space was cleared in the garage until the deer could be cured and butchered properly.

Of the over 300 missionaries that served with the Horiuchis all but three have remained active in the church.

22

TOKYO TEMPLE

IN 1988, AFTER 27 YEARS of teaching, Russell announced his plans to retire. Annette thought she might continue teaching but Russell told her that he was going to travel and that if she were teaching she wouldn't be able go with him. While the thought of Russell saying he was going to travel is funny to those who know him (the man simply didn't care for it) he would indeed be traveling, though perhaps not in the manner intended.

In a letter celebrating the event, Russell's sister Namiyo wrote, "My kid brother, Nozomi, Bug, (the only name I used and loved), inched and wormed his way up the ladder, reached his carefully planned goal, not once losing course of his path to success."

Russell looked forward to spending free time in the garden and fishing. He wasn't the only one. His neighbors George Rohbock and Ellis Fox, both recently retired themselves, were eagerly waiting for Russell join them so they could all go fishing together.

But Russell would not be unpacking his fishing poles for long.

The call from Salt Lake came on a Friday. It was President Gordon B. Hinckley, then serving as first counselor to President Ezra Taft Benson, who told Russell, "You come to see me" next week. This time Annette was asked to come as well. The weekend gave Russell and Annette plenty of time to wonder what was in store for them. As before, Russell feared he might be disciplined for something said during a lecture, but with Annette being called up as well that didn't make sense. They had already served as mission president and wife. They tried to think if they'd ever heard of anyone being called twice.

Monday found the Horiuchis in the old granite church office build-ing. After clearing security and the secretary and a series of doors, they found themselves shaking hands with President Hinckley. President Hinckley invited them to sit down across from his desk. The room was spacious with deep wooden bookshelves lining the walls.

President Hinckley didn't waste any time. In a haunting echo of President Tanner's words two decades prior he asked, "What do you think of serving as temple president and matron of the Tokyo Temple?"

Russ and Annette were stunned. Both of them bowed their heads for a long time. Annette sniffled. Thinking she was crying Russell began to cry as well. Neither said a word for a long time. Finally Russell looked up at the waiting President Hinckley, "President . . . I just got my fishing license!"

For a split second the Apostle's eyes widened, then everyone laughed. "Well," President Hinckley continued, "You can go across the street to Arisugawa Park [from the temple] and do your fishing!"

This time around Russell actually consented saying, "We'll go." El-der Hinckley thanked them repeatedly. He asked, "Who are your fishing companions?" and Russell explained they were his neigh-bors, one was a retired florist and the other previously worked for the utility company.

The mention of a florist prompted Elder Hinckley to share how he loved orchards and planting trees and how he planted 150 trees in his own orchard. They chatted for about an hour, Elder Hinckley thanking them the whole time. Annette felt it should have been them thanking him but Elder Hinckley was the one who kept thanking them. Russell pitches in, "That's because we did not want that kind of work!" Elder Hinckley was also the one who set them apart, although that meeting was a later date.

Annette mentions their fishing neighbors were so disappointed.

Concerning the Horiuchis' retirement plans, the call was well timed. While they were in process of preparing for retirement, the actual date was a couple of years away, which meant Russell would still have some teaching commitment left after they returned from the mission. In his inimitable manner Russell told them, "Aw, forget it." Which means no. Technically the Horiuchis were both on hiatus from BYU during their temple mission even though there was never any intention of returning once they came back.

As before, finances were an issue. With their pay at BYU stopping things would again be tight. When Annette's parents passed away, they divided their land among the children and Annette was able to collect some income from rental use of her portion. This money not only allowed the Horiuchis to survive in Tokyo but also they were able to "recoup quite a bit of our whole," according to Russell.

Around the same time, Spencer and Shirley Palmer were called to preside over the Seoul Korea Temple, and Paul and Harriet Hyer were called to preside over the Taipei, Taiwan Temple the same spring. It was another example of the Berkeley group moving around the world at the same time and the Horiuchis felt it an honor to be serving in Asia with these longtime friends.

Interestingly the Palmers and Hyers both received their callings over the phone. Only the Horiuchis were asked to come to Salt Lake in person. When asked why, Russell shrugs and says, "Because I'm an oddball." The family speculates that, knowing Russell's character and propensity to decline, he was asked in person because it would be easy to say no on the telephone.

This time, the call came in early May and, unlike their first outing, the Horiuchis weren't due in Japan until the first of September, giving them several months to prepare.

A reception was held on campus for the three faculty members going to Asian temples, hosted by Jeffery R. Holland, then president of the university. Russell was also invited to be the commencement speaker by the College of Social Sciences, where he shared his funniest stories and reminisced on his years teaching for which he received a standing ovation. It was fitting closure to a celebrated career spanning a long, almost unbelievable journey from barefoot plantation boy to award winning university professor.

Looking back, Russell enjoyed his teaching experience. He earned great respect as a professor and found great satisfaction in his association with young people over the course of his life's work. But he was relieved to be finished. By his own account Russell admits he should have been a plantation worker. Russell gives full credit to Annette for pushing him in a forward direction. Annette demurs, giving Russell the credit.

The Horiuchis knew the Kuni Takahashi family when the couple was going to school at BYU and living in the Y-Mount apartments, where Kuni served as part of the bishopric. After finishing school, the family moved into the Starcrest Apartments nearby the Horiuchis' house, living in a small two-bedroom apartment with their five children.

When the Horiuchis received their call, Annette asked if the Takahashis were interested in living in their house. Kuni politely declined saying they couldn't afford it. The Horiuchis offered to bring down the rent to what the Takahashis were currently paying, which was just enough to cover the mortgage. By contrast, comparable four-bedroom, two-bath homes were renting for nearly four times the amount.

The Takahashis stayed the entire three years of the Horiuchis' mission and later built their own house across the street, becoming outstanding neighbors and an invaluable help to the Horiuchis in their later years.

Between applying for Social Security, farewell dinners with friends, resignations, purchasing temple clothing and other considerations, the remaining months flew by. Due to going barefoot as a child Russell had an extremely wide foot in a small size, which made buying shoes difficult. In order to get temple shoes that fit, he needed to go to Salt Lake to make a special order at the only store in the region which carried them.

Ellen and her husband, Stephen, were also in the middle of moving from Utah to Washington, D.C. where he specialized in oral pathology at Bethesda Naval Medical Center. While the couple drove eastward, they left their son, Scott, to stay with the Horiuchis in order to complete his orthodontic treatments. Scott enjoyed spending time with his grandparents, helping pack and clean the house and carpets. Annette later flew east with Scott to take him home and to see Ellen and Stephen's new house as well as take in some of the tourist sites. The thing she remembers the most was the solemnity of the Korean War Memorial.

In June, Shigeko and Iwakichi flew from Tokyo to California, meeting up with Hisa and Charlie and driving up to Utah, stopping at Zion and Bryce National Parks on the way. They stayed in Orem for a few days before all three couples drove to Yellowstone National Park together. It was Shigeko's first visit to the United States and they had a wonderful time. Annette's sisters helped her make alterations to her temple clothes as well.

On the way back they stopped in Logan, Utah, to visit with Russell's teacher from Lahainaluna High School, Mrs. Hattie Foster Munk. Hattie moved to Logan from Hawaii after remarrying Newel E. Munk, a dentist. Russell always referred to his teacher as a "great lady" who set the example about Mormonism. She still remembered her student's names, even the difficult Japanese ones. It was a real treat to be able to reconnect after so many years.

On August 22, coincidentally the anniversary of their sealing in the LA temple, the Horiuchis drove to Salt Lake together with the Hyers for temple training. The sessions took place over five days and they chose to stay in a hotel instead of making the commute every day. At the beginning of the conference, the Horiuchis were set apart by Elder Gordon B. Hinckley as temple president and matron. Elder Wm. Grant Bangerter was president of the temple committee and all training took place in the Salt Lake temple itself with the first presidency and the quorum of the twelve serving as instructors.

The highlight of the week for Russell and Annette was attending a temple session with the general authorities. Presidents Gordon B. Hinckley and Thomas S. Monson conducted the special ordinance in lieu of President Benson who was under the weather. The entire Quorum of the Twelve and their wives were there, in addition to the nine recently called temple presidents and their wives. Each of the apostles spoke and everyone participated in prayers with Russell asked to offer the closing benediction. It was a tremendous spiritual experience as well as a learning one.

After a week in Salt Lake, the Horiuchis hurried home to do some quick laundry and last minute packing before leaving for Tokyo the very next day. The Katanuma and Takahashi families both came to say goodbye and the Pynes drove Russell and Annette to the Salt Lake airport where they were sent off by several more friends including the Shinos, Mitarais, Nishimotos and Okazakis.

The flight was delayed for an hour and a half causing them to miss their connecting flight. They were reassigned and upgraded on a Japan Airlines flight, receiving "the VIP treatment."

The Horiuchis arrived in Tokyo on August 26, 1988. The airport was crowded with summer travelers, leaving the Horiuchis little space to maneuver their cart full of suitcases. They worried they might be difficult to find in the crowd but current temple president Sam Shimabukuro, who came to pick them up, called out Russell's name as soon as they exited from customs.

Again, someone from Russell's past was there to help the Horiuchis through a transition. Sam conducted the first church meeting that Russell ever attended, while still a youth in Hawaii and now Russell was replacing him as temple president.

Dedicated in 1980, the Tokyo temple is set in Azabu Hiroo, an exclusive residential area that also serves as home to thirty different embassies and consulates. Annette was pleased to find that an international grocery store had been built nearby.

In many ways Russell's life had come full circle. Only a ten-minute walk from the Hiroo train station on the Hibiya line, the temple was built on the property where the former mission home was located, the same property that Russell helped President Clissord obtain forty years before. The Horiuchis were the fourth to serve as president following in the footsteps of Presidents Anderson, Komatsu and Shimabukuro.

Russell and Annette were generally pleased with the set up of their apartment, which was attached to the back of the temple building. With two bedrooms and two baths it was very comfortable. They were especially pleased that it was already furnished and they didn't have to camp out like their previous mission.

Annexed to the temple complex was the Japan Missionary Training Center (JMTC), which was presided over by Roy and Uta Tsuya, more old friends from their Hawaii days, which helped the Horiuchis feel immediately at home. Roy was from Hawaii and Uta was from Salt Lake but both served as missionaries in Hawaii. The Tsuyas were also friends with the Hyers so when Paul and Harriet passed through Tokyo on their way to Taiwan, the Tsuyas, in true aloha style, fixed dinner for both them and the Horiuchis.

On September 1, 1988, the Horiuchis officially assumed the duties of president and matron of the Tokyo temple. The training they had received in Salt Lake suddenly felt very insufficient but the assistance of temple counselors Minoru Yamaguchi, a *Nisei* from Hawaii, and Kaoru Yamaguchi, from Kagoshima, Japan, made the transition almost seamless. Equally valuable was the help of Brother Yasuhiro Matsushita, the temple recorder. When it came to running the temple, Annette says, "He can do everything practically."

On the surface, temple work looks calm but making the sessions run smoothly involves a lot of hurry-scurry behind the scenes.

Days began at four in the morning with a prayer meeting before dispersing to welcome the patrons. At peak times they ran five sessions a day and would remain on their feet until 9:30 in the evening.

The Horiuchis were grateful to be blessed with consistent and hardworking missionaries. Most of the time the temple operated with ten couples. Sometimes, due to missionaries returning, there were as few as five couples. This made things particularly hectic and everyone had to pitch in above and beyond their normal duties, helping clean up, wash dishes and fold the seemingly endless laundry. At the time, patrons rented their temple clothes and everything was washed and stored in the temple. There were three sisters working full-time in the laundry but it was often so busy that there were not enough hands. During those periods everyone would go to the laundry room and help whenever they had a spare moment. The juggling of missionary and volunteer schedules seemed like a full time job in and of itself. Sometimes there was an overabundance of hands and other times it felt as if there weren't enough people to make it through the day.

Due to limited real estate, the temple, like most structures in Tokyo, was vertical in design. It had elevators but they were often occupied by patrons and the Horiuchis and their missionaries found themselves climbing the three flights of stairs up and down from the kitchen and laundry rooms to the veil and back again. It was very strenuous, especially for the more elderly.

Midweek wasn't usually as busy. Fewer sessions were held and the missionaries were able to catch their breath a little. Weekends were usually the busiest time, as were holidays when the temple remained open so the saints could attend on their days off. At the time, the Tokyo temple was the only temple in the country, so they kept very busy, especially when excursion groups came. Often two or three large groups of saints arrived together, traveling together from outside the Tokyo area to attend the temple. When a marriage or a new endowment was thrown in, things became especially frenzied.

Temple excursions could be expensive, especially for those saints traveling a long distance. Groups, like the ones from Osaka, travelled over night by bus, arrived early at the temple and went right into the morning sessions. Many saints weren't able to come often so they wanted to complete as much as they could in the time they had, going through consecutive session after session for two or three days straight. Even when Annette told them they should take a break for lunch they would decline, saying that they wanted to finish up their temple work.

When even larger groups showed up, like the one from Okinawa with 120 saints that came in November, local volunteers were called in to help out the full time missionaries. The burden of responsibility fell on the matron's assistants and counselors to fill in any gaps in personnel. The Horiuchis were constantly humbled by the sacrifices of the saints. It was tiring for the missionaries but they knew the saints were very tired too.

In the pre-computer era, the process for names was very slow. Even with two sisters typing everything by hand, people had to wait in line for fifteen to twenty minutes at a time. Eventually as the Horiuchis grew more familiar with the workflow of the temple the process was streamlined. One day they completed 240 endowments in one session. Their record was 1058 endowments and 715 sealings.

"They were very faithful people," says Annette of the temple going saints. The traveling groups reminded Russell and Annette of the time they rode overnight on a bus themselves, traveling from Berkeley, California to the Los Angeles temple to take out their own endowments.

When the excursion saints did take time to eat they had to go out. With Azabu being an exclusive area, the closest restaurants were rather expensive. Dining out also took a lot of time since the temple-goers needed to change into street clothes and back again.

There was a nice kitchen in the temple complex that wasn't being used so Russell and Annette spoke with their missionaries to figure out a way to provide meals for the excursion groups. Brother Matsushita said that he could cook. Not only could he cook, says Annette, he was fast. He bought ingredients at the nearby wholesale market in the morning before returning to the temple to begin cooking. Various dishes were served but it was usually curry rice because it was quick to prepare and good tasting. Rice was prepared in an industrial sized cooker overnight and was ready to go for the next day. Meals were very inexpensive, usually around ¥100 to cover the cost. It was a hit among patrons and temple missionaries alike, saving time and money and the kitchen was often filled with visiting saints.

Russell and Annette, like the rest of the missionaries, helped with preparations, rolling up the sleeves of their temple clothes and slicing vegetables until the bell rang, summoning them up to the veil to help finish a session. The idea of using the kitchen also gave Russell a new title—dishwasher!

With no evening sessions on Saturdays the last session let out around four. The missionaries cleaned up and headed home by about 5 o'clock. With no time to go shopping during the week there was little food left in the Horiuchis apartment so they would go out for *soba* noodles or *tempura*. Often wanting to rest a bit first, they would turn on the television, sit on the couch and pass out from sheer exhaustion only to wake a few hours later to find it dark and all the restaurants closed. They would scrounge up whatever they had left over for dinner. "It was so tiring. We were like slaves," says Russell before amending himself, "Servant is a better word. Work! Work! Work!"

Russell and Annette often attended other church meetings during the day. They worked in the temple in the morning, came home, changed clothes quickly and went to their appointments with various wards and stakes. When they were finished they headed back to the temple, changed back into temple attire and went back to work. Some days they changed clothes two or three times, laughing that they were like actors.

Work in the temple was demanding, but it was the weekend speaking engagements that often proved the most challenging. In order to encourage temple attendance among the saints the Horiuchis traveled to a different conference in a different stake almost every weekend, covering nearly the entirety of the country from Hokkaido to Okinawa.

Annette usually gave a nice talk as a prelude to the laughter that Russell would create. He was, as always, totally unconventional in his approach, not concerning himself with statistics but placing his emphasis on the hearts and spirits of the saints.

If the stake they were visiting was far away, Russell and Annette came home after work on Saturdays, packed their bags and headed out by bus, train or plane to their destination, absorbing the cost from their own pockets. When they had to fly, they took a taxi to Hamamatsu-Cho, then took the monorail to the airport. After a Sunday full of meetings, they would return home. Monday was their P-day and they headed back to Tokyo as soon as meetings were over, often taking night flights, in order to maximize the day. Often their return schedule wouldn't get them home until the day was half gone, making it difficult to do any laundry, shopping or cleaning. "It would take time and it was kind of hard. It was a good thing we were healthy and young," Annette said, "We were able to move around like that." It was difficult but the Horiuchis never refused an invitation to speak, knowing the sacrifices many saints were making to come to the temple.

President Horiuchi has a very practical manner when counseling missionaries and members. This was true when I was one of his missionaries and continued to be true years later. I was stationed in Misawa Air Base outside of Aomori from 1988 to 1991. During this time, President Horiuchi and Sister Horiuchi were serving as the Tokyo Temple President and Matron. We attended the Japanese branch in Misawa and during one of our district conferences President Horiuchi spoke as the Temple President. As you know, the Japanese are known for their ability to work hard and to accomplish a lot. Knowing that the Temple President was speaking, the congregation was prepared to hear an exhortation to increase its temple attendance. As it was a twelve-hour trip by car to the temple, they thought that they would hear how to fine-tune their time in Tokyo to maximize the number of sessions that could be attended during a single temple trip. President Horiuchi stood to speak and he had on his typical, serious face and the congregation was steeling itself to be told to work harder. After the usual short introduction, President Horiuchi leaned forward over the pulpit, looked into the congregation and said, "Now, when you come to the temple I do not want you to see how many sessions that you can attend in one day." You could almost feel a sense of shock go through the congregation. President Horiuchi went on to say, "Rather, I want you to attend the temple and then to take your wives out to dinner and to enjoy your time in Tokyo. Your life in the church is not a short sprint. It is a marathon. You have to pace yourselves if you are going to be able to endure to the end. You need to spend time building a strong, loving relationship with your wives and husbands. In the long run, this is more important than how many sessions that you attend on a temple trip." This was not what the congregation expected at all. He went on for the rest of his talk to speak about the importance of the marital relationship and working together to develop an eternal family. Rather than leaving feeling guilty for not attending enough temple sessions, we left with an understanding of the importance of the family. Numbers were never the object or goal of President Horiuchi's life. People were more important than programs. I had understood this before I listened to the above talk. More in the congregation understood this after listening to his talk on temple attendance that day.

—David Ludlow

23

LIFE IN TOKYO

THE TEMPLE WAS BUSY BUT calm compared to being a mission president. The temple workers were generally more mature, long-time members and the Horiuchis felt all they needed to do was make sure things ran well. Russell didn't set up a lot of changes, just ensured that things operated smoothly.

Russell made it a point to engage their visitors and patrons, and often came in early or stayed late chatting, laughing and smiling. As much as possible they tried to send everyone away with a positive and uplifting experience.

In November, they had the opportunity to attend the Sapporo West Stake Conference presided over by Bin Kikuchi, now serving as stake president. His calling as mission president over the Tokyo North mission came while the Horiuchis were still serving in the temple.

The Horiuchis arrived the night before the conference. Brother Satou Yoshinori's father owned a big *yakitori*, seasoned fried chicken, restaurant. In the evening after closing hours, they served *yakitori* for next to nothing to the local members. It was thrilling for Russell and Annette to be reunited with the people they worked with as mission presidents. And the *yakitori* was delicious too!

The Horiuchis were also able to attend a seminar presided over by Elder Dallin H. Oaks. The seminar was for mission presidents but the Horiuchis were invited since it was held in the temple annex. Elder Oaks spoke about loving the saints, 70% love and 30% feeling.

The Horiuchis began having potluck dinners for the temple workers after large excursion groups. Many of the missionaries were from Hawaii, so they pitched in and brought really *"oishii kau kau,"* delicious food.[1] Rice, noodles, chicken *hekka*, a Hawaiian dish like *sukiyaki, yakisoba* and *tsukemono* were common favorites. If there was a good deal on salmon, the missionaries ate it as a treat or sometimes splurged on Kentucky Fried Chicken instead (it's very expensive in Japan). The meals were a lot of fun for everyone and were a good way to express the Horiuchis appreciation to the hard working volunteers and employees.

The temple served as a meeting place for many faces from the Horiuchis life, both old and new. Occasionally Adney Komatsu, who served as a Seventy, and his wife, Judy, would stop by and everyone went out to grab a simple meal. The Horiuchis enjoyed these visits tremendously, feeling they could relax around their old friends without having to worry about setting an example. Elder Komatsu formerly served as temple president in Tokyo as well and was able to discuss things in depth with Russell and Annette. The massage chair in the temple apartment was a remnant from their tenure.

When Elder Bangerter, president of the temple committee, and his wife came by they began talking about Utah and Russell got homesick and teary eyed. To cheer him up Elder and Sister Bangerter sang *Springtime in the Rockies*. The Horiuchis describe them as very humble and down to earth, which made it quite easy to relate to them. Over sandwiches at lunch the Bangerters shared their mission experiences from when they presided in South America, which helped bolster Russ and Annette's spirits.

---

1. For lingua-philes out there: *oishii* is Japanese for delicious while *kau kau* is Hawaiian pidgin for food. Welcome to island speak!

One benefit of being in Tokyo on this mission was that Annette was much closer to her family. She was able to attend the memorials for her father's 19th year of passing and her mother's 17th. In Buddhist tradition certain dates, beginning at forty-nine days then one hundred and so on, are set aside as *hooji,* when the relatives gather and go to the *oterra* shrine.

Annette also spent more time with her older sister, Shigeko, and her husband Iwakichi. Annette and Russell took the couple to Ueno-Ameyoko, the district famous for its many wholesale stores. Even though they had lived in Tokyo all of their lives neither Shige nor Iwakichi had ever been. Ueno-Ameyoko was home to one of Russell and Annette's favorite shops, the Purple Store. Another favorite shopping haunt of theirs was Topos in Kita Senju.

The next year Annette was able to attend the 50th anniversary of her Yaguchi Nishi Elementary School. She was amazed they managed to contact her after so many years, especially with the devastation of the war having destroyed so many records. She enjoyed catching up and visiting with her classmates, most of whom she hadn't seen since they were in school together.

Another opportunity living in Tokyo afforded Annette was the chance to attend Kiyoshi Mori's family reunion. The son of her father's stepbrother, Kiyoshi was one of her oldest living cousins, nearly 90 at the time. He had a remarkable memory and was able to provide invaluable help to Annette in gathering genealogical information.

Even though the Horiuchis had spent Christmas in Japan before, the first Christmas in the temple felt a bit odd. Being a non-Christian country, for most of the Japanese it was merely another working day. The Horiuchis felt a tinge of homesickness but their busy schedule didn't give them much time to think about it. To celebrate the holiday they gathered together with the temple missionaries eating, singing carols and hymns and exchanging simple gifts.

In Japan, New Years is bigger than Christmas, a time when people make an effort to gather their families together, sometimes traveling to their ancestral homes. For many Japanese men it is one of the rare occasions that they get to spend time with their families. The day was surprisingly quiet and reminded Annette of the peace she experienced as a child in Tokyo. The Horiuchis visited the Tsukiji wholesale market and learned how to make tamales from Uta Tsuya. A *Nisei* like Russell, Uta learned to make them from her friends in Salt Lake City, her home town, and made them in the Japan Missionary Training Center (JMTC).

In 1989, Emperor Showa, who ruled during WWII, passed away after 63 years on the throne. Each Japanese era is named after the reigning monarch and Showa's passing signaled the epoch of the *Heisei Gannen,* Heisei period. Russell complained that all the TV stations aired nothing but the funeral for weeks. Day in and out, every channel literally showed only funeral coverage or pieces about the emperor and his life.

That same year, the Tsuyas were replaced in the JMTC by Ralph and Lily Shino, who were now living in Salt Lake. Ralph was converted at 19 years of age, the first male baptized in Maui. Throughout his life Ralph maintained contact with the elders who baptized him, one of whom Annette recalls was a boxing champion in Arizona. Lily grew up in Utah county and attended Orem High School. Working closely with more old friends from Hawaii was an enjoyable privilege for both couples.

The large number of the boys from Hawaii that ended up filling leadership positions in Japan is testimony of how the Lord raised these young men to serve the spiritual growth of his children in Japan.

In a personal letter to Jeffery R. Holland, still president of BYU at the time, Russell writes how his style of leadership sometimes differed with the Japanese view of how a temple president should act. "It has not taken long to realize that peasants like us have difficulty in transforming into the 'lord of the manor.' We feel like misfits. We get admonished for opening doors for patrons since we were not doorkeepers. We go out to do a little exercise in the garden and the whole physical plant crew is out working shortly thereafter."

Russell focused on the welfare of the saints in Japan, particularly the leadership, desiring to help them focus less on forms and procedures, a common practice, and more on love and people as individuals. Russell felt that the often obtuse bureaucratic mindset was a roadblock to the development of the wards and saints. He believed the high level of inactivity in Japan was no accident. The saints were overworked and over-stressed, often made to feel guilty for not engaging in all the activities which in turn drove them away to "save face."

One guideline stated that no land purchase for chapels or other church buildings was allowed to exceed 150 *tsubo*. One tsubo equals roughly 2.95 square yards. In Tama city, in the Tokyo East Stake, a 180 *tsubo* plot of land came up for sale in a location the church was interested in. Russell encouraged JPBO, the Japanese Presiding Bishopric's Office, now called the Area Offices, to purchase the entire lot, making provisions for future expansion or additional parking. Strictly following guidelines the JPBO purchased only 150 *tsubo*. The remaining 30 were subsequently bought and developed into a strip club making the church's original intention of building a chapel unfeasible.

Russell was concerned with the way Church interacted with Japanese members and culture. Policies that work well in Salt Lake didn't necessarily succeed in Japan. Decisions such as getting rid of full time custodians and having the members clean instead work well enough stateside but it was very difficult in Japan, particularly for the long time custodians who would have a very hard time obtaining full time work again.

Things such as church callings could interrupt careers, difficult for anyone but particularly for the Japanese. In the Japanese *kai-sha* corporate culture a career interruption was essentially occupational suicide with leave of absences rarely allowed and little or no chance of returning. He knew that the levels of organization were necessary to keep the church running as a whole but felt that the needs of the saints at ground level were often overlooked, even if unintentionally.

The Horiuchis were asked by the temple committee in Salt Lake to close down the temple so that some new audio equipment could be installed. No one in Salt Lake ever consulted with anyone in Tokyo about it and the shutdown was scheduled during one of the temple's busiest periods. Despite protesting the dates, the Horiuchis were forced to cancel several excursion groups and a handful of weddings.

Russell's journal from February 2, 1990 conveys his feelings: "It was a bit distressing with four weddings scheduled and nine excursion groups coming. . . . Needless to say, the people were unhappy . . . We carefully endeavor to encourage temple attendance and we get the rug pulled from under us. Why do [they] have to subject us to all this? Feel like throwing in the towel and going home. Yet we have to maintain a stiff upper lip and keep morale high." And later, in conclusion to the whole debacle: "This too will pass."

Such inconveniences were rare, however, and the Horiuchis praised the overall leadership. "It may be difficult to find a group more dedicated, committed, and determined to serve the Lord than many of our leaders in Japan," wrote Russell, "They are obedient, sustain the General Authorities fully and are willing to make sacrifices. They are happy to spend long hours on the job, and attend their meetings even far into the night. A visitor cannot help but be impressed."

Many wonderful stories and memories come from the Horiuchis' time in the temple. With a fond smile, Annette relates how one young man was so excited about getting married that he forgot his wallet, arriving with no money for temple clothes and no recommend! He was given some Yen, a few phone calls were made and he was taken care of in time for his sealing.

The young man wasn't alone in his overeager forgetfulness. Another couple, traveling from far to be married, forgot their certificate from the bishop. So the temple had to catch both the bishop and the stake president at work to get approval.

Brother Akira Igawa was an award winning rose grower in Hokkaido and always brought a large box of the incredible flowers all the way with him when he'd come to Tokyo. It was extremely kind and the beautiful flowers were placed throughout the temple.

The people who handled finances knew that Russell did not like to spend from temple funds and chose instead to pull from his own pocket when expenses were encountered. The use of their own funds reflected the Horiuchis ideal of the importance of respecting the Lord's money.

Once several large excursion groups were scheduled at a time when missionary numbers were low. The Horiuchis asked for as many local volunteers as they could muster but it still wasn't enough.

One couple, Kiyomi and Yaeko Akagi, planned to be released and go home to Hawaii. Sister Akagi had a heart condition and had a medical check up scheduled shortly after their return. The Akagis realized the temple was understaffed at a busy time and were willing to extend for half a year but wanted Yaeko to have her check up with her doctor to make sure she was all right. Russell paid for her round trip ticket himself. She was deemed healthy and the Akagis were able to serve out their extension.

Brother and Sister Nara, the same couple Russell worked with reorganizing the church after the war, were both over ninety years old by now and the oldest living members in Japan. Ever the example, they traveled by bus and train all the way from Saitama Ken to volunteer at the temple even though they could barely lift their legs enough to climb on the bus. They both walked so slowly that it took about two hours to make the journey.

Another example of great faithfulness was Sister Misao Toma. On her own initiative she commuted from her home in Nerima-Ku, west from the temple, to help when they were short on missionaries, staying in the temple annex. One time Sister Toma was making *miso* at home and the pot needed stirring. As a volunteer she could leave any time but she made it a point to politely get permission from Annette before doing so.

A widow from Okinawa, Sister Toma lived through some very difficult times during the war. Her son remembers times when there was no food in the house. His mother gathered the children and said, "Children, let's sing." If she couldn't feed their bellies, she could at least feed their souls. Her example of humble perseverance paid off, and her children have all grown into equally humble and successful adults. One of her sons, Kenji, eventually served under the Horiuchis in the Japan East Mission.

When the Horiuchis were too busy to eat, Sister Toma would make *obento* for them. "*Obento motte kita yo, yuhan tabenasai.* I brought obento, please eat some dinner." "She was so nice," recalled Annette.

Very sincere people, the Japanese saints treated their temple visits respectfully and often came to the Horiuchis with questions or concerns. One sister came to the veil where Annette was standing. The sister confessed she might have dozed off a bit during the session and worried that it might disqualify her from going through the veil. Annette assured her it was all right and the sister was greatly relieved. Another sister was concerned whether she was allowed to attend or not since her husband wasn't a member, which was, of course, fine.

In October, the Horiuchis flew for the first time to Okinawa, where many of the members were second or third generation with very strong families and religious ties. Finding a little free time the Horiuchis went shopping for ham, corned beef and meat, shipping it back to Tokyo as a New Year's gift to the temple workers. Meat was extremely expensive when it was even available but everyone was so happy, including the givers.

On November 9, 1989, they heard the news that the Berlin Wall was being torn down! The world rejoiced as the 165 km wall that divided the city and the hearts of her people finally came down after 28 years.

Russell's journal entry for January 1, 1990 reads: "Annette is someone special. Can't help but getting to love her more and more each day. Without her prodding and arguing where will I be?" He also mentions how glad he was to see the faithfulness of the saints and to receive letters from Ellen writing that "she warms the heart of old dad."

While serving in the temple, Russell had the opportunity to seal himself to his mother and father. He was saddened to note that he was the only one of his siblings to be able to do so.

All the temple presidents worldwide were invited to attend General Conference in Salt Lake and attend special training. Russell, perhaps only half jokingly, said he was afraid to go since he wouldn't want to come back. Young missionaries aren't the only ones who keep track of how much time they have left until they go home, as many of the notes in Russell's diary will attest.

Arthur and Grace Nishimoto picked the Horiuchis up when they arrived in Utah. The two couples joined the Tsuyas, dining at the Kyoto restaurant in Salt Lake while catching up on all the latest.

While in Utah, Russell and Annette wanted to visit with their grandson who was attending his senior year in high school in Dugway and also to check on their house in Orem. For the first time in their lives they decided to rent a car and were surprised to learn that in order to do so they needed a credit card, something they had never owned. It was frustrating that they couldn't rent a car even though they could have bought the same vehicle in cash. They were pleased the rental company was willing to accept their debit card, which was unused and buried so deeply in Annette's purse that they forgot they had it.

With the rental car secured, the Horiuchis headed to Orem. There were some things that they had packed for Tokyo but weren't using so they brought them to store in their basement. They hoped to visit with some of the neighbors but were disappointed to find many of them weren't home. The Horiuchis swung by BYU for a pleasant visit with friends there, then met with the Komatsus and Nishimotos again, this time at Arthur and Grace's home.

The Horiuchis' grandson came in from Dugway to stay with them at their hotel in Salt Lake for a few nights. Scott remembers walking to General Conference with them. There was a big rock concert going on in the Salt Palace at the same time. The sight of all the Aerosmith fans walking up one side of the street and all the suit and tie conference goers walking up the other was a memorable exercise in contrast.

The temple presidents gathered in a solemn assembly with all the General Authorities in the Assembly Hall. Russell and Annette described it as a very humbling experience, especially when the twelve apostles themselves blessed and passed the sacrament.

The next day, special sessions were held in the Salt Lake Temple with the First Presidency and their wives acting as witnesses. President Monson and his wife witnessed the session that the Horiuchis attended. Russell and Annette were grateful to be able to participate in such a wonderful experience.

The night the Horiuchis returned, the sister missionaries, including Ethel Young, Ethel Kurihara, Francis Tengan, Shirley Arima and Margaret Larsen, prepared a delicious turkey dinner. Being temple president was a great responsibility and busy, but the quality of the people the Horiuchis were blessed to work with helped make the burden light.

A week later, Russell's sister, Kay, and cousin, Bernice, arrived in Tokyo, staying a few nights with them in the temple apartment. It had been several years since they last saw each other and they had a wonderful time catching up.

July 4, 1990 brought the sad news that Harriet Hyer passed away two days previously in Taiwan. Harriet occasionally suffered from emphysema related problems and died in the hospital. The Hyers also notified Spencer Palmer in Korea with the news. Harriet and Paul had been there at nearly every pivotal point in the Horiuchis' lives. It was difficult to see one half of that partnership pass on.

Temple work was busy but not so busy that the Horiuchis couldn't take in a few simple pleasures. With summer break came the cleaning period for the temple and two days with no hot water while the boiler was being serviced.

Russ and Annette took a private trip to Enoshima to visit the seashore near Fujisawa, at the southern end of Tokyo. They stopped at Kamakura on the way to see the huge bronze *daibutsu,* statue of Buddha. Once mentioned in a poem by Rudyard Kipling, the nearly forty-four feet tall statue is one of the most famous icons in Japan.

The visit to the beach reminded Annette of her happy days as a youth when her family would travel to Katase in Kanagawa prefecture, located on the other side of Enoshima. She has many fond memories of swimming and playing all day long. Now crowded with beach houses and people, Katase was a quiet swimming area when she was young. The trip was enjoyable and a welcome diversion.

Another time the Horiuchis went to see Brother Kanai's exhibition at the Ueno museum. One of their missionaries from the Japan East Mission, Brother Kanai was now an up and coming artist and gave them tickets. Annette, who was coming from her sister's, planned to meet up with Russell at Ueno, one of the busiest stations in Tokyo. In a pre-cell phone-days miscommunication, Annette waited on the north side of the station while Russell waited for an hour on the south. Finally Annette gave up and went to the exhibit alone; Russell never saw it.

During winter recess, Annette and her sister Shigeko went to Hakone-Yumoto and stayed at the Okada-ya *ryokan,* inn. Hakone-Yumoto is a resort area near the Izu Peninsula, near where Annette and her family stayed during the war. There were *ofuro* in each room but they went to the *iwaburo,* outdoor baths, essentially an outdoor hot tub made of stone, and separated by gender. Annette liked it because you could see the stars.

After relaxing thoroughly, the sisters returned to their room for a traditional style dinner consisting of many small dishes including sugar coated *umeboshi,* salted plums and tea. The two ate until they couldn't eat another bite.

While still at the *ryokan,* Annette received a call from her cousin, Kimiko Mori. Her husband, Aiba san heard that Annette was interested in research on Tanaka Mitsuaki, her blood grandfather, who held a connection with the Mito clan. Aiba san was somehow connected with the Mito clan and was as much the historian in his family as Annette was in hers. The two promised to stay in touch with each other. Regrettably, that was the only time Annette was ever able to speak with him before he passed away.

Many church members expressed a desire to do something similar to the Japanese tradition of visiting family shrines at midnight on New Year's Eve. So on New Year's Day in 1991 two extra sessions were held first thing in the morning, drawing people from near and far. Even though the extra hours of work were hard on the missionaries, it was a very gratifying experience.

That afternoon the missionaries had a feast, celebrating the New Year with traditional Japanese holiday dishes of *ozoni, nishime, namasu* and beans. Sister Toma, the volunteer who would stay in the annex and help, generously provided the food for the party.

During the middle of the dinner, an excursion group of roughly 100 saints arrived from Hokkaido and were invited to join the festivities. There were no restaurant or stores open, so the Horiuchis gathered whatever leftovers they could find. Perhaps it was the miracle of the fish and the loaves because they managed to feed everyone without any planning.

In May, President Hinckley had a long conversation with Russell about the possibility of extending his call as temple president. In his inimical manner, Russell told the President that he would rather go fishing back in Utah. It didn't help that in an earlier phone conversation Reiny Liechty,[2] who recently lost his wife, told Russell he was lonely and ready to go fishing. The phone call came early in the morning. President Hinckley was actually calling to discuss possible replacements in anticipation of the Horiuchis eventual release. President Hinckley put a name forward asking what Russell thought about that person. Russell knew that some of this person's financial dealings had been a little shady. So President Hinckley suggested a second name. Again they had been less than honorable in some aspects. The President mentioned a third candidate and was again met with concern about some of their dealings. (It should be noted that Russell was emphatic to make sure the word "dishonest" was never used in context with any of the men initially suggested by President Hinckley.)

Out of options, President Hinckley said, "Well, if we can't come up with anybody you're going to have to be extended."

Annette remembers hearing Russell exclaim, "No!" and knew immediately that they were likely being asked to extend.

President Hinckley then asked if Russell knew of any good candidates. Russell suggested maybe finding someone from Hawaii, perhaps a *nisei*. So the first presidency looked around and eventually called Tomo Abo and his wife Lorraine. President Abo was already in the early stages of Parkinson's disease by this time, but

2. His real name was Wilhelm, but everyone affectionately called him Reiny. He was a botany professor at BYU and part of the Horiuchis' monthly dinner group.

he accepted the call. A short time later the Horiuchis received a phone call from their friend Bill Evanson asking, "Did you extend?" No, they hadn't.

On June 16, 1991, shortly before the Horiuchis were scheduled to return home, the Sapporo and Sapporo West Stakes held a special conference at the Shimin-Kaikan with over 1,600 saints in attendance. The Horiuchis took great joy in witnessing the marvelous growth Hokkaido had experienced since their pioneer days twenty years before.

At the conference, Russell was reminded of the counsel that he gave to the saints in Hokkaido decades before. While still young as a mission president, Russell stood before a similar congregation and encouraged the members to purchase their own homes. Russell remembers the words coming out of his mouth but never felt that it was him speaking. Japan was struggling economically and for most of the saints buying their own homes would be difficult at best. It was challenging but the saints followed his counsel and by saving carefully were able to purchase their houses. As a result when the housing crash hit Japan later on, the saints in Hokkaido weren't affected as badly.

When the temple closed for the last summer cleaning of the Horiuchis mission, they were visited by Ellen, Stephen, Scott and Stephen's mother, Bonnie Williams. Russell stayed in Tokyo but Annette traveled with the family to sightsee in Kyoto. From Kyoto, Annette returned to Tokyo while the family continued southward to Miyajima and the Peace Memorial in Hiroshima. After returning north again, the entire family went to visit with Shigeko and many of Ellen's cousins in Ota-Ku.

August 31, 1991 marked the last day of the Horiuchis' temple mission. Leaving a mission is such a bittersweet experience and Russ and Annette were emotionally torn between excitement over returning home and sadness at saying good-bye to beloved friends. The temple was a marvelous experience and the Horiuchis were thankful for the opportunity to work closely with so many of the saints in Japan.

Before leaving, Annette visited with her sister one last time and paid a visit to the ancestral cemetery in Yaguchi where her parents are buried. After bidding Shigeko good-bye, Annette hurried back to the temple to attend the welcome lunch for the Abos. The Horiuchis knew the temple was in good hands with their old friends.

As before, Russell and Annette avoided farewell parties, not wanting to make anyone feel the need to make an extra effort. They did have a small get-together with the missionaries for a goodbye dinner. The only people to see them off at the airport were the missionaries who drove them there.

Annette: I think grandpa's [Russell's] life is kind of self made life.

Russell: No, grandpa's [referring to himself] life is a directed life. The good lord is directing us.

Annette: Yeah, but self made, *yo, dakara."*

Russell: Self made *janai yo.*

Annette apologized for the stream of visitors that consistently showed up at their house while being interviewed for this book.

Annette: Sorry for the constant interruption.

Scott: It's not your fault at all. You're fine. This is Grand Central Station.

Annette: Especially that day was very busy.

Scott: It's hard because I'm trying to interview a celebrity.

Annette: Yeah, that's true. Hard to. You are very privileged to get time like this.

Scott laughs.

Annette: Hey, don't laugh! (She laughs too.)

— Excerpts from interviews for this book.

Excerpt from a letter from Russell to the Tsuyas:

Dear Tsuyas,

Received your postcard with the trophy fish on it. After carefully looking things over and checking the tell tale signs, I remember now it was the fish I let go because it was a bit too small to keep up with my "meijin" or expert standards. But I am glad that Roy got a chance to catch a minnow or two for a change. Maybe I had better do a lot of rethinking, and note that perhaps he can and does catch a fish or two now and then. It is your chance to take in a few little ones before we get back.

24

GOLDEN YEARS

UPON THE HORIUCHIS' RETURN, TOM George, their neighbor across the street declared, "Now we'll finally be able to catch fish!" Fishing definitely remained a part of the Horiuchis' lives but, despite Russell's constant joke that you couldn't retire from doing nothing, the pair kept very busy and involved in many interests.

Not surprisingly, many of these activities revolved around food. Once a month, the Horiuchis gathered with friends for a dinner group to try out different restaurants, and catch up on the latest while deciding where to meet the following month. This dinner group is a continuation of the group that has met for over thirty years. Regulars include Janet and Dennis Shiozawa, Bill and Nancy Evanson, Fred and Gladys Takasaki, Reiny Liechty, Robert and Eda Lim and their son Evan, Dwayne and Kaye Jeffery and many others. Once a year the Evansons hosted a potluck for everyone in their home.

Russell and Annette frequently joined Wally and Bonnie Allred (when they weren't traveling) and Bob and Beth Foutin for lunch at Chuck-a-Rama, one of Russell's favorite restaurants. Of his friends Russell wrote, "Friends are very critical—we need them. They are good solid people—family oriented. We certainly have been blessed with good friends."

Annette met often with Naoko Monson, Kitty Muranaka, Toshiko Mori, Shizuka Okawa and Oriye Webb, all very close friends despite the fact that they were actually closer in age to Ellen. It was a refreshing respite for these women, all Japanese expatriates, to be able to spend hours laughing and talking in Japanese.

Mondays and Thursdays, Annette attended Tai Chi and Qi Gong classes at the Provo Senior Center.

In between luncheon engagements and Tai Chi, Annette worked diligently on her family history and enjoyed the privilege of taking her mother's and sister's names through the temple. When she emerged from the baptismal waters, the tears streamed down her face so heavily that she was unable to see and had to stand there a moment. The sister helping commented that she must have been doing work for someone very special and that her tears of joy weren't only Annette's but theirs as well.

For Christmas, Ellen and Stephen sent their mothers season tickets to the Hale Center Theater. Annette and Bonnie enjoyed seeing the shows together.

In 1992, Annette went with Ellen on a cruise to the eastern Caribbean. Russell was invited but was content to stay home and work in the garden. The two women met up with Mel and Jeneal Petersen, who were serving a mission in Puerto Rico. The Petersens took some time off to pick them up from the ship and take them around the island. With the captain's permission to bring guests aboard, Annette and Ellen invited the Petersens to a memorable dinner on the ship.

For his part, Russell kept busy working in his yard and garden, mowing the lawn twice a week, sometimes three times. Dressed in his favored plaid flannel shirts and cotton pants, Russell earned clearly etched farmer tan lines on his hands and neck. He was such a familiar sight that the neighborhood bevy of quail, which usually ran away at the slightest provocation, would come around when he was there. Russell could imitate their calls and elicit a response. They knew they were safe when he was around but if anyone else stepped into the yard they scattered quickly.

Russell delighted in sharing his garden produce. He once planted thirty tomato plants, excited at the thought of giving them away.

At Thanksgiving time he brought turkeys to neighbors and friends such as the Astles and the Fa'alafua families he home taught.

The spirit of giving was strong among the neighborhood vanguard and the Horiuchis' neighbors delivered goodies as well. Freshly baked salmon or grape leaf dolma from Tom George or apples from the Pyne's orchards were always welcomed gifts.

The Japanese tradition of *omiyage,* souvenir or gift giving, was alive and well in the Horiuchi household. When visiting friends, Russell and Annette brought a gift or food. When friends came to visit, the Horiuchis would send them home with something as well. Scott still laughs remembering the time his friend Duane Andersen stopped by the house and Annette, caught off guard, searched frantically and presented him with a half stalk of celery as a parting gift.

If Annette ever lost track of Russ, she knew he was somewhere around the block discussing the day's weather, politics or other current issues with a neighbor. He found simple joy in serving by taking their trashcans out for pick up on garbage day. George Rohbock wrote "Lawns are cut, bushes pruned, snow shoveled, and something delicious to eat is delivered to those in need . . . Russell [has] been a friend at the times we needed one most."

Fall was Russell's favorite season. He enjoyed the serenity of the changing colors and cooling weather and the anticipation of the upcoming Thanksgiving and Christmas seasons. Although, he writes in typical tongue in cheek fashion, "with fishing season closed there isn't much else to do but stay home and get nagged at."

Blending his continued intellectual pursuit with his spiritual interests, Russell devoted a lot of time to the study of the writings of Isaiah, his desk often covered with open scriptures, several texts, and piles of papers and notes that he'd written himself.

Another pastime was watching video copies of different Japanese *Jidaigeki* television serials, the Japanese equivalent of American westerns like *Bonanza* or *Gunsmoke.* Titles like *Abarenbo Shogun* and *Mito Komon* were particular favorites and the entire family would walk around the house quoting dialogue from them.[1] The shows even made mention in Russell's journal. "Simple predictable plot," he writes, "but the background scenes were nice."

Russell kept in touch with his sister, Kay, calling her regularly. Active in her retirement home community in San Francisco, Kay often spent her evening downstairs watching television with the other residents, which made it difficult to catch her but Russell persisted and the two remained in close contact. For Russell, notoriously wary of phones and known for his extreme brevity when using one, it illustrates how much he cared for his older sister. Kay flew in to join Russell and Annette when they visited Ellen and Stephen in Texas in March of 1998. Ellen pampered Kay and her mother taking them for a tour of the governor's mansion and then going to a day spa for massages.

In his journal, Russell wrote that the best thing about retirement "is good health," something he enjoyed throughout his life. Outside of a tonsillectomy when he was six and a fractured right ankle earned playing basketball as a GI in Tokyo,[2] Russell never spent any time in a hospital until he had a pacemaker implanted at almost 87.

One of the more curious roles Russell fell into was speaking at funerals. If it were close friends that asked him it was no problem. Russell gave great tribute to the power of long lasting friendship when Mack Hughes' family asked him to speak at their father's funeral, even though it had been nearly four decades since the two men associated closely. Hattie Munk, Russell's elementary school teacher, making preparations while she was still in good health at 83 years old, personally requested he speak at her memorial service. Hattie passed away in 2005 at the grand age of 101.

---

1. *Kono mondokoro ga me ni hairanu ka? Zu ga takai!*
2. His discharge papers mention a fractured rt. lat. malleclus. He was treated at the nearby Seiroka Christian Hospital. He didn't have to wear a cast or brace.

The task was more difficult if Russell didn't know the person or the family well. Once he attended the funeral of a less active man whom he visited twice as a home teacher. When he arrived at the funeral home, he was informed not only was he speaking but that he was the only speaker for the services.

He was asked to speak by friends, neighbors, ward members and prominent community families. He estimated having spoken at over 30 funerals.

Perhaps Russell's experience with George Haraguchi's funeral might explain some of the reasons he received so many speaking requests. George was the youngest son of Ann, a widow who moved to Provo because her oldest son was attending BYU. George, who contracted encephalitis, drowned when he had a seizure while swimming.

Russell began preparing his talk with a good idea of what he wanted to say but a "cold feeling" swept over him as he started to write. He stopped then started over only to be barred by the same sensation. After some pondering, Russell changed his approach and this time was met with a warm impression. As he wrote, he sometimes felt the hairs on the back of his neck rise. Russell says it was as though someone were standing over him guiding the words of his talk.

Very different from what Russell had first envisioned, his talk began with, "Sorry, mom, that I went so quickly." The Horiuchis had tickets to a basketball game after the funeral but Russell felt they should visit the Haraguchis instead. The family looked like they'd been expecting him. Right away they asked, "How did you know things that only our family knew?" Russell's talk had been right on target. Sister Haraguchi expressed what a comfort it was and felt that her son had been speaking through Russell.

Russell has always felt close to his ancestry and placed continued emphasis on work for the deceased. He confesses it might be a bit morbid but Russell spent time preparing himself for the next life, expressing the feeling that he will be called upon to serve his kindred dead and teaching the gospel to his ancestry. Speaking on the subject Russell says, "Something tells me that, Brother Horiuchi, you have a purpose after this life . . . Life is not my own now. I know why I have been guided to do this and that . . . The responsibility, at times, it frightens me."

It was fascinating to Russell that his patriarchal blessing declared him to be of the House of Israel with Annette being adopted into the same house when most of his family was of Ephraim. "Why are we from Israel, boneheaded lineage? It's no coincidence."

He studied *Doctrine and Covenants* 138 diligently trying to understand the great work that lies across the veil, spending hours discussing the topic with his neighbor, George Rohbock. George also felt a similar calling among his German ancestors. They agreed that whoever passed first would figure the situation out and then catch the other one up to speed when they arrived.

1997 was a hallmark year in many ways. It was the year of the Horiuchis' 50th Golden Wedding Anniversary. Russell, in his own obdurate way, nixed any plans for a celebration. Coincidentally, this was the year that their grandson Scott graduated from college and Ellen cunningly planned what was ostensibly a graduation party but conveniently invited all of the Horiuchis' friends and associates to the gathering, held in their backyard in Orem.

Word spread and friends and family from near and far came in for the occasion. Auntie Kay flew all the way from California. Shige and her grandson Kazuma, who just graduated from Waseda University in Tokyo, were visiting Kyoko in California. They came to Utah to visit Annette and Russell as well, although they arrived after the day of the party. Kazuma went on to visit Yellowstone National Park where he was given a private tour of the park as a graduation gift.

Around this time Russell was diagnosed with prostate cancer and began daily radiation and chemotherapy, leaving him drained and fatigued. After an exhausting month he was declared clean. He had to vigilantly monitor his PSA and receive biennial shots that would leave him tired but alive and kicking. Miraculously, Russell was able to return more or less to his normal routine, including fishing with his neighbors and his son-in-law, Stephen, who helped Russell take out his boat when he was in town.

One journal entry records a trip to Scofield reservoir with George Rohbock. "In the morning things were slow," writes Russell, "but had limit by noon. George took till 2:00"

On the eve of the Horiuchis' 60th anniversary, their grandson asked, "What is the secret of being married for so long?"

Russell, giving his best resigned-look sighed, "Just do what the woman tells you to do."

"That's right," Annette laughed in agreement.

Even though he was a noted geography professor with an encyclopedic knowledge of the world—he could tell you the capital of every country in the world, its gross national products, its terrain, its history and people—Russell hated to travel, preferring the comfort of familiar surroundings at home. Affectionately dubbing her father "The Armchair Geographer," Ellen tried in vain to remind him that no country could be understood strictly from a textbook; they had to be smelled, touched, and experienced. Russell maintained that he'd already done his share of travel by troop ship and that he would miss his own bed too much.

Despite Russell's aversion to travel, whenever Ellen and Stephen, now a lieutenant colonel (he eventually made full colonel before retiring himself), transferred to a new location the Horiuchis made it a point to go visit their new home.

This included a trip to Europe while Ellen and Stephen were stationed in Landstuhl, Germany. Russell's only request was to visit Normandy where D-Day took place.

The skies were appropriately gray the day the little band of Americans walked the sands of Omaha and Utah Beaches and among the tidy rows of white crosses and stars of David standing monument to the ultimate sacrifice made by so many valiant young men. Russell wordlessly stared intently at the still daunting cliffs.

Russell asked if they might also go to a German cemetery. Years later he spoke of the visit and how he envisioned the concourses of soldiers on the other side of the veil who needed to hear the gospel.

Annette contended with ghosts of her own. The family's travels brought them past Ramstein Air Force base, located near Landstul. Many of the aircraft could be seen from the autobahn as they drove past, particularly the large bombers. Though a generation removed from the planes that flew into Tokyo, the sight stirred up old memories, and Annette awoke in the middle of the night haunted by images of the B-29s that rained fire over the skies of her youth.

Annette had an interesting linguistic encounter in France. At a restaurant she excused herself to use the restroom. After being gone an unusually long time she returned and confessed to the family that she could find the men's room but not the women's. Ellen went with her downstairs to look. Annette knew the door marked *homme* was the men's room but repeatedly walked past the one labeled *dame*. In Japanese *dame*, pronounced "dah-may," means bad or broken. Ellen gently informed her that in French it was pronounced "dawm" and meant woman. Chagrined, Annette slapped her forehead before going in.

Another time, Russell took it upon himself to fly to Texas alone, once again to visit Ellen and Stephen, now stationed in Austin. Russell claims he wanted to see Miki dog, their brown and blue eyed Australian shepherd. Russell packed everything himself, forgetting one detail—he didn't bring any underwear!

When Ellen and Stephen transferred to Tripler Hospital in Hawaii in 2006 it seemed more than natural for the Horiuchis to visit the islands. Ellen spread word of their coming to everyone she knew who had connections with her parents. When it came to spreading news, Annette described Hawaii as the biggest small town in the world. Sure enough, Russell and Annette's trip turned into old home week with visitors pouring in from all corners of the islands. The Horiuchis had a great time, meeting and speaking with old friends and dining on generous amounts of island style *kau kau*. Ellen reports that Russell happily just talked and talked.

After his grandparents returned to Utah, Scott asked Russell, "How was the trip?" Russell, displaying his typical stoicism and knack for understatement answered simply, "Oh, it was all right," before adding, "I guess."

While the Horiuchis were enjoying their time in the Aloha state, their neighbors, members of their dinner group and several former missionaries pitched in to install a much needed and overdue sprinkling system in their yard in Orem. Several of the elders wouldn't agree to come until they were reassured that the *Buch* was safely away, fearful of catching an earful about fussing with his garden. Russell would have opposed the idea for several reasons, one being that he didn't want to hassle other people on his behalf and the other being a sense of pride at being able to handle such a large yard by himself. But with him out of town there was no one to stand in the way.

After several weekends of work, the system was installed making lawn care much easier for the Horiuchis, both well into their 80s by this time. Upon his return home Russell was surprised and thankful to everyone involved in the laborious undertaking. Watching the sprinklers at work he often repeated humbly, "Can you believe all these people would go through such trouble for an old fuddy-duddy like me?"

Janet Shiozawa, who helped initiate the project, said that, "it was a tribute to the Horiuchis that after all these years, the missionaries wanted to help their old mission president."

Russell disliked being financially obligated to others and hated borrowing money. The few times the Horiuchis did borrow money, they returned it as quickly as possible, even when it meant tightening their belts and going without for a while.

"Save your money" and "live within your means" are a few of the financial mantras Russell shared copiously. His three question advice when buying anything is still echoed in the family to this day: *Do you want it? Do you need it? Can you afford it?* If you can't answer yes to all three questions, you don't buy it. He emphasized knowing the difference between needs and wants. The priority was on staying out of debt.

The Horiuchis practiced what they preached. Even when they started out, living on the GI stipend for $125 a month they were saving what they could. Each time they received a pay increase or extra income, instead of expanding their spending habits they put the additional money into the bank. By the time of their retirement they were saving almost 75% of their paychecks. Russell never relied on the stock market. Some of his funds, invested by his retirement planners had been affected in a downturn and he considered the market too much of a gamble.

Their careful and continuous financial wisdom left them financially secure in their retirement years with enough to help out those in need. This feat was twice as impressive when compared to the poverty where Russell began.

The Horiuchis credit their comfortable living to the Lord, feeling any blessings they enjoyed were direct results of having been diligent and careful in their responsibilities.

While Russell and Annette's adage of service to others may not have made them millionaires, ultimately it left them with far, far greater riches in form of strong friendships. Literally hundreds of them. On any given day former students, missionaries, friends and neighbors could be found stopping by for a visit with many more keeping in touch by phone or mail.

Russell and Annette poured their hearts into the lives of those around them and in the end it is these friends, neighbors, and loved ones—not silver or gold—that have become their greatest wealth. The quality and strength of their relationships, forged over a lifetime of service, stand as monument to the character of the Horiuchis, whose lives in turn bear testimony to the truthfulness of the words of the Savior when He said, "For where your treasure is, there will your heart be also."

EPILOGUE

An old man stands in his meticulously cultivated garden, favoring a left foot lately troubled with gout. He is removing the golden autumn leaves from his trees by hand, pulling them off one by one and placing them in bags, preferring this to letting them fall and raking. For several years his family has tried to convince him that nature will take the leaves off herself but the man is content in his work. He has spent a lifetime diligently harvesting the fruits of his labors and in this respect plucking leaves from a tree isn't much different.

An aged woman, face still radiant with energy belying her age, the sparkle of curiosity undiminished in her eyes, emerges from the house. The yellow bricks and shingled roof are a far cry from the plantations of Hawaii and the cobbled roads of Tokyo but it is comfortable and it is home. She carries a glass of water to the man, encouraging him to drink and not over do it in the warm sun. His protests of her coddling pale next to the depth of his love and appreciation.

He takes her hand in his, the rice paper texture of her skin contrasting and complimenting the dark calluses of his own. "Mama," he speaks softly in the pidgin of his youth, "*Me you ga suki, ne?*" I sure do love you.

THOUGHTS, QUOTES, AND OTHER MUSINGS FROM FRIENDS, JOURNALS AND LETTERS

"This is a success story of two people who have accepted life's bumps and detours, but who would never give up. They have overcome everything, and have given completely of themselves to their family, to their friends, to God and the Church."

—*Charlie and Hisa Shibata, from a letter celebrating the Horiuchis' retirement 1988*

"Looking back 50 years—it was pretty good experience for us. Aiko really played a major role in our life. Much of what happened came about because of her. It could not have been otherwise."

—*Russell's journal July 25, 1998*

"I did not know then that Aiko was going to be my eternal companion—a twosome made in Heaven—she had to be—as I look at subsequent events."

—*Russell, undated note*

"Life's journey has come hard for me. The odds I have had to battle have been severe. I have had my share of success, and plenty of lumps along the way. It has been my ethnic background, my religious affiliations etc., that have tripped me. I have fallen flat on my face time and time again, but I have had friends to help me get up, and if I was down I was in a good position to offer supplication unto the Lord. I do not think that I felt so strongly about the Gospel, as I do now. My reversals have made me feel thankful that

I have the Lord to turn to. My testimony is strong. I do not know to what extent, but I have been very much blessed."

—*Russell, private letter March 26, 1961*

[During our] young time I wasn't member. I thought wow he [Russell] has direct connection with Heavenly Father because . . . when I have a worry he say "It's okay. [It will] work out in the end, and [everything would] turn out ok. So I trusted him [in] all things.

Even later years when I was going to school and class was very difficult and I thought, "I don't think I can make it." So I talk to him and he always gave me a different direction, different ideas. I never thought that way. [He would] calm me down and relieved me. That's why I was able to keep going. He was very optimistic I think. He always said, "It will be ok. Turn out all right." And [things] turn out usually ok.

—*Annette speaking of Russell*

PARAPHRASED FROM SPEAKING WITH CYRIL FIGUERRES

Russell had ways to capture attention. He showed up in Akita with no announcement. Fig was companions with Ludlow at the time. The other set of elders was Katayama, a *nihonjin* and Owen. The apartment didn't have a refrigerator. They had put in a request. The Horiuchis were trying to get all of the apartments fixed up for all the missionaries and things were pretty tight. It was mid winter and they asked the elders to be patient and suggested they could use the window (remember that is what the Horiuchis were doing themselves at the time). Owen didn't like that and told Ludlow, the DL, to write and ask for one. Russell asked them to wait. Owen said that if the mission home wasn't going to buy one that he would. None of the four missionaries had met the Horiuchis in person yet.

Fig and Ludlow were teaching a lesson in the room. So it was Owen and Katayama that answered the door to be quite surprised to find Russell on their doorstep, unannounced. He was acting rather unconversational, making them nervous. Asked a few questions but not much.

The apartment was pretty beat up. Fig remembers snow blowing in through the cracks in the window frames. Annette remembers it being right across from a cemetery and rather gloomy. Owen kept peeking his head in, "Fig, hurry up. It's the president. I think he's upset!"

As soon as the elders were all thoroughly intimidated Russell warmed right up and said he wanted to take them out to eat.

"He won our love," says Fig. He empowered the missionaries.

Because the mission was so spread out most missionaries were lucky to actually see the president once a quarter or so. Most things were word of mouth about the president. The *buch* was mysterious. He knew how to disclose his feelings so that they would last a long time. He had a warm way of showing and validating people.

FROM SCOTT HURST

This is silly. There are so many things I could share about my grandparents. Yet I share the following because it shows a bit how much grandpa loved little children and enjoyed teasing them.

Grandpa was always a very solemn and imposing figure to me as a child. The first joke I ever remember him telling, we were sitting at breakfast at the table in the kitchen of Orem house. Very seriously, Grandpa asked, "When you go to the bathroom which hand do you wipe with?"

I thought about it long and hard. "My right." I wasn't sure if I had given the proper answer.

He looked at me. "Really? I use toilet paper."

I immediately knew I'd been had but I was so shocked I didn't know if I was supposed to laugh or not.

Of all the silly things, it left such an impression on me that I remember it to this day.

After a visit to Annette's house Ellen writes

G'ma mentioned tonight that in the fall before G'pa passed away he commented about three times that he could hear people crying, especially children's voices. In a dream he stood and this mass of people came towards him. He could not see their faces, but it was a large group. It bothered him enough that he mentioned it three times to G'ma.

G'pa passed away January 15, 2011. The tsunami hit Japan six or seven weeks later March 11, 2011.

Also when Jan Komatsu called to tell my mother that her father had passed on, her comment was "Well, your husband called my father home!" I also felt that exact feeling when I heard that Pres. Komatsu had crossed the veil. He died Feb 23, 2011 barely over a month after G'pa went.

Chieko Okazaki passed away August 1, 2011. Mom asks about the coincidence that these great Japanese American pillars of the church all left the same year.

FROM STEPHEN B. WILLIAMS

One day, during the final week I could visit with Russell, as I sat across from him lying on the couch not feeling that well, I remarked that he had truly, in my estimation, endured to the end. With that he arose from the couch slowly with a gasp and leaned and pointed to me and said, "There is no end!" I wasn't sure what this meant, until he expounded—"There will eventually be a resurrection, and a millennium, and even another season when Satan will be loosed." And, "Even after that, if you persevere, there is really no end."

So I am to surmise that there is a lot more awaiting us beyond this life, but he had really felt it. The Spirit was strong with him after all he had given. If there is no end, then he really understood the text from "If you can hie to Kolob."

RUSSELL'S ACADEMIC HONORS:

Inducted into the National Scholastic Honor Society.

Earned Phi Eta Sigma as a freshman.

Phi Kappa Phi, one of the nations oldest honor societies

Pi Sigma Alpha, American Political Science Fraternity

Phi Alpha Theta, Honorary History Fraternity

MITSUTAKA AND KIKUYO HORIUCHI

Children:

Kay (never married)
Misao (Masayuki Sodetani)
Namiyo (Fujimoto Masaki—divorced, Mike Oyama)
Nozomi Russell (Aiko Mori)
Takashi (June Ohta—divorced, Eva Williams)

YOSHIZO AND HATSU MORI

Children:

Yae (never married)
Ichiro (Kazuko Naitou)
Hiroko birth name Miyoko[3] (Tomoya Kikuchi)
Shigeko (Iwakichi Mori)
Aiko Annette (Russell Horiuchi)
Hisa Jeanne (Charlie Shibata)
Kyoko (Tanaka Fujiyama Motohiko-divorced, Michael Partovi)

---

3. She was weak when born, so their parents changed her name. They believed her name was affecting her, so they chose a new one based on the characters.

EXCERPTS FROM MISSIONARY LETTERS

When our group arrived at Mission head-quarters in May of 1973, it was a joy to see Pres. Horiuchi again [Elder Raymond had been in one of his classes at BYU]. My first assignment was in Sendai to serve with Hull Choro, and Pres. Horiuchi said that Hull Choro would "walk my feet off" and teach me how to do missionary work. It was a true statement, and I appreciated the opportunity to serve the Lord in the Sendai ward.

My next assignment was in the city of Hirosaki in a very small branch—we called it a "twig" instead of a branch. There was only one active kyodai in the branch, and we held church in the missionaries' home. Dendo in Hirosaki was very difficult, but I do remember the beautiful castle in town, and enjoyed learning about the Japanese culture immensely. Part of the blessing of serving a mission is learning more about the culture and the people.

An opportunity to learn about the traditions, celebrations, and culture of Japan came to several of the missionaries in the Iwamizawa branch when we were invited to participate in the planting of rice to help an investigator's family, and to learn first-hand regarding the "back-breaking" work of agriculture for many of the residents of Hokkaido. I understood after this activity why so many of the older Japanese were quite "stooped" over in posture, and gained greater appreciation for their sacrifices involved.

If was always a joy to attend the many "taikais" held in the mission, and to hear our dear President speak to the missionaries and to the saints in the Japan East Mission, and to see Pres. & Sis. Horiuchi speak of their love for the Savior and for us as missionaries. It helped us overcome times of discouragement and loneliness, and overcome our feelings of missing our families back home.

Since returning it has been a blessing to visit with the Horiuchis' in their Orem home on a few occasions, even bringing my young son once to display a large rainbow trout caught that day. I knew Pres. Horiuchi would be excited.

— Michael Raymond

One of the missionaries, Craig Middleton, later served as bishop in the ward attended by Wayne and Marianne Scott, Ellen's in-laws from her first marriage!

— Stephen M. Scott

As I was attending general priesthood meeting . . . the spirit whispered to me that I should express gratitude for my wonderful mission assignment to Sapporo, Japan. Thank you so much for your dedicated service as mission president and the great example you have set for so many people over the decades since.

(Shields son, Colton, served in Torono West mission under Craig Middleton and his wife. Craig was one of the Horiuchis' missionaries as well.) Much of President Middleton's training as mission president, I believe, came from his service under both of you. So your influence is affecting another generation. Some of the things I specifically appreciate learning from you include working hard, doing what needs to be done and not expecting praise or honor.

I remember that the missionaries who worked the hardest with the least recognition seemed to be appreciated the most by both of you. I am also grateful for you helping me to raise my level of commitment to the gospel. I know serving as a mission president was not easy or fun for either of you, yet you did what you were asked to do with full conviction and energy.

Thank you for all you have done for me and my family.

I still fondly contemplate my mission days. Mission life in the Japan East Mission was hard but enjoyable. I have used stories from my mission during my entire life and still continue to do so.

— Jeffrey L. Shields.

President Horiuchi gave us one of the greatest gifts. His love and concern have sustained us not only through our mission experience but our lives.

— Randy and Margo Johnson

Our lives are forever better because of his influence and your sustaining support.

— Steve and Cathy Peterson

I'm Evans Shimai. I haven't been to a reunion in years. Almost made it to the last one but my daughter went in labor early and we had to go to her house. My funny memory happened at an activity in Sapporo. I was a very new missionary and fairly new in the church–not much experience and I thought people like mission presidents were like apostles or something. Pres. Horiuchi came up to me with a bowl of sugar coated soy nuts and asked if I would like some rabbit turds. I was so surprised yet I thought it was kind of funny too.

Another time he called me into his office and said he was sending me home early. I was shocked and then he asked me why I looked so guilty. I didn't know what to say. He was just joking but I didn't know enough then. He had just received word that the sisters missions were changed from 2 years to 18 months.

After my mission I felt so blessed to be able to go to BYU but after a year of school and still no husband in sight, I wanted to join the airlines and travel. I wrote for his advice as I didn't have any family that were members. I told the Lord I would do what ever he counseled. He wrote a short letter back and said "stay in school and get married" I recommitted to going to all my classes and doing better in school. Within 6 weeks or so of that time I met my now-husband and was engaged! We've almost been married 36 years and it just keeps getting better. I loved Pres. and Sister Horiuchi and how the mission blessed my life for eternity. I have 5 kids and 4 of them have served missions too. Life is good!! BUT don't ask me to speak Japanese. I speak much more Spanish now.

—Carol Evans Speaker

I remember a particular time as a district leader when we had some problems with an elder who was a junior companion and was bucking the leadership and had an attitude. Out of the blue, President Horiuchi was at sacrament meeting the next day in our branch. I was a little nervous and wondered why he was there. He asked us why he was there also. We each told him how we were doing and how things were going. He could immediately see the problem was with the junior companion and told him to shape up and that he supported me fully. I felt alot of confidence and appreciation for him for that support he gave when the junior didn't have that respect for the mission or what we were there for. He was transferred shortly thereafter and I got one of the best companions of my mission at transfers.

— *Robert Killpack*

Follow the Spirit. President and Sister Horiuchi followed another mission president who was extremely strict. In contrast, President and Sister Horiuchi were extremely kind and understanding towards the missionaries. They emphasized the Handbook of Instructions from Salt Lake instead of all sorts of added rules and procedures. President Horiuchi was more into "following the Spirit" rather than follow a bunch of precise rules. We, as missionaries, were very impressed with that type of attitude

No ego. President Horiuchi really didn't have an ego. He didn't care to stay in the nicest hotel in town when he came to visit us. He would rather pull out a Futon and sleep with the missionaries. That emphasized to us an extremely humble attitude. He made us as missionaries more effective in following his great example.

Service to others. At times the grass at the Sapporo chapel got way too big. Rather than wait for somebody else to mow it, he would frequently go out there and mow the grass. He set a great example to the members at that branch that no matter how prestigious your title is, no job was below him. That sure got a reaction from the members there—all of them wanting to serve in whatever capacity to get the work done. Additionally, when we had mission conferences, he would be the first one to go to the kitchen to wash the dishes. I don't know if he was trying to set an example or if that was just his way but it sure set a good example for us and made all the missionaries want to immediately stand up and do whatever it took to cleanup.

Great supporter. Sister Horiuchi was practically a wonderful supporter. You can't get anymore sweet and loving than her to her husband and to the other missionaries. She was a great example for all of us of a wonderful woman.

Cultural activities. Rather than avoid unique cultural activities in our own areas, he would encourage the missionaries to appreciate the culture around us. When the Sapporo Ice Festival happened, he encouraged the missionaries to appreciate that wonderful event and we did so.

High expectations. He didn't dictate to us exact requirements on doing things. Rather, he would build us up about our special abilities and responsibilities and let us "govern ourselves." Success with missionaries happened because he trusted us and let us lead ourselves rather than him dictating to us detailed instructions along the way.

Reluctant leader. When they first called him and he arrived in Japan, he would frequently comment that he didn't really want to be there. He was very much a reluctant leader. He was content with his job at BYU and only came because he was called to do the work. He never aspired to that or any other calling. He was very humble and laid back about it all. Even though he was in a very important calling and we all recognized that, he didn't make a big show about it at all. But what he did show was a great deal of dedication and devotion and was a great example to all of us.

Power of the Priesthood. I remember one time on my mission, my companion and I opened up a new area in Aizuwakamatsu. One of our investigators was a young man with a very rare skin disease. He wore gloves as water on his skin would cause a bad reaction such as boils or something like that. He wanted to be baptized but was concerned about his medical reaction to the water. So I called President Horiuchi and asked him for his recommendations so he asked me, "Elder, do you hold the Priesthood?" I said, "Yes, I do." He then responded, "Then use it by giving him a blessing and then baptize him." This renewed the faith of us, we did as he said and he suffered no bad reaction to the baptism.

Love for the missionaries. I worked in the mission home towards the end of my mission and was in charge of the mission magazine. I received interesting pictures of a missionary and his companion visiting a local zoo in which the monkeys kind of ran wild and had contact with the visitors. I thought it would be cute to use these photos as missionaries who are contacting "golden investigators" (the monkeys) It made for a funny article. I learned later that there had been some comments about it or he may have gotten into a little bit of trouble with LDS authorities, which I felt bad about it later. I now can see how it may have been bad form to use monkeys to act as investigators. But he never criticized me or called me to task over it as he perhaps could have. I appreciated that.

Patience and love. There were several Elders in my group who continually had problems being on a mission. They really wanted to go home. It was only because of the extreme love and patience of President Horiuchi with those Elders that they stuck it out.

Local leaders intrigued. I know that local leaders were very intrigued with him. He certainly looked like the typical Japanese on the street but because he learned his Japanese at a young age in Hawaii, the way he said things and the words that he chose would not have been exactly the standard way of saying it. The local leaders respected him quite a bit but were quite mystified by his background.

—*Don Sessions*

RUSSELL AND ANNETTE HORIUCHI

Mission President of the Japan East Mission 1970–1973
A Tribute

Who of us does not love President and Sister Horiuchi? We all love, admire and respect them. They loved us. They taught us. They sacrificed for us. For all they have done for us, we are eternally grateful.

Whenever President Horiuchi spoke we were laughing one sentence and crying the next. He tried to make us think he was "trunkie," but he was so dedicated to the cause of truth and righteousness, that we all worked our hearts out even if he told us he'd rather be fishing.

Thanksgiving, Christmas and other special American holidays made us all homesick. Our homesickness was less acute for mom's homecookin' in the states than it was for Sister Horiuchi's lemon meringue pie. The worst thing that could happen was to be serving in a distant town not able to get to Sapporo for the holiday celebration at which the "melt-in-your-mouth" pie was to be served. Winning the last piece of pie in a "junk-en-po" contest was the ultimate finale of all taikais.

Of all the wise counsel I have received from President Horiuchi, perhaps the wisest were these: treasure great friends, stand solid on firm ground and lead with the power of knowledge. Excerpts from my mission journal reveal his wisdom.

First meeting

Monday, November 9, 1970

While waiting to be instructed by Elder McConkie, President Horiuchi talked with us "greenbeans" and welcomed us to the mission. He is a tremendous person, and in just the few minutes we were together, it was easy to see why he is loved by everyone.

A year later, while serving in the Sapporo Branch, President Horiuchi played a trick on me. My journal record reads:

Tuesday, November 18, 1971

Just as we were kneeling in companion prayer last night about 9:45 pm, the phone rang. I didn't believe my companion when he came back and told me that it was the President calling us for transfers. "The President has never called out transfers, besides, not ever, since I've been here, has the President called us," I said. I picked up the receiver, and the person on the other end, having over-heard our dialogue, said in his gruffest voice, "As your companion told you, this is the President!" He inquired about our schedule for today and ordered us to be in his office for a chat as soon as possible. That was it, and he said "goodnight!" What have I done wrong? Have I juggled the books wrong? Talking too much to too many shimais? or haven't I been working hard enough? The only hint he gave me was that he asked me if I had a driver's license.

About 1 pm today Sled Choro and I timidly stepped into the office. The President invited us to sit down and then proceeded to give us the good old scare treatment. It didn't last long, when suddenly he asked Sled Choro how fast he could pack. He talked with Sled Choro just a bit longer, then called to an assistant—"OK, you can take him now." I thought he was talking about Sled Choro, so I said, "Well, we'll see you later, dod." The President said, "No, not him, you." "Why? Where am I going?" I inquired. "Bennion Choro, tell him when you get him outside," ordered President Horiuchi. As we rode in the mission car, Bennion Choro and Gailey Choro told me all about transfers, and that I was to be the new Assistant to the President."

With in a few days, my eyes were opened to a whole new vision of life and my mind to a new way of thinking about the world.

Thursday, November 20, 1971

President Horiuchi's philosophy of missionary work has always been to have few if any rules. He allows us to use our own ideas and programs, within the framework of the church's standards. So, true to form, he has said little, if anything to me concerning my duties and responsibilities other than a basic outline.

In short order, I became a student of the sensei.

Wednesday, November 24, 1971

Certainly, being in the mission office in close quarters with the president has its advantages. Today, we were enlightened concerning church government. In response to my inquisitive questions, the President stopped what he was doing, and I received one of the best, most thorough explanations on priesthood and church government and organization I've ever received. Some of the more meaningful thoughts: The organization of The Church of Jesus Christ of Latter-day Saints is perfect. Each calling has its definite purpose and set of responsibilities, each General Authority knows precisely his role and carries it out. However, never will he tread into another's area. We must work through the channels. Although this takes time, in the long run it is the most effective way—it is the Lord's way.

President Horiuchi included us in everything, even the assignment of missionaries at transfers.

Monday, December 20, 1971

Another interesting, beneficial night with President and Sister Horiuchi at their apartment. He quizzed us—Why did so-and-so go here?" Why did so-and-so go there?" His thought process and intelligence is astounding.

We soon learned that being a Mission President is not all that fun. A lot of stress comes with the calling.

Monday, December 27, 1971

It's impossible to even try to describe the pressure, the strain, and the delicate responsibility a mission president has—so many problems and so much to consider in searching for solutions.

Today the President shared a grave problem with us, then asked for a solution. We both kind of floundered around, not knowing what should be done, and the best solution was beyond us. Not to worry, the President seemed to know the end from the beginning. He had already analyzed, synthesized and organized the issues and come to a profound solution. I think he was either teasing with us, or using us to try out his conclusions to see if his logic was sound. In either case, I felt both totally overwhelmed by the problem and grateful to learn from the sensei how to think through problems to a logical solution. What a gift.

The office had its perks.

Saturday, January 28, 1972

The President has been extremely talkative and instructive the past few days. I really enjoy being under his tutelage. Tonight Sister Horiuchi invited all of the office staff over for dinner. What a fantastic meal, topped by a dreamy lemon meringue pie. The President and his wife are truly examples of the living gospel—full of love and charity for all. They are a marvelous example for all of us.

The president taught me to enjoy a good argument, but I was never a match for him.

Thursday, February 3, 1972

The President has been talkative lately and I'd much rather spend a few minutes with him that go to the Olympics. We always learn so much and I'm beginning to see much improvement in my ability to keep up with his thinking. Still, I'm far behind him, and there is one thing he is trying to teach me—I must stand on my ground firmly, be more confident, and fight when I know I'm right. The President is a brilliant debater—and he loves it—guess I should have learned to use more brain and less brawn when fighting with my brothers.

Wednesday, February 23, 1972

I've always thought that arguing was a vice. Certainly, arguing in anger with intent to hurt someone is not good. But today I discovered that if I want to become a half decent lawyer, I'm going to have to learn to like arguing, or should we call it "intelligently discussing." I am also going to have to learn the tricks of the trade and how to use them skillfully. The President is a great debater, and he loves it. We got going today in a fairly uneven battle—he picked me to pieces. But as always, after he walked all over me, he picked me up and turned the two hours into a great learning experience. Some of the things he taught me"

Start from a solid base—a true hypothesis

Be sure of yourself and convinced of your case—don't be persuaded too easily (my big problem).

Have a plan. Know your conclusion as well as your introduction and body.

Think ahead of the opponent.

Retain.

Never qualify yourself using such words as "if," "extreme case," "about," etc. etc. Learn to use words.

More heartache
Monday, March 6, 1972

I have never felt sorrier for anyone than President and Sister Horiuchi. No matter how hard they tried to show love and offer help, our pouting friend refused to shake hands or even talk to them. He even accused them of trying to poison him when they offered him a contact pill for his cold. Truly, the President and his wife have lived through hell this week.

On leadership
Friday, April 14, 1972

Another thing I've learned to appreciate even more is the type of leadership that President Horiuchi employs. He gives an assignment and puts all of his trust in you, then no matter how much he'd like to help, he lets you go through with your own ideas. Yes, the President is using this same approach with me again too. He simply said, "We're having a Taikai," and I knew from that exactly what my assignment was. I'm sure he'd really like to pitch in and help when he sees me floundering, but I'm glad he lets me grow.

More training

Tuesday, May 2, 1972

Knowledge is power! I enjoyed another hour of personal tutelage today as the President and I discussed several matters of importance concerning the church, especially the church in Japan. The President explained again how his policy of "loose control" was turning out to be much more effective in building strong leaders and good church members than the very tight control tactics of other mission presidents. The President explained to me that although it may appear as though he has no control over his mission because he dictates no huge policies and programs, he actually has more control because then the members must govern themselves. He said he is able to do this because he has knowledge of each person in his organization. He showed me some of the information he had on a few missionaries, and I was astounded. He then made the statement: "knowledge is power!" He then said that he didn't have nearly as much information as most of us think he has, but just the fact that we think he knows everything about us makes us be even more careful and honest with ourselves. President Horiuchi is certainly a magnificent leader. He knows how to gain knowledge, and how to use it. It is days like today that I love to be in the office.

More heartache

Thursday, May 25, 1972

The President absolutely amazes me. Two nights in a row an elder has taken off on his own—an act which could send him home. Yet the President still has trust and confidence in the young man. I'm sure I can't possibly appreciate the pain that is tearing up the President inside, yet he seems to have enough control and power over the situation (in other words, knowledge of the young elder and his problems) that he can still show trust and love toward him. Again, the President commands my respect.

More training needed

Thursday, June 15, 1972

When the President is displeased and disappointed with your efforts and lets you know it, you feel about two inches high. It is not so much that you didn't perform well that gets you, it is the thought that you've betrayed the trust placed in you by him—trust so highly sought for. But then, as you think about it, it is like he says "We haven't let him down, we let ourselves down."

Sayonara

Sunday, August 27, 1972

In my final interview tonight, the President again gave me some wonderful counsel and advice. In essence, this was his message:

Learn to have patience in leadership positions.

Get good, close friends—people you can call "eternal friends."

Work hard in school. Get good grades.

When planning, learn to step back and take a good perspective view of the situation.

Truly, the President has taught and loved me as a son. I'm proud to call him my "second dad."

Always the friend . . . ever the teacher.

When President Horiuchi was released and returned to the classroom as a professor of GeoPolitics at BYU, I signed up for his class. He was a master teacher—a true sensei. Fortunately, he was easier on me in the classroom than in the mission office. He gave me, or, dare I say, I earned an A in his class.

Some months after taking his class, and after many long conversation in which he counseled me against going to law school,

I showed up at his office dejected because of my score on the LSAT. He said, "Dudley Choro, how many times have I told you that you'd be a terrible lawyer? You shouldn't go to law school. Your gifts and talents lie elsewhere." Rather than feeling belittled, I accepted his gentle jab and then he spent an hour reviewing other alternatives with me. When he said, "have you ever thought about hospital administration?" it was as though a bell rang in my head. He told me more and introduced me to an administrator at Utah Valley Hospital. The more I learned the more I knew this is what the Lord wanted me to do. I thank God for speaking to me through President Horiuchi.

Through the years, though separated by time and distance, I have enjoyed calling on President and Sister Horiuchi with our children when we were in or near Orem. The two of them have always shown Michelle, our children and me great love and kindness. I know that our sons have loved their mission presidents because they first loved President Horiuchi just as much as I love him.

My dear President and Sister Horiuchi, please forgive this lengthy and somewhat self absorbed tribute. I know you'd have preferred a much shorter, less detailed history. However, your family deserves to know of the profound and lasting influence you have had on me and so many missionary sons and daughters. So, if this history seems to be over done for you, please forgive me.

May the Lord's countenance shine upon you and be gracious unto you. May you know His amazing grace and Divine joy for having offered a lifetime of service. May you feel peace for having lifted others with love. May you rejoice in the knowledge that your offering is acceptable to the King. And, last but not least, may there always be a big fish on the end of your line.

With a grateful heart,

I am, and will ever be, your humble friend,

Michael M. Dudley

JAPAN EAST MISSIONARIES 1970-1973

Sister missionaries are listed by their maiden name. Their married name follows in parentheses. Two surnames interspersed with an "or" indicates a mukoyoshi or taking of the wife's surname.

A

Bruce D. Abrams
Allan R. Adams
Eric Adams
Michael J. Akagi
Ryan Val Alder
Randall W. Allred
James W. Alverson
Gregg Alvord
Alton Anderson
Sherman F. Anderson
Stephanie Anderson (Kean)
Vaun Blair Andrus
Michael Ard
Nobuyoshi Araki
Robert D. Armstrong
Takehiko Asakawa
Bruce Ashton

B

Brent K. Bailey
Max William Barker
Leonard Jay Barney

Kent Ray Bascom
Stephen Beckstead
Max Behling
John W. Bennion
Alan Call Bingham
Susan Bird (Marcrum)
Randy Howard Black
Robert Donald Bledsoe
Joseph Robbins Boud
William Brent Bradshaw
Gordon W. Branstatar
Alan Bridge
C. McKay Brown
Howard Brown
Keith Sherman Brown
Michael Larson Brown
Paulette Brunger (Park)
David Kim Burnam
James Russell Burrows
Robert T. Burton
David Wayne Bush
David Buys

C

Reid Call
Todd Foster Claflin
David Walter Chambers
Reid William Chambers
Keith Chaston
Takeshi Chiba
Forrest B. Christensen
Scott Clark
Michael Colton
Bryan P. Crandall
Curtis Ralph Crane
Douglas Franklin Crigger
Craig Cutright

D

Michael G. Dahle
Richard Dalton
Richard Dart
Charles LaMar Davis
Ronald Davis
Darrell Jay Decker
Wesley G. Dewsnup
Marvin W. Dixon
Monte Dodge
Michael Dudley
Joseph Dunlop
Ernest Sterling Durrant

E

James Ellis Eager
John M. Edmunds
Kenneth E. Edwards
George E. Ellsworth

Marilyn Louise Erd
Carol Evans (Speaker)
Richard Chauncey Evans II

F

Cyril I.A. Figuerres

G

Joe Ronald Gabrielsen
David Craig Gailey
Dennis Harding Gaither
Brian Galbraith
Richard D. Garrison
Gary D. George
Robert Gibb
Michael Glenn
Eugene Hale Goodsell
James Graham
Gay Grant (Moon)
Rodney Lee Griffin
Lee Groberg
Dennis Dale Grow

H

John Kerby Hall
Virgil Hammond
Robert Hanamaikai
Curtis Hancey
Setsuko Haneda (Erickson)
Grant Hansen
Bill Hanvey
Mitsuo Hara
Gordon Hardcastle
Jeffrey W. Harris
Roger Harris

Dennis Harward
Hideo Hayashi
Joseph K. Head
Daniel G. Heiner
George Hellewell, Jr.
Reed Johnson Henderson
Dennis Nick Hendrickson
Kiyoshi Hisaka
Kevin Lee Hopkins
Linda Noel Houser (Hoseman)
Wayne Hull
Gerald M. Hunter
Lee Roger Hyde

I

Genji Ichikawa
Jay D. Inouye
Satoshi Ishizaka or Kanai
Misako Ishizawa(Matsui)
Kazuko Iwanishi (Kimura)
Kikue Izumizaki (Yomogida)

J

John Mark Jacob
Mark Jensen
Charles Dean Johns
Holly Johnson (Hopkins)
Jeffrey K. Johnson
Randy C. Johnson
Richard D. Johnson
Robert N. Johnson
Steven G. Johnson
Creed A. Julian

K

Toshiaki Karino
Mark Nathan Kartchner
Masateru Kasada
Hiroshi Katayama
Ikuko Kato
Joseph Kettenring
Robert Kimball Killpack
Dan A. Kimball
Scott G. Kimball
Akira Kina
Michael M. King
Paul R. King
Roderick Leon King
Alan Kenji Kira
Fumiko Kitamura (Miyazaki)
Betsy Michiko Kiyabu (Itoga)
Jay Emmett Komatsu
Frederick L. Kunz

L

Paul Wilson Landerman
Larrance Larson
Jeffrey Lee Leavitt
Clayton Michael Lefler
Bud Arthur Little
Jeff Lords
Brent Ludlow
David Emil Ludlow
Gregg Ludlow
Lorin Lund
Richard J. Lyon

M

David Mansius
Mariko Matsuda
Masako Matsuo
Steve Reuben May
Robert R. McCann
William D. McCook
Richard Alan McGraw
Kathleen McKee (Dastrup)
Robert McKinnon
John McNeel
Grady McNett
Craig Middleton
Raymond Milefsky
Kenneth D. Miles
Richard Kent Milligan
Mark T. Mitarai
Glenn Monson
Alan Keith Morgan
Haruyuki Morimoto
Paul Frederick Morrison
James Murray
Makiko Murui
Richard Musick
George Rulon Myers

N

Yoshitoshi Nakamura
Dean Katayoshi Nako
Keith Alan Nelson
Keith L. Nelson
B. Kelly Nielsen
Scott "Q" Nielsen
Veigh Moyle Nielson

Tsutomu Nishime
L. Dee Nord

O

Michael Ohlin
Kenneth Oka
Jerry Masaru Okabe
Theodore Okawa
Max Oldroyd
Sachiko Onda (Kira)
Teijiro Onuma or Wakatsuki
Frank F. Owen, Jr.
Dean Elliott Owens

P

Mark Hanson Packer
Ralph Keith Parker
Bryce Passey
Stephen N. Peterson
David F. Platt
Douglas R. Pohl
Robert Pontius
Charles Pulsipher
Richard Kirkmen Purdey
Dallan Leffler Purser

R

Kenneth Rapp
Michael Raymond
Curtis James Redd
Robert James Reese
Elizabeth Ann Rich
Kenneth Rich
Ryne Richards
Michael Roberts

Brent J. Robertson
Reed F. Robinson
Douglas Brent Rose
Mark E. Rowley
Sally Sue Roth (Lyle)
Gordon Stephen Russell

S

Douglas Kiyoshi Sakaguchi
Kyoko Sakurayama (Sairenji)
Toshiko Sasai (Mori)
Toshiko Sasaki (Matsukawa)
Cynthia Schoonmaker (Bowers)
John Michael Scott
Don D. Sessions
Mark Whiteley Sheffield
Val R. Shelley
Jeffrey Lane Shields
Daniel Albert Skinner
Gregory Sled
Quentin M. Steele
Treve R. Stephenson
Chris D. Stevens
Douglas L. Stevens
Benjamin David Stitt
Albert Stone
Paul Stuart
Haruko Sugimoto (Reese)
Yasuo Suzuki
Dean J. Swalberg
Bradley Don Swenson
Raymond T. Swenson

T

Greg Taggart
Sachie Takeda
Ronald B. Talmage
Hideko Tasaki (Okide)
Harold John Taylor
Kimball J. Taylor
Steven Taylor
David Y. Thomas
James R. Thompson
Kenji Toma
Joseph Toronto
Owen Scoville Tucker
Timothy William Tuitele
Robert Earl Turner
Darrell R. Turpin

U

Lorna Masako Uemura
Hisako Umino

V

Kenneth VonForell

W

Van Wai
David Martin Wakefield
Daniel Garth Walker
Grant James Walker
Eileen Walton (Bridge)
Stephen R. Warner
David Lynn Warren
Mark Watanabe
Gordon Dean Weatherbee

Mark Henry Weight
Karen Welch
Layne Westover
Steven Wheeler
Sherman White
John K. Wiggill
Mark William Wilcox
Alan J. Willes
Frederick F. Wolters
Gary Lorenzo Wright

Y

Tota Yaguchi
Yasuko Yamada (Oman)
Nobuko Yamaguchi (Azekura)
Shunichi Yamamoto
Hiroshi Yanagihara
Anthony G. Young
Lowell Young

Z

John Bruce Zimmerman